ELITE CADRES
AND
PARTY COALITIONS

Recent Titles in
Contributions in Political Science
Series Editor: Bernard K. Johnpoll

White House Ethics: The History of the Politics of Conflict of Interest Regulation
Robert N. Roberts

John F. Kennedy: The Promise Revisited
Paul Harper and Joann P. Krieg, editors

The American Founding: Essays on the Formation of the Constitution
J. Jackson Barlow, Leonard W. Levy, and Ken Masugi, editors

Japan's Civil Service System
Paul S. Kim

Franklin D. Roosevelt's Rhetorical Presidency
Halford R. Ryan

"Jimmy Higgins": The Mental World of the American Rank-and-File Communist, 1930–1958
Aileen S. Kraditor

Urban Housing and Neighborhood Revitalization: Turning a Federal Program into Local Projects
Donald B. Rosenthal

Perforated Sovereignties and International Relations: Trans-Sovereign Contacts of Subnational Governments
Ivo D. Duchacek, Daniel Latouche, and Garth Stevenson, editors

New Approaches to International Mediation
C. R. Mitchell and K. Webb, editors

Israeli National Security Policy: Political Actors and Perspectives
Bernard Reich and Gershon R. Kieval, editors

More Than a Game: Sports and Politics
Martin Barry Vinokur

Pursuing a Just and Durable Peace: John Foster Dulles and International Organization
Anthony Clark Arend

Getting the Donkey Out of the Ditch: The Democratic Party in Search of Itself
Caroline Arden

ELITE CADRES AND PARTY COALITIONS

*Representing the Public
in Party Politics*

Denise L. Baer
AND
David A. Bositis

Contributions in Political Science, Number 218

GREENWOOD PRESS
New York • Westport, Connecticut • London

Library of Congress Cataloging-in-Publication Data

Baer, Denise L.
  Elite cadres and party coalitions : representing the public in
party politics / Denise L. Baer and David A. Bositis.
      p.   cm. — (Contributions in political science, ISSN 0147–1066
; no. 218)
  Bibliography: p.
  Includes indexes.
  ISBN 0–313–26153–9 (lib. bdg. : alk. paper)
  1. Political parties—United States.   2. Political leadership—
United States.   3. Elite (Social sciences)—United States.
4. Political participation—United States.   5. Social movements—
United States.   I. Bositis, David A.   II. Title.   III. Series.
JK2261.B28   1988
324.273—dc19   88–5703

British Library Cataloguing in Publication Data is available.

Library of Congress Catalog Card Number: 88–5703
ISBN: 0–313–26153–9
ISSN: 0147–1066

First published in 1988

Greenwood Press, Inc.
88 Post Road West, Westport, Connecticut   06881

Printed in the United States of America

The paper used in this book complies with the
Permanent Paper Standard issued by the National
Information Standards Organization (Z39.48–1984).

10 9 8 7 6 5 4 3 2 1

Copyright Acknowledgments

The author and publisher are grateful to the following for granting the use of their material:

The Consequences of Party Reform by Nelson W. Polsby. Copyright 1980, Oxford University
Press, New York, New York. Used by permission of the publisher.

Party Reform by William J. Crotty. Copyright 1983, William J. Crotty. Used by permission
of the author.

For Demelza and Hallie

Contents

Figures and Tables

FIGURES

TABLES

Preface

This book was begun out of a sense of frustration with the tenor of the debate over the health of the party system. Our theory seemed to us to be mired in a series of duopolies: responsible parties versus indigenous ones, pro-reform versus anti-reform, atomized mass society versus pluralism, pluralism versus elitism, party decline versus party resurgence, centralized party organization versus decentralized ones, pragmatism versus ideology. The times they were a-changing, and yet our party theory formed a theoretical straitjacket providing little understanding of the transformed contemporary party system.

To materially redefine the terms of this debate, we have divided our argument into two parts, each of which complements the other. In Part I, we review the history of party reform and contemporary assessments of its meaning. Following this, we present our own theory in which we argue for a group approach; one in which we combine political science interest group theory with the body of scholarship on social and political movements. We argue that political action both within and outside of the party system is group based. It is the group concept that incorporates and accounts for elite-mass *inter*dependence. Elites and nonelites act independently, yet are linked through groups. We do not argue for elitism; we do, however, assume that elites—however recruited (and, of course, recruitment structures representation)—occupy the leadership positions. Discrimination is not individual, but group based. We offer what we term a *Party Elite Theory of Democracy*. This theory provides what we believe is a more satisfying resolution of the seemingly insoluble controversies in political party theory.

In Part II, we turn to an examination of these issues using survey data from the Party Elite Study.[1] This data set provides over-time comparisons among four elite cadres in both parties: nominating convention delegates, national committee members, state chairs, and county chairs in office in 1980 and in 1984. This data set was not specifically developed with the express intention of testing the hypotheses of our Party Elite Theory of Democracy.

This may leave some readers of our book unsatisfied. We do, however, use these data to strategically test assumptions and hypotheses derived from existing theories and explanations. To the extent that these theories are refuted, we believe that our explanation becomes more plausible. We do not expect all party scholars to embrace our interpretations; we would be quite satisfied to broaden the theoretical debate beyond narrow subfield controversies.

By theory, we mean all of the various propositions used in explanations (whether encompassing the whole of the party system or only one part) that seek to explain change in the parties. In assessing the current status of "party theory," we have occasion to consider many different explanations—most of which are widely known in their subfields as a theory (e.g., social movement theory, mass society theory, pluralist theory, rational choice theory, interest-group theory, etc.). To erect some formal definition of *systematic* theory unnecessarily limits our considerations to a quite small subset of party scholars. Those who do so miss the crux of the controversy over party—the question of linkage between elite and mass—that lies at the heart of our argument. Peter Natchez (1985) makes this point most persuasively concerning criticisms of voting behavior research, and we will have occasion to address this dilemma in the more general context of party theory. For those troubled by this indiscriminate use of the term "theory," we wish them to bear in mind that this reflects the state of political party theory, and not our inability to distinguish between "seat-of-the-pants" theorizing and formal theory.

A word is in order concerning our use of the women's movement (as a social movement) to test the effects of party reform. We argue that social movements comprise an antidote to elite oligarchy. The black civil rights movement was, of course, the first contemporary social movement. It was the black civil rights movement that defined the meaning of the term "social movement" and offered a theoretical point of departure from the early literature focusing on collective action qua the craze, the panic, the riot, the mob (e.g., see Smelser, 1963). In order to make our case that social movements are grass-roots phenomena that seek to make changes in all social institutions, we could certainly have used blacks as well as women. However, there is very little disagreement among scholars that blacks comprise a legitimate social movement and that blacks experienced discrimination that resulted in organized group pressure within the party system (as we should expect, because the civil rights movement provides the paradigm case study from which social movement theory developed). As we shall point out, there *is* a disagreement about women—whether or not they have experienced discrimination and whether or not they actually comprise a social movement. Women, therefore, present a harder test case for us to make, precisely because the women's movement represents an *extension* of social movement theory. There are practical considerations as well. While the gender gap results in greater Democratic identification among women, blacks are overwhelmingly Democratic. Even if we wished to limit ourselves to delegate analyses (where most black party activists are concentrated), the number of blacks at the elite levels of the Republican party is so small as to preclude interparty analysis. While it may be arguable which group (women or blacks) made the most gains from party reform, women's gains are the more recent. For these reasons, we believe that a focus on women in Chapters 5 and 6 provides a sufficient test of the more general argument we make in Part I concerning the characteristics of social movement groups and their orientation to party activity.

No theoretical and empirical work of this scope develops in a vacuum. First, we acknowledge our intellectual debt to Roberto Michels, Maurice Duverger, and E. E. Schattschneider. These scholars wrote about party, elites, and the dynamics of political change in such a timeless fashion that one is rewarded with each new reading of their works. We are not the first to benefit from their wisdom, and surely not the last.

We acknowledge a considerable debt to John S. Jackson III of Southern Illinois University. He began the Party Elite Study in the 1970s with surveys of Democratic midterm conference delegates and later national convention delegates. In 1980, he and his coinvestigator Barbara Leavitt Brown expanded the study to include national committee members as well as state and county chairs of both parties. In 1984, he invited us to join him as coinvestigators in the expanded Party Elite Study. We have long valued John Jackson's substantial personal commitment to the systematic over-time observation of party elites as well as admired his considerable commitment to supporting political parties as fundamental institutions of representative government.

Several of our colleagues have commented on the manuscript and offered useful suggestions for improvement. We owe special thanks to Cornelius Cotter of the University of Wisconsin and William Crotty of Northwestern University. Both carefully read the manuscript and called our attention to points and references that might bear reconsideration. Neil Cotter, in particular, read the manuscript with consideration for the larger theoretical questions. We share his admiration for Michels' work and the significance of elite recruitment and elite circulation as issues of fundamental importance. Precisely because we approach parties from complementary, albeit somewhat different, vantage points, his criticisms were all the more provocative. Thanks also to Nancy McGlen of Niagra University for her comments on an earlier draft. And as we cannot claim to have taken all their good advice, we must bear final responsibility for what remains here.

NOTE

1. The Party Elite Study is an over-time study of party elites. The study began in 1974 when John S. Jackson III of Southern Illinois University at Carbondale surveyed

delegates to the Democratic midterm conference. The Party Elite Study provides the most comprehensive data set available on *national* political party elites; other studies have limited their study populations to either one elite cadre (e.g., delegates or county chairs), or to only one state or region.

PART I

THE PARTY COALITIONAL APPROACH

In Part I, we introduce a new theory of democracy. We begin by examining the current crisis in party theory and the attempts that have been made to cope with it. The crisis stems from an inability to agree on the nature of the new party system resulting in a disagreement about whether the parties are in a period of decline or growth. There are those who redefine the parties to be something new, a "Super-PAC" or a service organization, and come to the conclusion that the parties are much stronger than in the recent past. Those who view parties in the more traditional sense view the decline of the party-in-the-electorate and the proposed redefinition with alarm. Thus, there are those who would divorce the empirical study of parties from the normative tradition represented in past scholarship, and there are those who strenuously oppose this. The crisis has resulted in two opposing groups of scholars who have begun to speak past each other, not even using the same concepts and terms.

We next examine this "unraveling" of party theory and the significance of the unraveling of party research into a tripartite system with specialized researches into each of the three parts. This focus on constituent parts has resulted in three bodies of scholarship, each with its own focus, methodology, and conclusions as to the status of the party system. This focus on the parts has generally resulted in a diminished concern for the dynamics of the party system as a whole.

We then return to the origins of party systems and examine the concomitant development of social movements and political parties, the historical relationship between social movements and political parties, and the unique contribution each has made to modern democracy. In this context, we likewise examine the modern variants of these social movements, in particular—the civil rights and women's rights movements.

Finally, we introduce our reconceptualization of democracy. The political parties are a necessary element to this new conceptualization. The pressure group system is biased toward in-groups (in E. E. Schattschneider's terms "sings with a strong upper-class accent"). The new party system however is not one with an homogenous in-group party elite. Rather, in the democratized party system, the parties are ruled by a coalition of elites sprung from many social groups. We do not equate democracy with simple mass-level participation. Our conception of a democratic system is one where there is no exclusion from the elite class based on social category. A political elite stratum that is permeable to elites of all social groups is inherently more democratic in our view than one that is not. While we articulate an elite theory of democracy, we do not endorse an *elitist* theory of democracy. We do not argue that elites should rule because they possess more or better information (and values), but rather that they possess such information because of their elite position. Therefore, excluding some groups from elite status disadvantages those groups in terms of obtaining their policy goals. Our theory places great stress on the recruitment of elites and the recruitment of elites formed within social groups—and especially important for democracy, the recruitment of elites *formed within social out-groups*. This not only democratizes the political system at the policy level, but offers a wider and more meaningful range of opportunities for mass-level political participation because such participation is more meaningful in the context of these intermediate associations.

1

The Current Crisis in Party Theory

INTRODUCTION

We are currently experiencing a crisis in party theory. Whether dated from Walter Dean Burnham's 1969 essay "The End of American Party Politics," or from David Broder's 1971 conclusion that *The Party's Over*, we have been aware that the party system has been undergoing a metamorphosis for over a decade and a half. But what we do not know is what will come out of the chrysalis—a truncated and deformed party system or a resurgent and strengthened one. Our book is based on a simple argument: the crisis is not in the party system, but in the party scholarship.

Other scholars have noted the crisis in party theory. Burnham (1985) describes the current era (which he dates from 1968 to the present) as an "interregnum"—inexplicable under current party theory. Joseph Schlesinger argues that our party scholarship has been "piecemeal" in its focus. "We cannot predict how a political scientist might go about answering the question: 'are parties declining?' not because students of politics are incompetent, but because they have no agreed upon way to approach such a question" (1984:372). Schlesinger attributes this result to the "dominant, textbook mode of analysis" that separates party research into different "images" (Eldersveld, 1964), or "pieces" (eg., V. O. Key's identification of the "party-in-the-electorate," the "party-in-government," and the "party organization" [1964:371]. Similarly, Alan Ware sharply criticizes the "model of the 'unholy trinity'—a device which avoided theorizing about parties" (1985:7).

While we agree with these theorists that as political scientists our current party theory is inadequate to explain the dramatic changes in the party system, we diverge quite sharply in our assessment of both the causes and the results. Burnham, for example, argues that the contemporary change in the party system represents elite manipulation of the masses, while J. Schlesinger resuscitates rational choice theory to develop a theory of the party organization—a definition that excludes the voters from the party concept. Our approach is diametrically opposed to these analyses. We have no quarrel with the corpus of party theory developed by the first generation of party theorists (writers such as Roberto Michels, Maurice Duverger, Charles Merriam, Harold Gosnell, E. E. Schattschneider, V. O. Key, and Samuel Eldersveld). The first generation of party scholars provided a comprehensive explanation of party dynamics—it is the extensive derivative research of the second generation of party scholars that has dismembered political parties and treated the party system as static that we are critical of—not the body of traditional party thought from which they derived their hypotheses.

In making this argument, we base our definition of the party squarely in the mainstream tradition of political party theory. As stated quite succinctly by William Nisbet Chambers, a political party is

a relatively durable social formation which seeks offices or power in a government, exhibits a structure or organization which links leaders at the centers of government to a significant popular following in the political arena and its local enclaves, and generates in-group perspectives or at least symbols of party identification or loyalty. (1967:5)

The political environment over the past two decades has not been static— and it is our argument that one cannot understand the current party system without incorporating the changes in what Gerald Pomper (1975) terms political modernization, and in the development of the new social and political movements arising in the 1960s. The configuration of the pressure group system has been fundamentally altered—and democratized, we believe—with the rise of the new citizens groups (G. Wilson, 1981). The party system described by the first generation of party theorists rested on the firmament of a demographically homogeneous political elite. Ironically, at a time when elites are increasingly demographically representative of the diversity of groups in the mass public—our theorists are interpreting these changes as reflective of an increased separation between the political elites and the mass public in terms of political influence. This is occurring because these party scholars have neglected the increased diversity among the mass public, and they have misunderstood the increasing links between party elites and the increasingly divergent groups they represent—and belong to.

The most dramatic change in the party system is not the rise in campaign technology, the increasing reliance on campaign consultants, or the decline in party support among the electorate—the critical change is that the party system is based on a coalitional structure at the *elite* level, not *only* at the mass level as was in the case in the prereformed party system.[1] The decrease in internal party discrimination against women and minority groups is due to the reform process in the Democratic party dating from 1968. The consequent introduction of women, blacks, and other minorities to the elite levels of influence and power in both parties has altered the basis of party organization in a more democratic direction.

Other observers, noting the increasing heterogeneity among party elites, have not come to such sanguine conclusions as ours. Nelson Polsby (1983a), for example, argued that the result of the party reform process has been to increase factionalism in the parties (and particularly among the Democrats)— rather than broadening the coalitional structure of the party system. Polsby's critique is fundamentally a normative one that follows William Kornhauser's 1959 analysis of the volatile and demagogic potential in a mass society in which the traditional economic and communal groups become less inclusive (see also Hayes, 1983). In contrast to J. Schlesinger's argument that party theory must be based on empirical realities, we agree with Polsby that there is a normative element to our assessments of party functioning. Rather than tailoring our party theory to a "truncated" party system (i.e., an elite organization divorced from a mass base), our party theory must retain the capacity to compare different types of party systems in terms of their capacity for democratic government.[2] For this reason, we turn to a consideration of the parameters of the debate over party decline versus party resurgence.

PARTY DECLINE OR PARTY RESURGENCE?

During the early 1980s, most party scholars held that the party system was in decline (e.g., Crotty and Jacobson, 1984; Wattenberg, 1986; Polsby, 1983b; Kirkpatrick, 1979; Ladd and Hadley, 1975). In a 1983 survey of the state of the discipline in party research, Leon Epstein concludes that "the relative *ineffectiveness* of contemporary American parties is now our field's principal concern" (1983:146). However, some recent research on party organization indicates that this assessment may have been premature. In words reminiscent of Mark Twain, one group of party scholars remarked that "for at least twenty years, political scientists and journalists have been conducting a death watch over the American parties . . . [with] . . . some of the more impatient watchers . . . [conducting] . . . the obsequies without benefit of the corpse . . . " (Cotter, et al., 1984:168). In fact, by mid-decade a number of party scholars were either identifying signs of a resurgence of party (e.g., Cook, 1986; Frantzich, 1986; Herrnson, 1986; Kayden and Mahe, 1985) or arguing that parties had never really declined, but instead evolved from "episodic voluntary associations" to "modern institutionalized parties" (Cotter et al., 1984:168; see also J. Schlesinger, 1985).

The concern for the decline of the party system did not develop without good reason. The weight of earlier research focusing on the party-in-the-electorate concluded that the party system was dealigning. The proportion of party identifiers had gradually decreased, and ticket splitting became common even among strong identifiers (Crotty and Jacobson, 1984). Scholars amassed a great deal of evidence detailing the unraveling of the New Deal coalition—with no new realignment readily apparent (e.g., Ladd and Hadley, 1975). Writing in 1970, party realignment theorist Burnham focused on the phenomenon of electoral disaggregation by highlighting the "exceptionally rapid erosion of the behavioral hold of the old major parties on the American electorate" (1970:92). Phillip Converse dates the decline of the party-in-the-electorate from 1966 (1976; see also Nie, et al., 1976). Public support for the party system as a whole has decreased (Dennis, 1975). These findings, considered with the decline in voter turnout, led William Crotty and Gary Jacobson to identify a "nonvoter party" (1984). Martin Wattenberg argues that the American electorate is not negative toward the parties—they are simply neutral (1986).

Other changes in the American political system raised concern among many that the party organization itself was declining. While there are some notable dissents to the notion that parties perform essential functions in a democracy (e.g., Epstein, 1967:8; King, 1969; Sorauf, 1984:442), most party scholars have endorsed Schattschneider's characterization of party functions, " . . . whatever else they may or may not do, *the parties must make nominations*" (1942:101; emphasis in the original). Both the Democratic party and the U.S. Congress were extensively reformed in the early 1970s, with results that appeared to reduce this crucial role.

The reforms in the Democratic party began with the 1969 appointment of the Commission on Party Structure and Delegate Selection, popularly known as the McGovern–Fraser Commission after its two chairs, George McGovern, succeeded by Donald Fraser. The McGovern–Fraser Commission guidelines were incorporated in the Final Call to the 1972 Democratic Convention, issued in October 1971. In doing so, the Democratic party fundamentally reformed the presidential nominating process by implementing reforms that opened up the delegate selection process to all interested parties. The major reforms included provisions requiring due process in delegate selection (e.g., by requiring public notice of meetings and abolition of proxy voting), provisions requiring timeliness in delegate selection (the provision of a "window" for caucuses and primaries, requiring that the process be completed in the calendar year of the convention), abolition of the "unit" rule (providing for the proportional representation of candidate preferences), and provisions banning discrimination in the delegate selection process (e.g., by promoting the participation of disadvantaged minorities).[3] These reforms have been altered substantially with succeeding reform commissions for each Democratic convention since 1972; however, the fundamental result of the initial, and succeeding, reforms was to render the Democratic party more permeable to party activists.

We will discuss these party reforms in more detail in later chapters and make the argument that the fundamental consequence of reform was to democratize the party system. This has not been the view of traditional party scholars. Actually, since the 1972 Democratic National Convention, when many reforms were introduced and ratified, most scholars working within the traditional party perspective have agreed with the assessment of Byron Shafer that "at bottom, the result of all these reforms was *the diminution, the constriction, at times the elimination, of the regular party in the politics of presidential selection*" (1983:525; emphasis in the original).

Perhaps the most extensive series of reforms undertaken during this era were those enacted in the U.S. Congress beginning in 1970. In terms of the party, the most important single reform was the passage of the 1974 amendments to the Federal Election Campaign Act (FECA). FECA provided for public subsidy of presidential campaigns and limited individual and organizational (including party) contributions to congressional campaigns. The limitation on party contributions, according to some party scholars, enhanced the contributions of organized interest groups (and gave rise to political action committees or PACs) to the detriment of the party organization (Price, 1984:239–262).

The remaining reforms, which altered internal congressional organization and procedures, were enacted throughout the 1970s (Rieselbach, 1986). Some of the reforms affected both houses; some only the House and others the Senate; others still were enacted only within one party caucus. The reforms include redistributed committee power (e.g., by restricting the powers and resources of committee chairs, mandating [in the House] a "Subcommittee Bill of Rights," and limiting the number of committee and subcommittee chairmanships permitted), democratized decision making (e.g., by weakening the filibuster in the Senate and placing restrictions on the House Rules and Ways and Means Committees), increase congressional accountability (the "sunshine" reforms that opened committee hearings to the public and provided for recorded teller votes, television and radio coverage of committee hearings and House—and more recently, Senate—floor debate), and reassert congressional prerogatives (e.g., the War Powers Act, the Congressional Budget and Impoundment and Control Act, creation of the Office of Technology Assessment, and increased use of the legislative veto). While some reforms were implemented that were designed to strengthen the power of the party leadership (particularly among House Democrats, who enhanced the Speaker's power to make committee assignments and refer bills), the major consequence of the congressional reforms of the 1970s was to decentralize power in Congress. Not only were members of Congress less constrained by the party leadership's monopoly of power than in the past, but the "electoral connection" (Mayhew, 1974) was changing as well. The increasing importance of "home style" in legislator-district relations (Fenno, 1978) and the rise of incumbency as a voting cue in congressional elections— with party identifiers crossing party lines to vote for the incumbent (Jacobson, 1983)—further increased the independence of each individual member of Congress. As a consequence, party voting was declining in Congress (Crotty and Jacobson, 1984).

Concomitant with both sets of political reforms was perhaps the most fundamental of changes affecting the parties: the proliferation of primaries. Primaries remove the party's control over candidate nomination and allow outsider or insurgent candidates to run under the party label. The initial turn to primaries was a direct offshoot of the Progressive Era, with the first primaries adopted in 1901. By 1916, twenty-six states required presidential primaries. However, with the ebbing of reform sentiments, states began to repeal their primary laws such that by 1936, only sixteen states required primaries (Price, 1984:206–207). The use of primaries continued at this level until the 1968–1972 period. In 1968, seventeen states required Democratic primaries and sixteen required Republican primaries—each party selecting slightly over one-third of its delegates that way. By 1972, however, over one-half of the delegates were selected through primaries (twenty-three Democratic and twenty-two Republican primaries).

Some have attributed the rapid increase in primaries to the Democratic party reforms, citing the difficulty of complying with the complex McGovern–Fraser guidelines. "The result was an explosion in the number of primaries, quite unforeseen by most McGovern–Fraser Commission members—from seventeen in 1968 to twenty-three in 1972 to thirty in 1976" (Ladd, 1978:54; see also Polsby, 1983a; Kirkpatrick, 1979; Ranney, 1978). Others (e.g., Bode and Casey, 1980), however, have disputed the direct relationship, arguing that the increase in primaries resulted from a number of idiosyncratic reasons (e.g., a favorite son candidacy). David Price (now the Hon. David Price, D-NC) gives what we think is is a very thoughtful and judicious assessment.

In the wake of the 1968 Democratic contest (and before the adoption of the McGovern–Fraser Commission guidelines), primary laws were introduced in 13 states; some of the six primaries that eventually were added might have been established even without the new rules. Nevertheless, it is impossible to separate the proliferation of primaries from the workings of reform. The stress on participation and on reducing the control of party leaders created a climate favorable to primaries as the simplest mechanism for involving large numbers of people and responding directly to their preferences. (1983:207)

He points to the reform era (which resulted in changes in the U.S. Congress as well as in the Democratic party) as a major factor, and not simply the undeniable fact that the party leaders looked "favorably on primaries as the simplest way of achieving compliance" (1984:207). However, even if we exonerate Democratic party reform from initiating primaries, "there is little doubt that the current number and role of primaries sap party strength" (Price, 1984:211). Thus, for party scholars working within the traditional party paradigm, the party as an organization was less able to fulfill its traditional functions—not only was it less successful (than before) at structuring the electorate but it was apparently less active in recruiting and funding party candidates and in conducting campaigns (Ranney, 1975; Kirkpatrick, 1979).

These changes have been described by some (e.g., Salmore and Salmore, 1985) as resulting in a fundamental shift in electoral politics—shifting from party-centered campaigns to candidate-centered campaigns. The decline of the party has made room for a new power in American politics: the political campaign consultant (Sabato, 1981). In a profile of over twenty consultants, journalist Sidney Blumenthal argues that the result of this is that it is the consultants who "are permanent; the politicians are ephemeral" (1982:17). The doctrine of the consultants is the "permanent campaign." "The permanent campaign is the political ideology of our age. It combines image-making with strategic calculation. Under the permanent campaign governing is turned into a permanent campaign. . . . It seeks to restore the legitimacy of the state by maintaining the credibility of politicians" (1982:23).

Burnham incorporates Blumenthal's critique of the consultant corps in his analysis of the Reagan "revolution." According to Burnham, the Reagan realignment of the 1980s is fundamentally different from the earlier partisan realignments, "it was a *policy* realignment without *electoral* realignment" (1985:250). By this terminological distinction, Burnham focuses on the tandem appearance of partisan decomposition and electoral volatility at the mass level *and* an increasing ideological (and conservative) politics at the elite level. He terms this an *interregnum* era, marking a sixth electoral era (which, following Blumenthal, began in 1968). Burnham's analysis captures the main contours of contemporary politics, echoing *Washington Post* reporter Thomas Edsall's incisive analysis, *The New Politics of Inequality* (1984). Yet, Burnham's classification of the contemporary state of affairs as an "interregnum" also marks an interregnum in party theory.

One of the more thoughtful analyses of the negative changes deriving from the decreased role of parties is provided by Polsby (1983a). He argues that a central feature shared by traditional interest groups and party institutions is their *intermediary* role in linking the mass public to public officials. What is particularly problematic in the current era is that this intermediary role is now performed by the media—based on a new class of media elites and information specialists. According to Polsby, the media promotes a new type of (artificial) group that is oriented toward symbolic politics (i.e., the manipulation of symbols). These groups are artificial because they have no significant mass base. We find the "steady replacement of face-to-face, primary and geographically proximate interest groups with distant, symbolic and noninteractive mediation mechanisms" that Polsby argues results in declining political participation and mobilization among ordinary citizens (1983a:141). Consequently, they rely on mass persuasion in the media to obtain their goals, as opposed to the face-to-face contact of traditional communal and economic groups. According to Polsby, the promotion of these groups by news media has resulted in a decline in party coalitions, the heightening of factional interests, and a crisis in governing. Whether one attributes the source of these changes to "changes at the elite level" rather than to changes at the mass level as Polsby does, or to some other cause, his analysis, if correct, raises important normative issues about the capacity of contemporary parties for democratic governance.

With the reelection of Ronald Reagan in 1984, some scholars have begun to identify a resurgence of party. Yet, if Burnham and Polsby are correct, this resurgent party is a truncated one—divorced from any mass base. Warren Miller and M. Kent Jennings (1986:180–81), in a survey of convention delegates found an increase in ideological differences between parties from 1972 to 1980. Yet, convention delegates—compared to other party elite cadres—are *most* sensitive to the groups and activists participating in any single presidential nomination contest. According to the party resurgence thesis, the *sine qua non* indication of party resurgence is the dramatic rise in partisanship in the U.S. Congress. As J. Schlesinger concludes,

> the ultimate test of party linkage is the behavior of the party member in government. . . . Since 1968, . . . there has been a rise in cohesion scores for both parties. . . . In 1983, the Democratic Party reached a cohesion level impossible to find in the history of the party. This is truly remarkable for a party lacking the earlier mechanisms of discipline, and for a party we are so often told is coming apart. (1985:1168)

Party cohesion has increased not only among rank-and-file members, but among committee and subcommittee chairs—in part a reflection of the democratization of leadership recruitment (Smith and Deering, 1984).

Timothy Cook points out that in 1986 the level of party voting is reaching such high levels that, if continued, it will "rival the highest party voting since the New Deal Congresses" (1986:18). The proportion of party unity votes (defined as occurring when a majority of Democrats vote in opposition to a majority of Republicans) has indeed increased from 1970 (the pre-party reform era) to 1986, as seen in Figure 1.1. In recent years, over one-half of the recorded votes in Congress find Democrats and Republicans on opposing sides. While this remains much less than the proportion of party votes at the turn of the century, it does represent a significant increase over the 1950s.

An additional measure of the growing importance of *national* party unity— as opposed to *sectional* party unity—is the decline in the appearance of the "Conservation Coalition" (see Fig. 1.1). This is defined as occurring when a majority of southern Democrats vote with a majority of Republicans in opposition to a majority of northern Democrats and reflects the sectional ideological split in the Democratic party that has existed since the Civil War. The proportion of votes in which the Conservative Coalition has appeared has been nearly halved since 1969[4]. The increasing party responsibility among the "party-in-government"—despite the weakening of the centralized control of the institutional party leaders due to congressional reforms—supports the

Figure 1.1

Proportion of Party Unity and Conservative Coalition Voting, U.S. Congress, 1970–1986

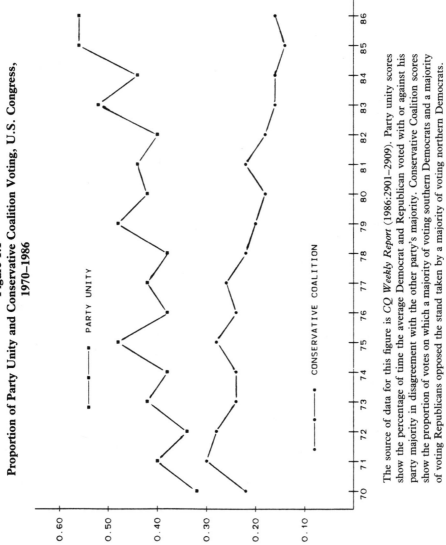

The source of data for this figure is *CQ Weekly Report* (1986:2901–2909). Party unity scores show the percentage of time the average Democrat and Republican voted with or against his party majority in disagreement with the other party's majority. Conservative Coalition scores show the proportion of votes on which a majority of voting southern Democrats and a majority of voting Republicans opposed the stand taken by a majority of voting northern Democrats.

argument made by scholars heralding the newly strengthened party organizations (Frantzich, 1986; Herrnson, 1986; Cotter et al., 1984; Kayden and Mahe, 1985; J. Schlesinger, 1985).

UNDERSTANDING THE "NEW" PARTY SYSTEM

What is the meaning of these new developments in terms of party theory? The contradictory data—increasing ideological and organizational coherence at the elite level, electoral disaggregation at the mass level, and the increasing professionalization of campaign consulting—have engendered a diversity of interpretations. Some still identify a decline of party (Crotty, 1985). Others have begun to study candidate campaigns as the central variable (Goldenberg and Traugott, 1984; Hershey, 1984; Jacobson, 1983). Many argue that what we have witnessed is a "new" party system—whether based on a "policy" rather than a "party" realignment (Burnham, 1985), or on a "realistic" party theory (first introduced in 1966) based on the office ambitions of candidates (Schlesinger, 1966; 1985). These latter approaches, which recognize a "new" party system, represent extensions of contemporary party theory that we review in Chapter 2. We now turn to the views of those who argue that we need a new conceptual framework to understand a new party system.

Redefining the Party: The "Truncated Party" Solution

Scholars who have studied the campaign activities of the national parties argue in favor of a redefinition of the political party. Xandra Kayden and Eddie Mahe (a political consultant and former deputy chairman of the Republican National Committee) describe the party system as a "phoenix . . . risen from the ashes" (1985:3)—a new political species. While little direct supporting evidence is offered, Kayden and Mahe argue that the selective application of national party resources can influence government policy, "if the party recruits and trains candidates and provides the backbone of their campaigns, they are likely to end up as a more homogeneous group and more inclined to be team players" (1985:196).

Paul Herrnson (1986) identifies a new model of the party based on his interviews with the professional staff of the three national committees of each party (i.e., the Democratic and Republican National Committees (DNC and RNC, respectively), the Democratic and National Republican Senatorial Campaign Committees (DSCC and NRSC, respectively), and the House campaign committees (the Democratic Congressional Campaign Committee [DCCC] and the National Republican Congressional Committee [NRCC]). Herrnson proposes that following the demise of the "party-as-machine" model (late nineteenth and early twentieth century United States) and the "party-as-peripheral" model (the contemporary image of the declining party), we should define the party as a "broker." The party-as-broker proposed by

Herrnson focuses on the diversity of campaign resources selectively distributed by the campaign committees of the national parties.

Stephen Frantzich (1986) proposes that parties be reconceptualized as a "service-vendor." For Frantzich, the new role of the parties incorporates a new component of the party, the party-in-the-campaign. "The party-in-the-campaign refers to those candidate support activities provided or coordinated by the party and which involve other than those individuals involved in the other components" (the party-in-the-electorate, party-in-organization, and party-in-office) (1986:2). These activities include candidate recruitment, candidate and campaign staff training; voter lists, registration, and get-out-the-vote drives; opposition research; opinion polling; campaign advertising; and postelection assistance. Frantzich, among others (e.g., Cotter et al., 1984; Salmore and Salmore, 1985), conceives of these changes as "Republicanizing" the parties. This refers to the notion that the "Republican model" of reform has been to concentrate on "competitive" reforms—reflected in their electoral success—while the Democrats have concentrated on "expressive" reforms, encouraging internal party participation (Salmore and Salmore, 1985:212–213).[5]

Christopher Arterton proposed a "PAC model" of parties (1982:132). This party-as-PAC model represents an ideal type toward which Arterton suggests parties might evolve. The increasing role of the parties in channeling funds toward candidates minimizes the deleterious effects of single-issue groups, PACs, and the candidate-centered campaign. He specifically cautions against the possibility of an ideological based "responsible party system" such as implied by Kayden and Mahe (1985). A strengthened national party may take advantage of "economies of scale in the technologies of communication," but they are not able to ignore or eliminate the diversity of state and local parties, serve as the instruments of citizen involvement in politics, or promote face-to-face contacts (1982:136). Arterton here acknowledges the "truncated" nature of the party-as-PAC model.

The Normative Dilemma Posed by Traditional Party Theory

The "truncated party" offered by the party organization perspective defines away the normative problem posed by traditional party thought. According to traditional party theorists, modern political parties are inextricably linked with democracy (Epstein, 1983). In the oft-quoted words of Schattschneider, "political parties created democracy and . . . modern democracy is unthinkable save in terms of the parties" (1942:1). The rise of parties, according to Schattschneider, occurred through the ever "expanding universe of politics." Parties compete for support, and thus have expanded from merely an organized caucus contained entirely within the legislature to include a "party organization in the electorate." Hence, "the enlargement of the *practicing electorate* has been one of the principal labors of the parties" (1942:48–49; emphasis in the original).

Similarly, the work of Key makes a sharp distinction between "factions" and "parties." In his study of southern politics (1950), Key argues that the one-party politics of southern states did not provide democratic competition. Instead, the factions are "multifaceted, discontinuous, kaleidoscopic, fluid, [and] transient" (1964:302). Lacking continuity in their name, and in the makeup of their inner core of professional politicians or leaders, "they also lack continuity in voter support which, under two-party conditions, provides a relatively stable following of voters for each party's candidates whoever they may be" (1964:303). Because of this distinction, Chambers points out that the "Federalists and Anti-Federalists in the years 1787–89 were also not parties, but rather congeries of local groups, factions, leaders and cliques, or other molecular elements of politics" (1967:5).

The central contribution of parties to democracy is their simplification of the alternatives in their organized attempt to win control of the government. While Schattschneider points out that parties are not "vast associations of partisans" (1942:58), they do involve a working collaboration of "ignorant people and experts" (1960:137). Thus democracy, according to traditional party theory, is both produced by parties and is the genesis of parties (Schattschneider, 1942, 1960; Key, 1950, 1964). "Democracy is a competitive political system in which competing leaders and organizations define the alternatives of public policy in such a way that the public can participate in the decision-making process . . . " (Schattschneider, 1960:141).

The criticisms of the new party system posed by party scholars working within the traditional party theoretical paradigm focus on the decline of "democracy." Hence, these new conceptions that propose a (truncated) re-definition of the party do not deal with the most pointed of Polsby's criticisms: the apparent decline of grass-roots politics and the growing gulf between elite and mass. Redefining the party to be a new political "animal" (e.g., Kayden and Mahe, 1985:4) does not tell us whether the prospects for democracy have diminished. And it is the parties' role as the linchpin of democratic polities that has fueled the scholarly commitment to parties as unique institutions (Epstein, 1983). As Schattschneider pointed out many years ago, the pressure group system is flawed as a mechanism for representation because "the flaw in the pluralist heaven is that the heavenly chorus sings with a strong upper-class accent" (1960:35). It is only the party institution that can expand the scope of the conflict to the public sphere and represent those who have no other avenue of representation.

The normative issue remains: can parties still serve as a vehicle for dem-ocratic politics? The dilemma of the proposed redefinition of the party system is that it is based on a truncated party and a party system that includes voters only as consumers. Whether our party theory should be scaled down to accommodate the twin phenomena of apparent (mass) party decline and (elite) party resurgence is an empirical question as well. Resolution of the normative issue revolves around just how one defines democracy and the proper relationship of elites and masses. We shall address both of these issues in more detail in Chapters 2 and 3. For the present, we turn to other—empirical *and* conceptual—reasons for refraining from a wholesale redefinition of political parties.

Limitations of the Truncated Party Solution

We view the proposal to redefine the political parties as campaign organizations dominated by professional staffs as unnecessary for four reasons. First, this proposal seems a drastic solution to dissatisfaction with contemporary definitions of the party system. Clearly, as we show in Chapter 2, there are serious problems with current party theory. But, we believe that reconceptualizing the parties as a "Super-PAC" or as a "Super-consulting firm" is empirically inaccurate because it ignores the gradual organizational development and nationalization of the national parties since the 1920s. As Cornelius Cotter recently pointed out,

party records in the presidential libraries indicate many of the party practices of today are reflected in the party experience of the 1940s and 1950s. The Democratic National Committee (DNC) was, by the mid–1940s, investing in congressional campaigns ... and in the early 1950s the DNC was allocating funds to the Democratic Congressional Campaign Committee. The DNC may have pioneered direct mail sustaining fundraising under Mitchell's leadership in the 1950s. ... In summary, the tendrils of today's "modern" parties reach back into the 1950s. ... (1986:672–673).

The increasing organizational vitality of the party organizations is not a new phenomenon—as the party resurgence thesis implies—but merely an intensification of a secular trend evident since at least the 1950s. As Epstein concludes, it is the "previous absence" of strong national party organizations rather than their relatively recent arrival that was "an anomaly in a political and social system already predominantly national in so many other respects" (1986:238).

Second, we believe that this redefinition of the party does a grave misjustice to the goal-oriented nature of the party organization. Parties *may* represent a relatively issueless psychological attachment at the mass level, but it most certainly is an issue-based attachment at the elite level. At their core, parties are comprised of individuals who share similar views of the world and of the proper role of government in addressing social and economic problems. Focusing primarily on the organizational attributes of the parties ignores the essential purposive, ideological, and representational nature of the party organization. Of course, we do not wish to overstress this point. As Schattschneider pointed out in considering the motives for which party elites seek power, "a thousand men want power for a thousand different reasons" (1942:36). Yet, the critical fact about parties is that *"parties are mutually exclusive, whereas pressure groups are not"* (Schattschneider, 1942:198; emphasis in the original). Because parties compete against each other, the simple fact is that one must choose sides. One cannot be both a Democrat and a Republican.

Political parties are unlike any other large bureaucratic organization in this regard (Eldersveld, 1964). Political parties do not merely wish to survive and prosper vis-à-vis other political organizations, but to prevail by implementing their own political vision. To accomplish this, parties must remain permeable to new members at all levels—from the volunteer worker to the elite apex. The growing issue and ideological basis of the party attachment (discussed in Chapter 3) represents a sea change in American politics—present among the attentive public as well as among elite activists and party regulars.

The porous nature of the parties is antithetical to the bureaucratic structure. Max Weber conceived of bureaucracies as based on the principles of hierarchy, expertise, task specialization, fixed rules of behavior, and impersonality (rather than individual discretion) in the handling of individual cases (Gerth and Mills, 1953). These characteristics allow no room for political processes. In Weber's view, "the absolute monarch is powerless opposite the superior power of the trained bureaucrat" (quoted in Gerth and Mills, 1953:234). Parties are in conflict with bureaucracies (Shefter, 1978) and, in this conflict, parties should not be confused as an analogue or organizational copy of the bureaucracy.

Although party leadership cadres may indeed have some *esprit de corps*, this is quite different from that of a bureaucratic cadre. In the latter case, *esprit de corp* rests heavily on vocational security, professional associations, expectations of permanency, and a desire to protect the group from its environment. The party, however, is an open structure; tenure is unstable; personal relationships are uncertain. Thus power vanishes easily within a political party. . . . (Eldersveld, 1964:11)

The essentially political nature of the successful, permeable, and adaptive party is not compatible with bureaucratic organization and norms.

Third, discussion of the strengthened national parties invariably focuses on the increasing levels of education and professionalization among party staff—almost to the exclusion of party committee members. It is well to remember that at least two-thirds of the members of the Democratic and all of the members of the Republican National Committees are comprised of individuals appointed by the state parties.[6] The congressional campaign committees (the DSCC, DCCC, NRCC, and NRSC) are composed of members of Congress. These party committees are not dominated by a permanent in-house staff—but are run by officials with regular positions within the party.[7]

Certainly, the party organization is strengthened and modernized insofar as the political party "hack" is being replaced by trained staff—but this has not changed who is in charge—the party elite cadres and elected officials.

Finally, the idea that the mere provision of services does anything more than assist in the chances of electing more members of one's party is undemonstrated. Interviewing professional staff who are in the habit of talking to the press and wish to put a favorable "spin" on their party's chances is insufficient evidence to prove influence. And that is the essential fact to prove. How else could we explain the increase in ideological cohesion in Congress under this model? The major criterion used by the party in supporting a candidate for federal office is electability, not ideological consistency. Once elected, incumbents do not require party support. And, of course, the congressional parties always support their incumbents. While the party committees may use their dollars strategically, rather than just relieving their incumbents of the onerous task of fund-raising, in no case have they supported challengers over their own party's incumbent. At this point, we have no evidence of freshmen senators or representatives supporting the party position out of gratitude (on this point, see Salmore and Salmore, 1985:223–236).

For these reasons, we do not find the proposed reconceptualization of the party an acceptable resolution for the apparent contradictions of party decline and party resurgence. Yet, the recent upsurge in party cohesion—and the decline in the appearance of the conservative coalition—is a phenomenon that still requires explanation. The old party system rested on the judicious use of "carrots and sticks" by the party leadership—logrolling and trading of votes, the granting of desired committee assignments, and the loss or threat of loss of committee assignments. As former House Speaker Sam Rayburn said, "to get along, one must go along." With the introduction of congressional reform, the availability of these leadership tools has been restricted. How else can one explain party cohesion? The party organizational approach has turned to the congressional campaign committees and their provision of election assistance. Yet, as explained above, we simply find this a weak reed on which to base leadership pressure. After all, with the rise in incumbency return rates (over 97 percent for the House in 1986) and the decline in marginal seats, there are no electoral carrots and sticks for the leadership to proffer. All that is left is simple gratitude—a notoriously unstable foundation in politics.

It is our argument that there are overall fewer external pressures to enforce conformity—and thus, the party organizational explanation is insufficient to explain the upsurge in party cohesion. Therefore, we are in agreement with the position advanced by Burnham and others that the increase in party cohesion rests on a true increasing ideological divergence among political party elites. This, however, returns us to the problem of the interregnum in party theory.

THE THEORETICAL CRISIS IN PARTY RESEARCH

Our rejection of the proposed reconceptualization leaves us with some unanswered questions. First, why did traditional party theory unravel? Why is it that the party theory of Michels, Duverger, Merriam, Gosnell, Schattschneider, Key, and Eldersveld—our first generation of party theorists—fail to explain the interregnum identified by Burnham and others? This is the question we seek to answer in Chapter 2. We will argue that the wealth of behavioral research on political parties that built on the theory provided by the first generation of party theorists separated into three distinct strands of research. These researches provided rich contextual understanding of only one aspect at a time of the tripartite American party structure—the party-in-office, the party-in-the-organization, and the party-in-the-electorate. Yet, this increased focus on the "trees" resulted in a lessened sensitivity to the "forest": as a discipline, we have lost sight of the *dynamism* of the early party theory. We aim here to focus attention on the relation of elites and masses, and on the bases of conflict of the party system—factors essential to a *dynamic* conceptualization of the present party system.

Second, we must next consider why we are left with this unacceptable dilemma: how can we explain the simultaneous appearance of increased ideology in the party system alongside continuing electoral disaggregation without recourse to a truncated definition of parties? We will address this problem in Chapter 4 by incorporating social movement theory into contemporary party theory. Our basic thesis is that previous party theory was based on a conceptualization of traditional interest groups based on pluralism. The appearance of new social movements, informed by a group consciousness, has appeared inexplicable. We will argue that these new groups represent an ideological revitalization of the Democratic and Republican parties that *provides the missing link—a mass base for the party system.*

We do not view the vast changes that the political parties have undergone as negative ones. On the contrary, we will argue—and produce empirical evidence to document—that the parties are both pragmatic *and* ideological, and that the reforms adopted by the parties were undertaken in a democratic response to pressure by social movements.

NOTES

1. We use the term "coalition" here in the traditional party sense. The new groups are not politically neutral—they are tied to one of the parties. Working within *a* party framework requires the groups to negotiate among themselves. This is different from a "faction," particularly in the sense used by Key in *Southern Politics in State and Nation* (1950). A faction, for Key, was fleeting because it depended on the strength of a particular leader or clique. By contrast, the new elite coalitions—while new to

the political scene—are not ephemeral, but, in Chambers's terms (1967), relatively enduring aspects of the social formation of the new party system.

2. We have adopted the term truncated from Kay Lawson (1978:174).

3. The unit rule resulted in "winner-take-all" primaries. A candidate who obtained a majority (or plurality) of the vote would receive all of the delegate votes from that state. This, in practice, provided for a southern veto of Democratic nominees and aided front-runners and candidates with sectional, as opposed to national, support.

4. For 1987 (through July 21), the proportion of conservative coalition votes was down to a remarkable 7.5 percent (Ehrenhalt, 1987:1699).

5. Jo Freeman (1986) critiques this notion based on the different political cultures of the two parties. Implicit to this comparison are beliefs that there is one route to electoral success (professionalization of campaigns), that the Republican model is the successful one, and that the major result of Democratic party reforms is electoral failure. We address these assumptions in a later chapter.

6. The RNC is composed of the state party chairpersons, plus one national committeeman and one committeewoman from each state and territory. The DNC has a somewhat more complex structure: the fifty-two state and territorial chairmen or chairwomen, the highest-ranking officer of the opposite sex, plus some 200 national committee members appointed to the states on the basis of population (each state has at least two committeepersons) and a small number of representatives of other party cadres (e.g., governors, county chairs, Young Democrats, and so forth).

7. Among the party committees, the committee meetings are usually held *in the absence* of the staff. As opposed to the notion of a "staff-dominated" committee, policy decisions are the prerogative of the committee, *not* the staff.

2

The Unraveling of Traditional Party Theory

INTRODUCTION

As Kenneth Janda observed, "party organizations are the leprechauns of the political forest, legendary creatures with special powers who avoid being seen" (1983). This apparently ephemeral nature of political parties has made defining parties an inherently unsatisfactory process. Early works on the party system (e.g., Key, 1950, 1955, 1959; Eldersveld, 1964; Schattschneider, 1942, 1960; Duverger, 1954; Merriam, 1922; Michels, 1915) sought to develop an integrated and overarching party theory. It is the work of these party scholars (the first generation of party theorists) that we refer to as *traditional party theory*. Some scholars (e.g., Sartori, 1976) have maintained that we have never had a party theory worthy of the name. Whether or not party theory is truly scientific, or only "prebehavioral" (Wahlke, 1979), is not the question we wish to pose. Our concern is with the unraveling of traditional party theory: parties themselves have not declined, they are transformed. Yet, we have been unable to recognize the nature of the transformation because the dynamic party theory of our first generation of party scholars has become ossified with the flowering of the behavioral revolution in empirical party research.

The vast outpouring of behavioral research in the 1960s and 1970s resulted in a splintering of *party* research into several specialized subfields of a more properly termed *party-related* research. While the independent development of these specializations added greatly to our understanding of individual variables, the immediate and critical consequence has been a decreased attention to how these variables interrelated. Traditional party theory, by contrast, paid as much attention to the dynamic interaction of party variables as it did to the mapping of each individual element.

Traditionally, political parties have been viewed as a distinctive social formation whose purpose is to link the elites who govern with the masses who do not. As such, they are essential to democracy in modern polities. Traditional party theorists focused on the ties between elites and masses, although they have disagreed on the actual process of representation. The work of traditional party theorists has culminated in two basic models of the party system: the empirically based model of *indigenous* or conventional *American parties* (e.g., Banfield, 1980b; see also Epstein, 1983) and the idealistic or normative model of *responsible party government* as outlined by the 1950 report of the American Political Science Committee on Political Parties, chaired by E. E. Schattschneider. Both of these models rest on a similar assessment of voters as *choosers* between the parties, differing primarily in the extent to which the party organization was held to be collectively responsible for the conduct of government. Both models of the American party system acknowledge an existing gulf between elite and mass, but one which the responsible party school sought to close.

The APSA Committee report (1950) was greeted with a round of criticism.[1] Except for a few isolated scholars (e.g., Pomper, 1971; Saloma and Sontag, 1973), the dominant reaction was to reconceive *is* as what *ought* to be. The derivative research built on this foundation—treating this gulf between elites and the coalitional groups they represent as a normative ideal, rather than simply an empirical description of the party system of the 1950s and early 1960s. Not only was it generally accepted that the United States Constitution, the federal structure of government, and the American political structure provide an inhospitable environment for "responsible" parties of the British model—but, for most, the indigenous American parties provided the *best* party system (Banfield, 1980b; see also Epstein, 1983). This dominant preference for the party system of the 1950s and early 1960s yielded a benchmark against which party decline may be measured (e.g., Polsby, 1983a, 1983b; Kirkpatrick, 1979).

The sharp contrast between the *empirical* indigenous American parties and the *normative* (and foreign) model of responsible parties obscured the fundamental characteristic of traditional party theory—its dynamism. As opposed to a static reflection of their relatively constant political environment, the first generation of party theorists (in particular, Schattschneider) viewed parties as part of a constantly evolving system that represented the dominant lines of political cleavage in society. Writing in 1960—notably well before the era of the "decline of parties" thesis—Schattschneider identified a trend toward the nationalization of conflict and a more ideologically based partisan cleavage, with the decline of sectional based conflicts. Yet, writers such as Nelson Polsby (1983a) and Jeane Kirkpatrick (1979) attributed an increase in what they viewed as ideological "extremism" not to basic secular changes in political cleavages, but to the party reforms first instituted by the Democrats beginning in 1968–1972. For Polsby and Kirkpatrick, change is not an inherent part of the party system (as Schattschneider argued), but rather, an extrinsic factor externally imposed. Against the benchmark of the indigenous American party system, change—any change—represented decline, not evolutionary growth. Thus, the idealization of the indigenous American parties rationalized the ossification of traditional party theory. Beyond the obvious satisfaction most party scholars felt toward the old party system described by the traditional party model, how did traditional party theory unravel? We believe that the answer can be found in the tripartite methodological compartmentalization of party research, to which we now turn.

THREE DEFINITIONS OF THE PARTY SYSTEM

It is a commonplace among party scholars to refer to the tripartite American party structure drawing on the work of Frank Sorauf (1984) and V. O. Key (1964). According to this conceptualization, the *party* consists of the party-in-the-electorate, the party-in-organization, and the party-in-office. The *party* is an abstraction, resting on an amalgamation of the three constituent elements, none of which can stand alone, but together, comprise the party. Sorauf, for example, describes the individuals who people the parties as follows. "The major American political parties are in truth three-headed political giants, tripartite systems of interactions, that embrace all these individuals" (1984:8).

A simplistic rendering of the tripartite party structure has given rise to a superficial model of traditional party theory—one in which the elite and mass distinction is erased. However useful in portraying the decentralized structure of the indigenous American party system, this commonplace "textbook mode of analysis" (Schlesinger, 1984:341) rests on a fundamental misunderstanding of traditional party theory. As we have argued above, the relationship of elites and masses is a central element of traditional party theory. In this context, Anthony King commented:

It is common in the United States for writers on parties to refer to "the party-in-the-electorate," sometimes as if it were on a par with the party in Congress or the party organization. The notion of party-in-the-electorate seems a strange one on the face of it. It is rather as though one were to refer not to the buyers of Campbell's soup but to the Campbell-Soup-Company-in-the-Market. (1969:114)

Following King, we term this conceptualization of parties the "Campbell soup" model of the parties (depicted in Fig. 2.1). The party concept is abstracted from the three separate constituent parts: party supporters, organizations, and elected officeholders. The theoretical concept of the party requires the "whole cloth," but each part may be considered as a separate unit, and it is precisely this separability that has given rise to three distinct freestanding lines of research.

Criticisms of the "unholy trinity" (Ware, 1985; see also Joseph Schlesinger, 1984) have focused on the Campbell soup model, not on traditional party

Figure 2.1
The "Campbell Soup" Definition of Party: A Three-Legged Stool

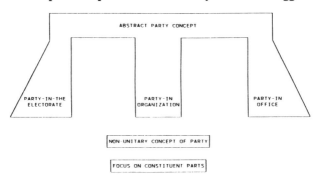

theory. We distinguish the Campbell soup model from traditional party theory, which we depict in Figure 2.2. As noted above, a major difficulty with the Campbell soup model is its distortion of the centrality of the elite-mass distinction contained in traditional party theory.

The traditional party definition is based on a dynamic conceptualization of the party system. In place of the "three-legged stool" capped by an abstract concept (the Campbell soup model), our theoretical understanding may be visualized as a "two-legged stool" in which the political elites are linked to a differentiated partisan electorate through strong party identification (the traditional party model). For elites, politics represents a phenomenon of immediate interest, whereas for the mass, politics is of distant concern. Party identification arises out of group identification, not through ideological concerns or issue preferences. Elites are elected to office through mobilizing their partisans in the electorate—independents comprise a small group usually irrelevant to electoral success. The partisans are mobilized primarily through local party contact, not through the media. Following Richard Jensen (1969), we term this the militarist campaign style. The strength of the party habit among the electorate permits the undifferentiated elites to govern through pragmatic compromise, not collective responsibility.

It is important to recognize that the traditional party model was a *conclusion* drawn from traditional party theory. In other words, it represented the *sum*, not the *substance* of traditional party theory. It is this model that party researchers have relied on as a common theoretical core in their party research, regardless of the particular study population they used (party-in-the-electorate, party-in-organization, or party-in-office) *in their research design*. Methodologically, most party research (at least on the national parties) has proceeded along the lines of the Campbell soup definition. With a few exceptions (Jackson, Brown, and Bositis, 1982; Montjoy et al., 1980; Kirkpatrick, 1976; McClosky et al., 1960), party research has not incorporated party elites and supporters *in the same research design*. In other words, party

Figure 2.2
The "Traditional Party" Definition of Party: A Two-Legged Stool

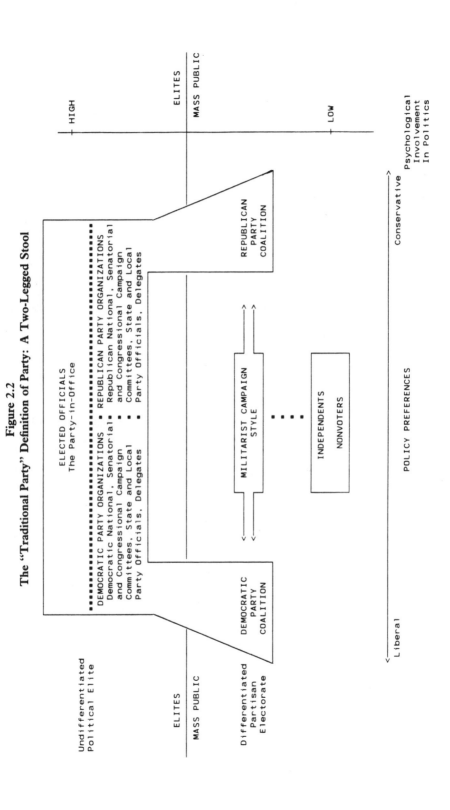

theory was based on a linkage of elites and masses (the traditional party model), yet in practice, party researchers studied elite and mass behavior as separate phenomena (the Campbell soup model). The separation of theory and methodology in party research has left party theory in a time warp. The party system has changed—but our theory has not. With the hypertrophy of compartmentalized party-related research, we have failed to revise our party theory to meet changing party circumstances.

We will document the unraveling of contemporary party theory by comparing the different conclusions drawn by party researchers, which depend in large part on which portion of the party they study. Our intent in this overview is not to comprehensively review all related research, but to extract conceptions of the party developed in each type of research and examine the perspectives adopted on elite-mass relations and on change in the party system. What we seek to show is that an extension of current party theory is insufficient. Extending present party theory will not resolve the proliferation of counterfactuals nor explain the changing group activity both within and outside of the party system. We will argue that what is required to understand the contemporary party system is a *synthesis* of the three types of party research. Only by doing so can we understand the metamorphosis of the party system.

Mass-Level Research

We turn first to voting behavior research. As indicated in the previous chapter, it is this definition of the party that has supported the decline of party thesis. The strength of this line of research—long considered the most scientific of political science subfields (Asher, 1983)—has rendered this approach a particularly attractive vantage point from which to study parties.

The Party-in-the-Electorate. Charles Merriam pointed out a half century ago that fundamental to any scientific study of parties is a focus on the role of social groups in politics. "The broad basis of the party is the interests, individual or group, usually group interests, which struggle to translate themselves into types of social control acting through the political process of government" (1922:2). Following Merriam, studies of the party-in-the-electorate have traditionally viewed the party as a coalition based in the psychological attachment of groups of voters to one of the two major parties (Kamieniecki, 1985; Petrocik, 1981).

The early voting studies of the Columbia school (Berelson et al., 1954; Lazarsfeld et al., 1944) included no direct measures of parties and instead analyzed the vote by inferring party affiliation from social and economic group memberships. The introduction of the individualistic social psychological approach in political science in *The American Voter* (Campbell, et al., 1960) did not undermine the coalitional interpretation of the parties. On the contrary, the authors of *The American Voter* explain the development of party identification through early socialization in the family and the social forces that differentially impact on community and group members (Campbell et al., 1960:146–167). Both the Columbia school and *The American Voter* assume that voters align themselves on a relatively permanent basis with one of the two established parties through their membership in social and community groups.

This definition of party, while focusing on the mass electorate, does not incorporate a positive construction of the capacities of the average voter. While *The American Voter* described the party identifiers as more interested in and informed about politics than those independent of party, the portrayal was of a "dependent" voter, not one "responsive" to changing government policies (Pomper, 1975). "Partisanship thus plays a useful role for party leaders: it gives them a base of support in the electorate which can generally (within limits) be depended upon to view their actions in a favorable light" (Wattenberg, 1986:12).

The opportunities for demagogic leadership and "flash" parties are much less when citizens identify with the established parties (Converse and Dupeux, 1966). The enduring attachments of identifiers to the parties, impervious as they were to the policies adopted by political elites in the party platforms and into law, allowed maximum flexibility for political compromise—a system many saw as desirable (Epstein, 1983). Note here the opposition between an undesirable (extremist) ideological party system versus the "American" (pragmatic) decentralized party system. The indigenous American party system was based in immediate social and solidary ties among mass-party supporters—with the party functioning as an intermediating institution linking individuals at the mass level to political elites. While this intermediation did not necessarily result in a quid pro quo in public policy, it did provide social cement for a stable society.

It is important to recognize that the coalitional approach incorporates both a theory of the relation of elites and masses, pluralism (Truman, 1958), and a theory of the probable consequences of the decline of intermediary groups, i.e., the theory of mass society (Kornhauser, 1959). David Truman argued that the political activities of interest groups only represent a stage of activity. The fundamental importance of groups lies in their ubiquitousness: groups are shared attitudes that are formed through habitual interaction. Thus, primary (or face-to-face) groups comprise the basic social units in society—all opinion is formed in this group context. Groups in the United States are characterized by *pluralism*, i.e., overlapping memberships that moderate their political goals. Groups are governed by leaders (who are in the functional position to make decisions for the groups); unorganized groups tend to be represented by "demagogic" leaders (Truman, 1958:441).

The *pluralist* society, according to William Kornhauser, is characterized by a citizenry "unavailable" for (remote) political involvement because their time and energy are monopolized by a variety of (proximate) concerns. Group memberships are essential for stability: individuals at the mass level are expected to be "indifferent or only superficially interested [in politics] unless they were involved in some sort of group activity *through which distant events are linked to proximate meanings*" (Kornhauser, 1959:65; emphasis in the original). The *mass* society, on the other hand, is characterized by atomized and socially isolated individuals who tend to be apathetic and ill-informed on public matters. However, "in times of crisis a greater proportion of people with few proximate concerns discard apathy and engage in mass movements outside of and against the institutional order" (1959:64). The strong, yet overlapping group memberships of the pluralistic society insulate the masses from the dangers of demagogic elite leaders, thereby restraining the potential for direct participation, and allowing elites to lead by "protecting the structure of authority" (1959:59).

Thus, the coalitional approach rests on a "trustee" conception of elite representation and change would normally be incremental.

There would be a high degree of continuity between administrations elected from different parties. Elections would not shake the nation to its foundation because the competing parties would be fundamentally in agreement. Agreement would be so built in by countless compromises within the parties a change of party would seldom entail complete reversal of policy in an important matter. (Banfield, 1980b:140)

The function of party elites was not to represent—either demographically or through the direct enactment of policy preferences—but to aggregate, and in doing so, moderate diverse political positions and demands. This approach assumes a differentiated electorate (tied psychologically and socially to one of the two parties)—but an undifferentiated elite. In contrast to the socialist working-class party, American parties have been dominated by the middle class. "Even though the Democrats have often had a heavy working-class vote, they have been a middle-class party in leadership and organization" (Epstein, 1967:130). Consider this description of the Democratic and Republican party convention delegations from the period covered by *The American Voter:*

They are as a group overwhelmingly white and male—about 90 percent male and 98 percent white in the 1952 conventions. They are Protestant, although less dominantly so within the Democratic Party. They are, furthermore, well-educated and well-off. A large percentage are lawyers (over 35% in 1948) and either public officials or high ranking party officials. As a group they appear representative of activists in the two parties. (Sorauf, 1968:260)

While this description focuses on convention delegations in the 1950s—according to William Crotty and John S. Jackson III (1985)—this description was accurate as far back as 1831–1832 and extending until at least the 1968 conventions. Cornelius Cotter and Bernard Hennessy (1964) document the same point in terms of the national party committees.

The coalitional approach allows for occasional and dramatic disruptions among political elites and reversals of government policy. While the "normal" election would maintain the current alignment of groups, a realignment could take place during a *critical* election (Sundquist, 1973; Burnham, 1970; Key, 1955). Although there is some disagreement whether a realignment occurs simply by restructuring the partisan distribution (or coalitional bases) of the parties—and thereby redefining the basis of conflict between the parties (Schattschneider, 1960; Campbell and Trilling, 1979:83)—or whether this restructuring must also reverse the majority status of the parties (Pomper, 1968), there is considerable agreement that realignment requires a rapid expansion of the electorate and issues of high intensity (usually tied to a crisis). The critical election is "an election type in which the depth and intensity of electoral involvement are high, in which more or less profound readjustments occur in the relations of power within the community, and in which new and durable electoral groupings are formed" (Key, 1955:4). Key later expanded the realignment concept to include a *secular* realignment based on a gradual but permanent change in the partisan composition of the electorate (1959). While a secular realignment takes place through nonpolitical demographic changes in the electorate (e.g., differential birthrates or migration patterns between political coalitions) that culminate in different political generations, realignments generally occur through the evolution of polarizing issues (Carmines and Stimson, 1984).

The critical or realigning election follows a period of dealignment. Party theorists assume that a realignment must be triggered at the electoral level: it is widespread and permanent dissatisfaction with the current party-in-office *at the mass level* that provides the causal impetus for change at the elite level. It is this emphasis that encapsules the weakness in the party coalitional approach as currently developed. Social change has undoubtedly taken place—but thus far without a party realignment—according to several of the newer coalitional theorists (e.g., Wattenberg, 1986; Ginsberg and Shefter, 1985).

Prominent realignment theorists agree. James Sundquist concludes that the major effect of the polarizing issues of the 1960s was to crosscut and weaken the New Deal alignment without producing a new party alignment (1973). Walter Dean Burnham argues that the stabilization of the economy via Keynesian economics has removed "an important stimulus or 'trigger' for partisan realignment in electoral politics"—in other words, the stabilization of the economic cycles has also stabilized the political "business cycle" (1985:252). The continuing electoral disaggregation at the mass level provides no explanation for the increasing ideological coherence at the elite level—the causal trigger is absent. It is for this reason that Burnham, citing Sidney Blumenthal (1982), recently adopted the awkward language of referring to the current party system as a realigned one—but one which has undergone a "policy" realignment at the elite level, rather than a "party" realignment at the mass level (1985:250). For Burnham, it is this which comprises the "interregnum" in the party system: elites have become differentiated, while the decline of the party in the electorate has led to an undifferentiated mass public. Following Burnham, we term this the *interregnum model* of the party, as depicted in Figure 2.3. This new model represents an inversion of the traditional party model: elites have changed, the mass has only responded.

The status of contemporary party theory based on party coalitions (the interregnum model) provides very little guidance about the process of elite leadership. Beyond the assumption that political elites will act as trustees, we gain little insight as to the motivations of party elite cadres. Martin Shefter (1978) argues that the party is no longer the primary arena of conflict among elites. As concisely summarized by Joseph Cooper and Louis Maisel,

Shefter argues that social change, which has been used to explain "critical realignments" in the American party system, is a contributing but not a sufficient cause for the changes he sees in parties and bureaucracy and the relationship between the two. Rather, Shefter maintains that the variables he examines have been used as tools in ongoing party struggles in the United States. He maintains that American parties are on the decline today in part at least because the major struggles for power are taking place outside of the party system. Party in this case is a dependent variable which can be explained in terms of the strategies of those struggling for power. Party is on the decline today because it is irrelevant to that more significant power struggle. (1978:27)

In viewing the public as having little capacity to analyze public policies, a party coalitional theorist is reduced to blaming "elite political maneuvering" for the concurrent phenomena of party decline and resurgence (Wattenberg, 1986:126; see also Burnham, 1985; Sandoz and Crabb, 1985; Shefter, 1978). The mass electorate has not changed—in Martin Wattenberg's adaptation of Key's phrase, the public remains an "echo chamber"—but the elite power struggle has altered its battleground.[2]

The Theoretical Gap in Voting Behavior Research. The party coalitional approach, from an early emphasis on the group support for parties in traditional party theory, is now firmly based in the sociopsychological concept of party identification. The focus on party identification treats the central variable as static—the decline of party is inferred by measuring the lessening influence of the long-term factor, party identification. Students of party organization (e.g., Cotter and Bibby, 1980) and critics of the voting behavior research (e.g., Natchez, 1985) have long argued that defining party as located in the electorate is reductionistic, ignores central issues of democratic linkage, and results in the absurdity of assuming that "the will of the people alone directed government and policy" (Natchez, 1985:46). We concur in this assessment; yet it is critical to also note that the inability to address the

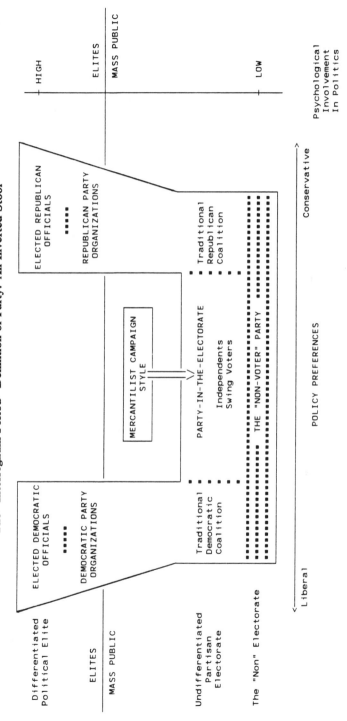

Figure 2.3
The "Interregnum Period" Definition of Party: An Inverted Stool

contribution of political elites also made it impossible to address the dynamic nature of partisan change in the electorate. This static approach that tracks *individual* partisanship renders *groups* invisible. Thus, voting behavior research has ignored the increase in interest group activity (both in number and in the scope of the participation)—what Jeffrey Berry has termed the "advocacy explosion" (1984)—as well as the composition of the interest group's structure and the growth and persistence of the new citizens groups, including both public interest and social movement groups (Walker, 1983).

The fundamental change in the party system lies in the fact that more and more citizens are becoming active in party politics for purposive incentives— party support has altered from a primary basis in socialization and partisan habit to a political commitment based on issues and values. Group consciousness and purposive goals provide a strong incentive for activism. Sidney Verba and Norman Nie demonstrated that group consciousness can provide a basis for activism among blacks that can overcome the deficit of their lower socioeconomic status (1972). Feminist consciousness has also been found to increase political participation among women (Klein, 1984; Fulenwider, 1980). Moreover, these groups are not politically neutral. They work within the party system: blacks are overwhelmingly Democratic, and feminists have tended to support more liberal policies (i.e., greater governmental activism) and the Democratic party. The significance of these changes in participation and partisanship have been ignored by contemporary party theorists.

By concentrating on the coalitional structure established in the realignment of 1932 and examining the decrement in habitual party identification, contemporary coalitional theorists have not recognized the need for theoretical revision. The coalitional approach has ignored the significance of the increase in discriminating issue voters and group activists, while focusing on what we acknowledge to be the simultaneous increase in those who are falling through the cracks of the party and the pressure group system. Our party theory must take account of both sets of changes in the party system, not merely the negative ones.

Most coalitional theorists have chosen to view the increase in citizens groups as an increase in *single-issue groups* (e.g., Polsby, 1983a; Everson, 1982). This interpretation allows these groups to be explained via Kornhauser's mass society thesis: single-issue groups, based as they are on issues rather than traditional communal or ethnic groups, derive from the erratic emotional concerns of socially atomized individuals. Therefore, the new citizens groups do not have to be understood as a new phenomenon—insofar as individuals at the mass level are not believed to be capable of informed issue judgment. These groups undermine political leadership—they are extremist, thereby making pragmatic compromise impossible.

Theorists of interest groups have belatedly recognized the implications of the new development of citizens groups. Jack Walker concluded recently that none of the major interest group theorists "offer convincing explanations of the changing composition of the group structure in the United States. The political system is beset by a swarm of organizational bumblebees that are busily flying about in spite of the fact that political scientists cannot explain how they manage it" (1983:397). Unfortunately, coalitional party theorists, despite their focus on the most purposive of groups—the party—have based their analysis of the changing group structure upon pluralist theory (which predates the rise of new citizens groups and social movements), not social movement theory (e.g., Oberschall, 1973) or the revised interest group theory (e.g., Walker, 1983; Moe, 1980; 1981).

We conclude that the coalitional approach of traditional party theory provides a rich theoretical framework to analyze mass level attachments to the parties and to relate social and political groups to party support. However, this approach—as developed in current behavioral research—has misunderstood the implications of the rise of citizens groups and lacks a complementary and concomitant analysis of political elites. It is to two-party theories of political elites that we now turn: the party-in-government and the party-in-organization.

Elite-Level Research

In this section, we consider two strands of elite-level research focusing on political officeholders and party organizational elites. We consider these two sets of research separately because they rest on two distinct theories. Theorists focusing on candidates have employed positive theory (or rational choice theory) and ambition theory, while those focusing on the party organization, per se, have employed theories of organizational incentives. As we shall see, the distinction will become an important one. The two theories (although both based on an assumption of rationality) explain different aspects of the party system: ambition theory and rational choice theory (the actions of individuals) and incentive systems theory (the behavior of organizations). And, as Mancur Olson (1965) demonstrated, what is rational for the organization is not necessarily rational for the individual. We will further argue that positive theory cannot explain the increasing ideological nature of the new party system, while organizational incentive theory cannot explain the increased development of the organized party.[3]

The Party-in-Government. The party-in-government generally refers to partisan cooperation among elected officials of the same party. It is this group that is theoretically held accountable for the conduct of government. In the words of Key, "at times party denotes groups within the government. Thus, all Democratic Representatives form a group within the House that acts with high solidarity on many matters. Similarly, Republican Senators form a party group. At times there may be a 'party-in-government' including the President, groups of his party in both House and Senate, and the heads of executive departments" (1964:164). The party-in-government has been studied by examining either the role of the party leadership in Congress (e.g., Sinclair, 1983), examining issue voting and party cohesion in congressional votes (Kingdon, 1981; Sinclair, 1977; Clausen, 1973), or by examining the influence of the president on Congress (King, 1983).

Our focus here is not on this research concerned with evidence of party cohesion, but rather, the impact of office holding and office seeking as separate variables within party theory. In particular, we will focus on the economic theory of Anthony Downs (1957) and the ambition theory of Joseph Schlesinger (1966; 1985). Both Downs and Schlesinger define parties solely in terms of their candidates for office and assume that political elites act solely out of self-interest—whether for "power, prestige and income . . . [or] . . . the love of conflict, i.e., the 'thrill of the game' " (Downs, 1957:30).

The positive economic theory of Downs is based on an analysis of the availability and costs of obtaining information in a democratic society. Elites and the mass public differ qualitatively on this dimension. Elites are those who seek to influence others. Each influencer must "produce arguments to counter any attacks upon him"; "assault the others' contentions with data of his own"; and "be informed enough to know what compromises are satisfactory to him" (Downs, 1957:253). Voters merely need to react to proposals formulated by others, while elite policymakers and influencers act in a competitive environment in which there is a high return compensating those who invest in information. The mass public (or citizens in Downs's model) have less compensation for their acquisition of information and less incentive as their only method of influence—the vote—is diluted by the votes of millions of others.

These characteristics of the Downsian model have important implications for the political system. We will consider here only the consensual two-party system described by Downs. Downs introduces a spatial analysis in which the political preferences of Americans are assumed to be normally distributed. The rationality of the political party is to maximize votes, while the rationality of the voter is to maximize his party differential (i.e., to vote for the party that gives him the most return for his vote). However, the competitive pressure for the most votes inclines the parties toward the center of the voter distribution: the ideologically passionate outliers have no alternative party to turn to. Policies are made to overlap those of the other party, and described as ambiguously as possible to attract the most voters clustered in the moderate center.

Naturally, this makes it difficult for each citizen to vote rationally; he has a hard time finding out what his ballot supports when cast for either party. As a result, voters are encouraged to make decisions on some basis other than the issues, i.e., on the personalities of the candidates, traditional family voting patterns, loyalty to past party heroes, etc. . . . Rational behavior by political parties tends to discourage rational behavior by voters. (Downs, 1957:136)

The essence of Downsian theory for our purposes is an undifferentiated consensual citizenry whose ideological center is moderate and a differentiated elite (or "influencers") who develop public policy out of the view of the electorate and in their own individual self-interest. This analysis, while ignoring the attachment of social groups to parties and the role of group political interests in formulating public policies, does flesh out the motivations and characteristics of political elites and is consistent with the traditional party model (see Fig. 2.2). Yet, it should be noted that these elites act not as representatives of groups, but in their own *individual* interest.

J. Schlesinger bases his analysis, not on economic postulates, but on the empirical behavioral consequences of office seeking. Schlesinger, like Downs, defines parties in terms of officeholders and office seekers, but he takes great pains to distinguish his own analysis of "complex electoral constituencies" from the "simple (or team) theory" of Downs (1966:121–125) and others, such as Schattschneider. Schlesinger bases his theory on the analysis of a "party nucleus" (the basic party unit consisting of the "cooperative efforts aimed at a single office" (1966:126). Whether different party nuclei cooperate or act in isolation depend in large measure on whether the electoral constituencies are *congruent* (facilitating maximum cooperation), *disjoint* (allowing maximum independence), or *enclaved* (i.e., a smaller constituency located within a larger one, which allows for diverse outcomes, depending on the competitive strength and organizational resources of each party nuclei and the distribution of political opportunities for elective office). *Progressive ambitions* for a "higher" office engender elite behavior compatible with the desired constituency, rather than the actual constituency.

Schlesinger's theory is useful in highlighting the diversity and variety of party organizations. Schlesinger points out that there are two aspects to the organizational tensions arising from the factors he considers: organizational cooperation versus competition within the same party and policy convergence versus divergence vis-à-vis the opposing party. Meaningful competition between the two parties for the control of the legislature results in greater organizational cooperation among party nuclei. "If one party has safe majorities in the legislature, its leaders or senior members will be less concerned about the fate of party members in competitive districts" (Schlesinger, 1966:136). Policy convergence between the two parties occurs only under certain circumstances. Downs's analysis assumes genuine two-party competition. Schlesinger's does not, and furthermore, the one-party dominant case is an important one because such dominance results in policy divergence across parties. Convergence occurs when (1) the two parties are competitive and (2) the career lines of the candidates become similar.

Consider Schlesinger's analysis of three hypothetical constituencies enclaved within a competitive state. X is a competitive enclave, Y is dominated
by the Republicans, and Z is dominated by the Democrats.

Note the conflicting pressures in these two arrangements. The nuclei in the state and
in the competitive (X) constituency are under pressure to converge. The cooperative
tensions above, then, tend to push the two parties together in terms of policy. The
distribution of resources, however, plays up the divergent tensions found in the Y
and Z constituencies. (Schlesinger, 1966:132)

J. Schlesinger recently updated his ambition theory in the context of the
new party system (1985). Schlesinger argues—contrary to the decline-of-party
thesis (citing Fiorina, 1980)—that it is precisely the increase of separatist
tendencies that has resulted in greater organizational cooperation among party
nuclei. Congressional and party reform, the increase in primaries, the expansion of the electorate, the demise of malapportioned districts, and the
introduction of campaign finance laws have all worked to increase flexibility
in the electorate, and hence, party competition. "The most striking difference
between the new and the old party systems is that there are no states in which
one party is completely unable to win any office" (Schlesinger, 1985:1166).
Schlesinger argues that the critical characteristic of this new system is electoral
insecurity—no margin is safe. Following his earlier development of ambition
theory, it follows that there would be an increased level of organizational
cooperation in campaigns among party nuclei. Indeed, there is increasing
evidence of organizational integration and a sharing of expertise and resources
(Cotter et al., 1984).

J. Schlesinger's 1966 formulation of ambition theory described a decentralized party system based on the candidate nucleus. He used the same
theory in 1985 to explain the growth of multinuclear candidate organizations
(e.g., state and national party organizations). How does he explain the sys-
temic change? Ambition theory is a theory of elite political behavior. And,
according to Schlesinger, elites have not really changed—they respond to
their environment just as they did in the 1950s. We have a new party system
because the mass public has changed. "Thus the essential difference between
the old and new party systems resides in the altered attitudes and behavior
of the voters" (Schlesinger, 1985:1167). The strong partisan identification of
the 1950s has eroded—and it is this environmental change that has provided
the stimulus for new organizational cooperation.

Thus far, J. Schlesinger has maintained consistency with his earlier theory.
The flaw in his analysis of the new American party system lies in his attempt
to explain the increasing ideology in the system. If elites—the essential political actors—have *not* changed in their motivations, then we must look
elsewhere for the change—to changes in the electorate. Schlesinger attributes
the increasing interparty cohesion to the increased competitiveness of the

two parties in his most recent work. Yet, his own ambition theory (circa 1966) predicts increasing *convergence*, not the increasing *divergence* that has taken place. As he concluded in 1966, "since the state nuclei are competitive, the two parties will tend to converge, as they would in simple party theory" (Schlesinger, 1966:132).

The Theoretical Gap in the Party-in-Government Research. The party in government research has focused on how running for office affects the party organization. The resurgent party is measured by examining increased competitiveness and the rise of candidate organization. In doing so, the dominant theoretical perspective among students of campaigns has obscured the purposive goals of public officials. Candidates and public officials do not merely act in their own self-interest (although this is a primary incentive), but take positions because they believe it is the appropriate decision to make based on their party and group ties. That is, elites are subject to purposive incentives as well.

Research on candidates and public officials has ignored the increasing heterogeneity of candidates and public officials. The proportion of women state legislators has tripled since 1969, and the numbers of women running for positions in the state house has increased dramatically. Similarly, the proportion of elected Hispanic and black public officials has increased as well. The critical issue is what happens to the party system when the elite consensus based on similar socialization and status (i.e., white middle class professional male) is shattered? Not only have the new female and minority public officials resulted in an increasingly heterogeneous leadership group for the parties, but they have been elected through the auspices of sponsoring groups (e.g., in the case of women, the Women's Campaign Fund and the National Women's Political Caucus [NWPC]), and they have organized similar caucuses to represent their group's interest in the U.S Congress (e.g., the Congressional Caucus for Women's Issues, the Hispanic Caucus, the Black Caucus). Not only have the members of these groups organized, but business has become more politically active on its behalf—in an aggressively ideological way (Edsall, 1984; G. Wilson, 1981). Elites have become more ideologically oriented, and this is not due to electoral competitiveness. It is an offshoot of the new social movements of the 1960s. This is ignored by the rational choice theories which only explain *individual* not group self-interest.

We agree with Cornelius Cotter and his associates' assessment of Joseph Schlesinger's contribution. "However fruitful Schlesinger's theory is, and replete as it may be with useful implications for the traditional party organizations in the form of local, state and national party committees, it is a theory of campaign organizations, not of party organizations" (Cotter et al., 1984:4). Schlesinger has provided us with a richer understanding of the diversity among political elites where their ambitions diverge and of the pressure to share campaign technology and organize more effectively when it is in their interest to do so. But, the rational choice theory employed by Schlesinger (and the earlier work of Downs) cannot be used to explain why the system has changed and why it is now more ideological. It is the demise of the monolithic elite party organizational cadres that theories such as ambition theory and market economic theory leave unexplained. It is to this research area that we now turn.

The Party-as-Organization. One characteristic that political parties indisputably share with other political groups is a palpable organization. Writing in 1887, German scholar Ferdinand Tonnies emphasized the importance of organization; "that parties will become organized is a natural law in the sociological sense. For essentially merely a union of those who strive for a certain aim, the party becomes, through organization, a corporation fit to fight" (Heberle, 1955; cited in Eldersveld, 1982:169). Quoting Tonnies's description of the party as "a corporation fit to fight," Samuel Eldersveld concludes that "the question for scholars, since Tonnies, has been what type of corporation, what type of organization?" (1982:169).

Unfortunately, the study of party organizations qua organizations has been ignored in recent scholarship, despite the fact that "the great theoretical tradition in the study of political parties was established by men with a distinctly organizational approach to the study of parties" (Sorauf, 1967:36; see also Cotter *et al.*, 1984:1–5). Sorauf (1967) and, more recently, Cotter and his associates in their study of state and local party organizations (1985), outlined two reasons for this neglect. The first constraint derives from the wealth of survey data produced by the biennial National Election Studies (what Sorauf refers to as The Law of Available Data). The richness of the "Available Data" for secondary analysis has given birth to a line of party research in which the party organization is only inferred from mass-voting behavior (the party-in-the-electorate). In those instances where research resources have been devoted to the elite levels of the parties, the study population has been state (e.g., Rapoport, et al., 1986) or national convention (e.g., J. Kirkpatrick, 1976; Miller and Jennings, 1986) *delegates.* However important their participation in the nomination of their party's presidential nominee, delegates (which may include party officials) have no formal organizational role within the party. Second, the attractiveness of theories fusing the *party* organization with the *candidate* organization has diverted our research, inducing a myopia in terms of the independent role of party organization. In this context, Cotter and his associates specifically reference the rational choice theories of Downs (1957) and J. Schlesinger (1966). More recently, however, Schlesinger (1984) extended the concept of the party organization qua candidate organization to include the party workers (a reformulation which we will shortly consider).

We would like to suggest a third explanatory factor for the neglect of party organizations: most party scholars, we believe, were on the whole satisfied with the available party theory on party organizations. Party organizations were not studied following Eldersveld's (1964) refinement of party theory because most scholars found extant party theory—the traditional party model—sufficient. The contours of the party organization (populated by an undifferentiated political elite) had been identified—the traditional party model as depicted in Figure 2.2. Thus, the thrust of research on party elites post-Eldersveld has been to study the *attitudes* of the newer party activists who were conveniently found within the ranks of the postreform convention delegates. The delegate studies (e.g., Kirkpatrick, 1976) surveyed delegates to determine their party organizational style—under the assumption that changes in the composition of party activists will affect the known (i.e., assumed) organizational characteristics (see Clark and Wilson, 1961). This emphasis is just as evident in more recent delegate studies. Miller and Jennings (1986), for example, base their entire over-time analysis of convention delegates from 1972 to 1980 on the delegates' convention year of mobilization, attachment to the party, candidate preference, issue preferences, and attitudinal proximity to the mass public. Hence, the delegate studies adapted and extended to party elites the individualistic attitudinal approach developed in voting behavior research, while the study of party organization, per se, became relegated to the intellectual dustbins of party research.

The strength of party organizations and their import for party theory now represent points of contention among party scholars. In Chapter 1, we rejected the notion that the party organization is isomorphic with bureaucratic organization. We now consider some conceptualizations of the party drawn from the study of party organizations: from the "great theoretical tradition" in party organizational theory (as well as the derivative scholarship); from the recent study of party organizations—the Party Transformation Study conducted by Cornelius Cotter, James Gibson, John Bibby, and Robert Huckshorn (1984); and from J. Schlesinger's (1984) revised theory of party organization.

The Theoretical Tradition in Party Organizations

Robert Michels, in his analysis of the German Social Democratic party (originally published in 1915), first posed the question of the relationship of party organization structure to the party system (Hennessy, 1968). Michels's answer to the question was to conclude that "power is always conservative"; with the development of the organization, "the struggle for great principles becomes impossible" (1962:366). Michels's description of the Iron Law of Oligarchy—"Who says organization, says oligarchy" (1962:32)—has been particularly persuasive among scholars given that the party of his study was based on a revolutionary and democratic ideal. According to Michels, the party gradually develops a leadership group as the organization increases in size. This leadership becomes increasingly professional and specialized—and increasingly separated and distant from the mass base. This growing gap between the leaders and the followers eventually culminates in the development of a cohesive elite whose primary incentive is to stay in power. They evolve into a self-perpetuating elite because they, as organizational leaders, control (1) the information available to the nonelites, (2) the organs of communication to their followers, and (3) the recruitment of new elites.

Michels's theory predicts an undifferentiated elite—even in parties whose *raison d'être* is to represent the masses. Organizational development, he argues, necessarily results in a new political class. New elites—those who do not threaten the interests of the established elite cadre—are absorbed. The interests of elites always diverge from the masses; the masses, for their part, wish to be led. For many, the idea of an inevitable closed political elite is undemocratic. Party theorists since Michels have reacted to the seemingly "conspiratorial" aspect of the oligarchical elite he described so well by emphasizing the historical developmental circumstances in which parties organize.

Maurice Duverger (1954) took issue with Michels's Iron Law of Oligarchy by proposing a distinction between the *cadre* structure (consisting of a set of leaders or notables active only at election time) and the *mass-party* structure (consisting of leaders and party members or adherents interacting in an ongoing organization in pursuit of common ends). While the American parties were characterized as "cadre," the socialist mass-membership parties represented the modern party of the future for Duverger. Duverger acknowledged that the parties were indeed run by elites. However, the socialist party elites were different in that they were "sprung from the masses." The mass-party leaders and their adherents each had reciprocal roles and responsibilities in the party—the relationship was not simply one of the elites exploiting the masses. Parties, according to Duverger, do organize to achieve competitive advantage—hence, the incentive to develop a mass-membership party following the organization of the socialist parties resulted in a "contagion from the left."

Eldersveld's 1962 study of Detroit area precinct committeepersons provided another important emendation of Michels's theory. Eldersveld attacked the concept of the oligarchic elite on two fronts. First, the organizational structure of American parties is not hierarchical. It is, instead a *stratarchy*, based on a "reciprocal deference structure" (1964:9). The basis for leadership is rapport, not expertise. The centralist leaders engage in "downward deference" to local interests, culture, and inertia. Contrary to the authoritarian or bureaucratic models of organization, the "critical action locus of the party structure is at its base" (1964:9).

Second, the party is comprised of diverse elites with different career patterns, not a single unified elite cadre. This pluralism derives from the quixotic nature of the party leaders' authority and the high level of turnover among party personnel. Some party personnel are motivated for power, but differ in terms of self-consciousness, belief, and communication. Turnover can result in a loss of power, or in a reconstitution of the party's subcoalition. "But this is not a *pro forma* turnover, as the oligarchic theorists would contend, a circulation resulting from the 'amalgamation' by the old elite of 'new elite' elements which are considered 'safe' " (Eldersveld, 1964:11).

The stability of the party, however, is maintained. Some party elites are primarily oriented toward the party, and not by a desire to wield power. "The saving grace is the existence of career groups of individuals who are not essentially aspiring to power. For many of these the party means 'status,' not 'power,' and the continuity of their commitment to party tasks contributes to stability in the face of constant flux and potential disequilibrium" (Eldersveld, 1964:11–12). Eldersveld's empirical findings substantiated that the Detroit parties were "incohesive"—no more than 10 percent of precinct leaders of either party were ideologically motivated. Instead, the party is a "social group," uniting "an agglomeration of people with a rich variety of motivations, drives and needs" (1964:303). While Eldersveld himself contributed to a party theory of organizations, the thrust of his approach and empirical research was to initiate a focus on the variety of organizational incentives and commitment among leaders and activists.

American scholars found Duverger's description of American parties as cadre in organization a useful one—it certainly is a categorization to be found in nearly every text on parties. However, Duverger's resolution of Michels's elite "conspiracy" (or, in more neutral terms, an elite unity) resulted in an unflattering characterization of the American party system as not typifying a modern society. Leon Epstein (1967) surveyed party systems in western democracies with a deliberate "Americanist" bias. "The aim is to show that American parties, so often regarded as underdeveloped by European standards, are really responses to American conditions which cannot, in their entirety, be regarded as marks of a backward nation supposed to eventually resemble Europe" (Epstein, 1967:6; see also 1986). In contrast to Duverger, Epstein analyzed parties not from their organizational development and complexity, but from the functions they fulfill.[4] In doing so, Epstein provided a theoretical focus that shifted the concept of party away from an organizational emphasis. There is no organizational imperative—the more developed party, for Epstein, is not necessarily the more modern.

Therefore, the picture of the party organization to be gleaned from traditional, theoretical works is that the American party system is decentralized and stratarchical rather than hierarchical, and pragmatic rather than ideological (again, consistent with Figure 2.2). The system worked quite well without a class consciousness and avoided the "conspiratorial" taint of the cohesive and hierarchical elite identified by Michels. Once the general contours of the party system were identified, the elite behavioral research following Eldersveld and Epstein built on this foundation. Parties performed indispensable functions for society, and party stability rested on the proper mix of party style among activists (or the "different career classes" in Eldersveld's terms).

Eldersveld was not the first to stress activist style in party work. Eldersveld's significance was in his singular focus on *party* organizations. Organizational theorists, with their analysis of incentives for organization, had long considered the political party a special case of group organization, subject to the same dynamics as other organized groups (e.g., J. Wilson, 1973; Olson, 1965, 1971).

Olson (1965, 1971) pointed out the limitations of large groups with latent interests. "Only when groups are small, or when they are fortunate enough to have an independent set of selective incentives, will they organize or act to achieve their objectives" (1971:167). Political parties, organized for collective ends, are at a disadvantage in the capacity for organization. Indeed, Olson finds David Truman's oft-quoted assessment of party organization in the 1950s—"the quadrennial creation of presidential parties is an exercise in improvisation"—Truman, 1958:532)—quite consistent with his "by-product" theory of groups.

... the average person will not be willing to make a significant sacrifice for the party he favors, since a victory for his party provides a collective good. He will not contribute to the party coffers or attend precinct meetings. There are on the other hand many people with personal political ambitions, and for them, the party will provide noncollective benefits in the form of public office. (Olson. 1971:164)

Therefore, beyond the individual benefits of office holding (or the selective benefits provided by the party machine via patronage), the logic of collective action is such that party organization will remain weak. Large groups will always be at a disadvantage compared to the strong organization of a primary or an intermediate group.

A similar set of arguments have been advanced by James Q. Wilson (1973). In an early article, Peter Clark and J. Q. Wilson argue that "all viable organizations must provide tangible or intangible incentives to individuals in exchange for contributions of individual activity" (1961:130). They identify three types of organizational incentive: *material* (tangible, easily transferred into monetary terms), *solidary* (intangible, including social status, group identification, socializing, etc.), and *purposive* incentives (intangible—the stated ends of the organization, resting on a change in the status quo). Clark and J. Wilson argue that incentive systems are central to understanding the dynamics of organizational change. "The distribution of motives throughout the society defines the potential contributors to various organizations. As motives change, so will organizations. Some organizations will grow or decline spontaneously as the particular incentives they offer become relatively more or less appealing ... " (1961:164). They offer the example of the decline of the political party machine as an illustration of the effect of the decline of material incentives for activism. The remaining incentives left for parties are solidary and purposive.

J. Wilson's study of three Democratic political clubs (in New York, Chicago, and Los Angeles) during the 1950s illustrates how these incentive systems are useful in analyzing party change. In *The Amateur Democrat*, he identifies a new style among party activists: those who believed that the party should be "programmatic, internally democratic, and largely or entirely free of reliance on material incentives such as patronage" (1962:340). Material incentives—in terms of patronage jobs — had declined in society as a whole. This left only purposive or solidary incentives to motivate activism. Purposive incentives (such as motivate the "amateurs") are problematic for party stability because "purpose and principle are . . . episodic in their salience and divisive in their impact" (J. Wilson, 1973:96). Candidate followings represent an intermediate type of organization. "Unlike the machine-style organization, the support of the followers cannot be easily transferred to a candidate other than one to whom they have given their loyalty; unlike amateur clubs, the followers will not be as inclined to insist on doctrinal orthodoxy" (J. Wilson, 1973:116).

Party Reform and Organizational Resurgence

The vast body of empirical research on nominating convention delegates in the 1960s and 1970s built on the foundation developed by Eldersveld and J. Wilson. The general conclusion was that the attitudes associated with the amateur status were no longer limited to "clubs," but were increasingly associated with party activists—at least as measured by studies of convention delegates (Jackson et al., 1978; Kirkpatrick, 1976; Roback, 1975; Soule and McGrath, 1975; Wildavsky, 1971; Soule and Clarke, 1970). J. Kirkpatrick (1976; 1979) argues that the "new breed" of convention delegates was detrimental to the party. With the decline of party "regulars" or "professionals," the party was increasingly prey to those with antiorganization values.

The party reforms undertaken by the Democratic party beginning in 1968 can only be understood to be irrational according to the rational choice theories. The emphasis by the Democrats on what have been termed "expressive" reforms, while the Republicans have undertaken "competitive" reforms (Salmore and Salmore, 1985), makes no sense when one assumes that elites act only to further their own private (or selective) benefits. For example, party theorists such as J. Kirkpatrick (1979) and Polsby (1983b) argue that the party reform undertaken by the Democratic party was self-destructive, as it increased the participation of those without ties to the party. According to this view, the Democratic and Republican parties have diverged in their activities related to candidates and campaigns. The Democrats have emphasized "expressiveness" ("the extent to which parties accurately and fairly represent the strength and ideas of their constituents") while the Republicans have emphasized "competitiveness" ("their ability to win elections") (Salmore and Salmore, 1985:212; see also Ranney, 1975). Under the rational choice assumption that elites will act to win elections, the Democratic reforms were an irrational act.

Ideological goals (or purposive incentives) were insufficient incentives for organizational maintenance, compared to the pragmatic self-interest considered to be the norm among party elites. As a direct result of the (Democratic) party reforms (J. Kirkpatrick, 1979; Polsby, 1983a), ideological elites were clearly on the increase. This posed a problem for the future of the Democratic party: Democratic presidential candidates were less competitive, outsider or insurgent candidates were advantaged, and a Democratic president was unable to govern (Polsby, 1983a).

Thus, it was assumed that the values of these new party activists were "predictive of the future of party organization, since the convention delegates of today are taken to be the organizational leaders of the future" (Cotter et al., 1984:143). The Party Transformation Study, conducted by Cotter and his associates, provided the first empirical test of this assumption. Cotter and his colleagues find several contradictions in current party theory. Contrary to the party decline thesis, electoral disaggregation is *not* associated with declining party organizations. On the contrary, during the same period of the apparent accelerating electoral decomposition of the parties, "the decade of the 1960s, which is generally recognized as a period of decline in popular support for party, witnessed what may have been a renaissance for state party organizations" (Cotter et al., 1984:157). State party organizations are more complex in *organizational structure* (professional staffing and division of labor, permanent headquarters, regularized budgeting) and in *programmatic capacity* (fund-raising, electoral mobilization, public opinion polling, issue leadership, newsletters, candidate recruitment, provision of financial and campaign services, and preprimary endorsements).

A second contradiction presented by their study is on the impact of increasing amateurism among party activists. They conclude that "generally, there are only negligible organizational differences between parties run by chairs having amateur role orientations and parties headed by chairs expressing professional role orientations, and this is the case for both parties" (1984:149). They speculate that the primary factor is the "organizational imperative" that causes "even amateur activists to engage in activities that recognize common organizational needs" (1984:150). Organization is an instrumental end that allows the pursuit of divergent goals.

What is the meaning of these findings for parties? Cotter and his associates suggest that it would be more fruitful to view the change between the electorate and the party as the successful adaptation of the party organization from the "militarist" to the "mercantilist" approach to campaigning (Jensen,

1969). The mercantilist approach involves a broad appeal to the electorate, without regard for party affiliation and is based on public relations. The "militarist" style is that of the party machine and depends on the mobilization of the already committed—the party adherents in the electorate. According to them, this adaptation has *both* counter-realigning and counter-dealigning effects. The party organizations have adapted to modern society and, in doing so, are no longer dependent on party supporters. They explain this change by focusing on the activities of elites within the parties. Thus, they return the party-in-organization research full circle, back to the Michels's description of the political elite. Parties are "vehicles for accommodating social change." As such, "they serve this function . . . by accepting and socializing elite representatives of groups which have previously been politically passive, or excluded from politics, or new entrants by way of age or immigration" (Cotter et al., 1984:165). Thus, Cotter and his associates here implicitly acknowledge the role of grass-roots based social movements in providing the impetus for a restructuring of elite party groups. They then go on to quote Michels with approval. "As Michels wrote some seventy years ago, it is likely that 'the struggle between the old leaders and the new' will result 'not so much [in] a *circulation des élites* as a *réunion des élites*, an amalgam, that is to say, of the two elements' " (Cotter et al., 1984:165; quoting Michels, 1962:182).

This conclusion is reminiscent of C. Wright Mills' analysis in *The Power Elite* (1959). Elites are cohesive not through a simplistic notion of conspiracy, but through the similarity of experience and an identity of political interest (i.e., their elite status). Burton and Higley stress that a major flaw of elite studies in general is the analytical focus on the characteristics of individual elite members, thereby trivializing elite theory by reducing "it to the banal observation that powerful and influential persons exist in each society and should be studied" (1987:222). From a theoretical standpoint, the contribution of the organizational focus of Cotter and his associates is to redirect our party theory away from the individualistic delegate studies to a group-level conceptualization of a unitary elite class among party elites. Their position on the role of elite consensus is supported by Eldersveld's finding that among local party activists who remain (regardless of their initial motivations for activism), "the party is a rewarding 'social group' " (1986:107). Elite cohesion represents an important insight in the study of political parties; yet Michels's monolithic elite by itself provides an insufficient framework for explaining both the diversity of party organizations and increased partisan conflict and cleavage.

J. Schlesinger's recent work (1984) is an attempt to reconcile the resurgence of the party organization with continuing electoral disaggregation. Using rational choice theory, Schlesinger deliberately excludes voters from the party definition to recapture the "reality of party"; "voters are choosers among parties, not components of them" (1984:377). Schlesinger expands the Downsian notion of teams of candidates who seek "to control government by winning elective office" to encompass those party workers recruited to assist in seeking the voters' support.

In the organizing and channeling of the activities of these individuals, the party becomes an organization. With reference to Olson (1965), J. Schlesinger then distinguishes between those recruited for selective and private benefits (i.e., solidary or material incentives), and those recruited in pursuit of collective benefits (i.e., purposive incentives). "Olson's logic removes one of the legs of the tripod of incentives constructed by Clark and Wilson (1961). . . . Purposive incentives are of course collective. While not denying that these [purposive] incentives do attract many activists, the logic indicates that such incentives, unreinforced by private benefits, have little staying power" (1984:387). Thus, in contrast to J. Wilson (1973), Schlesinger argues that the mix of incentives has not changed (e.g., J. Wilson's argument that material incentives were removed with the decline of the political machine), but has always consisted of selective incentives for the political elites.

Schlesinger concludes that only those with "relatively little information about the costs and benefits"—the inexperienced and the young—will participate for collective benefits. While parties are ostensibly collective groups, "the evidence points to a reality in which relatively few oligarchs or an 'active minority' run the organization" (1984:387). In doing so, J. Schlesinger is erecting a two-tier structure to describe the party organization: the relatively permanent elite stratum who participate for private benefits, and the volunteer worker stratum (necessarily characterized by high turnover), who participate for collective benefits. While basing his theoretical analysis on different assumptions (i.e., organizational incentives) than did Cotter and his associates, Schlesinger arrives at a quite similar conclusion concerning elite dominance of party organizations.

The Theoretical Gap in Party Organizational Research. The study of party organizations, long a concern of traditional party theorists, has been resuscitated in recent works. Earlier research measured the decline of the party organization by documenting the increasing proportion of party elites with antiorganizational values, a phenomenon usually attributed to (Democratic) party reforms. Recent work on party organizations has argued for a strengthened party system by reviving the institutional approach. What matters according to this latter perspective is the extent of organizational capacity to act in furtherance of party goals—an instrumental end that both "amateurs" and "professionals" agree on.

Both of these perspectives ignore the fundamental significance of party reform: the increasing heterogeneity of party elites in party organizations did not merely increase the relative proportion of "political amateurs," it provided for the representation of groups with an ideological understanding of group conflict. Leaders of these newly represented groups attained their elite status via group pressure and cannot be understood to be *simply* participating for private selective benefits. Further, little mention is made in party literature of the extensive nature of reform throughout this era. Similar political reforms were undertaken in all major political institutions—from the statehouse to the U.S. Congress—and not merely in the party system. By redefining parties to consist only of elites, the party organizational approach has restricted itself to an oligarchic interpretation of leadership and ignored the fundamental democratization of the political party system. The integration of formerly unrepresented women, blacks, and other minorities into elite party cadres has broadened the party base and now permits the representation of more diverse views in party affairs.

Focusing on party organization, per se, as the central variable in party theory makes sense only if it is reasonable to view parties as nonpolitical organizations and if the primary incentives for party participation and membership are selective ones. We argued in Chapter 1 that this perspective ignores the fundamental purposive goals of party organizations. Furthermore, we agree with interest group theorist Terry Moe's recent conclusion that "like it or not, people apparently do join groups for reasons ranging from ideological commitment to perceptions of efficacy, and rational theories of membership cannot forever pretend that this is not so" (1980:596). The organizational approach does not merely ignore issues of values, it is empirically inaccurate.

Organizational research on political parties, in sum, provides little assistance in understanding either electoral disaggregation, or in determining the meaning of the increasing variety of elite motivations. The value of the Party Transformation Study is to highlight the role of organization as an independent variable and to place renewed emphasis on elite cohesion in our party theory. Our party theory must acknowledge a distinct "organizational imperative" in party organization. And, as Schlesinger argues, party organization should be viewed as an instrumental end for political elites and one that is not without importance in the socialization of new activists. However, we still find the rich diversity of motivations among elites, as well as an increasingly heterogeneous political elite and increased partisan conflict and cleavage. And it is these important changes that are inexplicable under contemporary party organizational theory.

CONCLUSIONS

We argued that traditional party theory—developed as a dynamic theoretical system that was capable of explaining party change—has unraveled. Rationalized by a normative preference for the indigenous American party system, circa 1950–1960, party research elaborated on the traditional party model through a methodological separation of three strands of party research. While traditional party theory highlighted the linkage of elites and mass as the central distinguishing characteristic of parties, in practice, behavioral research treated party elites and party supporters as separate and distinct entities.

To document the unraveling of traditional party theory, we discussed in detail the views of a number of contemporary party theorists, according to the (methodological) party definition they have adopted. While relying on a common theoretical core (the traditional party model), party researchers adopted a definition of the party based upon the population studied—whether the party-in-the-electorate, the party-in-office, or the party-organization. In essence, the party stratum studied has structured the assessments of party strength and the explanation proffered for party change. We have summarized the views of these contemporary theorists in Table 2.1.

The compartmentalization of party research has placed traditional party theory in a time warp. Despite the extensive behavioral research on political parties over the past three decades, our party theory has not kept pace. Traditional party theory has clearly unraveled. Contemporary party theory is indicted on at least three counts. First, contemporary party theory lacks internal consistency. When the predictions of traditional party theory are compared to developments in the party system, we find a number of con-tradictions. Consider the following:

- Traditional party theory assumed that a decline in party support in the electorate necessarily results in a decline in party organizations. *Yet, organizations have become more cohesive.*
- Traditional party theory assumed that an increase in ideologically motivated party activists necessarily results in a decline in party organization. *Yet amateurs and professionals alike have worked to increase organizational strength.*
- Traditional party theory assumed that an increase in party competition resulted in greater organizational competition *and* greater policy convergence. *Yet, while we do find greater organizational cooperation and integration, the congressional parties display more intra-party cohesiveness and greater inter-party divergence.*
- Traditional party theory assumed that elites were motivated by a diverse set of incentives and therefore did not comprise a monolithic set of elites. Recent party organization theory—revised to account for strengthened party organizations—re-turn us full circle to the notion of a "conspiratorial" or "unified" elite class who control the information available to nonelites, and control entry into elite status. *Yet, this does not square with the increasing heterogeneity of American political party elites.*

Second, contemporary party theorists are unable to agree on the state of the party system—who is to be included as part of the party, and who is to be excluded—and whether, as a consequence, parties remain in decline, are resurgent, or never declined but have become stronger. There was consid-erable agreement on these questions in traditional party theory—but the segmentation of party research has led to divergent conclusions among con-temporary theorists.

Table 2.1

Traditional Party Theory Unraveled: The Views of Contemporary Party Theorists

LEVEL OF ANALYSIS	PARTY STRATA	ASSESSMENT OF PARTY STRENGTH	EXPLANATION OF PARTY CHANGE	THEORISTS
MASS	THE PARTY-IN-THE ELECTORATE	PARTY IN DECLINE	ELITES HAVE CHANGED: Mass public has only responded to a changed elite.	Wattenberg, 1980 Burnham, 1985
ELITE	THE PARTY-IN OFFICE	PARTY SYSTEM IS STRONGER - AND IT NEVER DECLINED	MASS PUBLIC HAS CHANGED: Elites have responded to this change to strengthen their position.	Schlesinger, 1985
	THE PARTY ORGANIZATION	PARTY SYSTEM IN DECLINE- PERFORMS FEWER FUNCTIONS	MASS PUBLIC HAS CHANGED: (Democratic Party) Elites have responded to their disadvantage.	Schlesinger, 1984 Cotter et al., 1984 Kirkpatrick, 1979 Polsby, 1983a

Third, there are a number of serious theoretical gaps in contemporary party theory. It is ironic that contemporary party theory has relied on a restrictive interest group theory (whether that of Robert Dahl or of Olson), which provides little scope for collective action for purposive goals, when the subject of our theory remains the most inclusive of collective groups whereas interest group theorists have taken the lead in revising their own theory to accommodate the empirical realities of social movements and purposive groups.

In the following two chapters, we outline our theoretical reformulation of traditional party theory to account for the linkage of elites and masses, the diverse motivations of party elites and supporters, and the impact of social movements on political parties, democracy, and representation. We first document the role of social movements in the process of Democratic party reforms, and Republican party nonreforms.

NOTES

1. Some immediate critics include T. William Goodman (1951); Murray S. Stedman, Jr., and Herbert Sonthoff (1951); and Austin Ranney (1951). One of the more comprehensive critiques is provided by Evron M. Kirkpatrick (1971). See also David H. Everson (1980) for an extended discussion.

2. Clearly, there have been a number of important changes in the electorate: an increase in the average level of education is the most dramatic. Some have argued that more educated voters are less willing to depend on parties to simplify their vote choice (e.g., Sorauf, 1984; Ladd and Hadley, 1975; Pomper, 1975). Wattenberg (1986) takes issue with this conclusion, arguing that the decline of party has occurred equally at all educational levels.

3. J. Schlesinger utilized both positive theory (1966; 1985) and the theory of organizational incentive (1984). However, as he did so on two separate occasions (without specifically integrating them), we will treat the two theories separately here.

4. For Epstein, the cadre style of party developed from parties with "primarily and almost entirely electoral functions" (1967:99). The mass membership parties began not as parties, but social movements under particular circumstances that were not the most "modern": "a pre-modern class consciousness, a delayed mass voting franchise, and widespread economic deprivation" (Epstein, 1967:165). Similarly, the American parties developed under particular circumstances. Epstein distinguishes at least three types of (urban) parties: the patronage (cadre) and the mass membership parties of the socialist working class and of the middle class.

3

Reform and Contemporary Social and Political Movements

The twenty year span from the mid–1950s to the mid–1970s was the crucible for the development of a number of social and political movements: the civil rights, the women's rights, the student and antiwar, and the new right movements are among the more notable examples that we wish to consider. The major efforts of these purposive movements were focused on working within the party system. Traditionally, protest movements evinced themselves via the third party route. However, as V. O. Key noted in 1964, "students of the topic seem to agree that the day of the third party, at least in presidential elections, is done" (1964:281). Beginning with the adoption of the Australian ballot in the late nineteenth century, the history of state regulation of parties has institutionalized the Democratic and Republican parties (Epstein, 1986). Following the passage of the 1974 FECA amendments—described as a "major party protection act" (Rosenstone et al., 1984:18)—third parties face even greater impediments. While FECA encourages the contesting of primaries by candidates with only a minimum of support, it does grant the Democratic and Republican parties a privileged position in public subsidies, while limiting the funds available to third parties. Thus, the third parties of the nineteenth century possessed a real organization apart from the candidates, while in the twentieth century, "the most prominent movements of the 1900s . . . are all more accurately labeled independent campaigns than political parties" (Rosenstone, et al., 1984:81).

The civil rights movement, the student and antiwar movement, and the women's rights movement focused on the Democratic party. In part, this derives from the dominant position of the Democrats. As William Crotty and John S. Jackson III noted,

the Democratic Party, as the majority party of the 1960s and as the more heterogeneous coalition, was the focus of pressures for political change. . . . In its influence on the Democratic party and the reform era, the civil rights movement was augmented by two other major social and political movements of the 1960s and 1970s: the protest over the war in Vietnam and the movement for equal rights for women. . . . Certain other trends, such as the increased role of television in national political life, augmented these movements. But the protest movements themselves stimulated an upheaval in American politics. (1985:27–29)

The Democratic party reforms, as we saw in Chapter 1, occurred in the context of society-wide reforms that affected Congress as well.

Reform, however, has taken different courses in the two parties. In part, this result was shaped by the different political cultures of each party (Freeman, 1986) and reflects the fundamental fact that the Republican party (unlike the Democrats) faced no internal crisis, and that the "national Republican Party . . . takes a states' rights view of its party units and their relationship to the national unit" (Crotty, 1983:227). More important is the fact that the two parties also have different philosophies of government: the Democrats generally view government as a positive force in accommodating social change, while Republicans generally take a *laissez faire* approach to social problems.

This has structured the partisan affiliations of contemporary social and political movements depending on their goals: *social movements* such as the civil rights movement wishing redress of racial discrimination, or the women's rights movement wishing redress of sex discrimination as women move into nontraditional roles find the Democratic party a congenial home, while cultural defensive *political* movements such as the new right (Guth, 1983) have an affinity for the Republican party's philosophy of *laissez faire* and its cautious attitude on accommodation to social change. Historically, the Democratic party's role as the avenue of upward mobility for new groups in American politics has made it relatively more supportive of the socialization of conflict (Edsall, 1984; Schattschneider, 1960). "Single issue" or political movements, however, comprise a perennial facet of American politics (Tesh, 1984; Cantor, 1979) —and they have permeated both parties. The student and antiwar political movements, for example, resulted in fairly rapid ratification of the Twenty-sixth Amendment guaranteeing the vote for eighteen year olds and in both parties seeking increased representation for "youth." For these reasons, we consider each party separately.

POLITICAL AND SOCIAL MOVEMENTS: A DEFINITION

Before doing so, it is necessary to clarify what we mean by our distinction between social and political movements. "Movements" may be of several types. Many trends are identified as "movements" toward something whether or not they are based on collective action (i.e., are the result of independent action among large numbers of people). Yet, from a social science standpoint, the organized collective action of large numbers of people is an essential characteristic of movements. Movements are to be distinguished from a *trend*[1] (the result of many similar but independent actions) and from *quasi- movements*,[2] which possess some but not all of the characteristics of a movement. Various types of movement include intellectual, social, political and religious movements, each of which seeks institutional change. Intellectual movements, such as the behavioral movement in political science (Dahl, 1961a), occur among elites and usually remain within the intellectual discipline or "high culture" within which it originated. Social and political movements are of particular significance here because both are directed toward political changes, while religious movements (e.g., Methodism and Pentecostalism) remain within nonpolitical and nonpublic spheres of society.[3]

Our distinction between political and social movements reflects an integration of two distinct literatures: that of organized interest groups (drawing from economic and political science literatures) and that of social movements (based in sociological literature). Interest group theory focuses narrowly on individual incentives for collective action. As we saw in Chapter 2, interest group theory, by itself, is insufficient to explain social movements.[4] Moreover, a narrow focus on the mix of organizational incentives can result in an exaggeration of the differences between social movement organizations, while ignoring the central fact of their presence in the same social movement[5]. Other observers, drawing primarily on the sociological literature of social movements, have used the terms "social movement" and "political movement" interchangeably. Herbert Simons and Elizabeth Mechling (1981:418), while noting that all social movements have political goals, define political movements as "social movements with a political agenda." While we seek to incorporate social movement theory as a means of broadening our comprehension of the party system, we do not wish to ignore the insights provided by the interest group literature that acknowledges that many groups of political significance may have only political or economic goals—in particular, Mancur Olson's analysis of the logic of collective action (1965; 1971). We thus reserve the term "political movement" for those interest groups that, while clearly increasing in organized grass-roots support, have only political goals.

Social Movements: A Distinctive Social Formation of the "Have Nots"

Social movements, in contrast to both political and religious movements, are not limited to one sphere of action. They rely on the organization of social out-groups, and as thus are directed toward change in both social and political spheres. Social movements are autonomous and are based on voluntary action. Just as parties comprise a "relatively durable social formation" (Chambers, 1967:5), so too, do social movements. Social movements do not have designated leaders who have the delegated authority to speak for the whole group. As Rudolf Heberle pointed out, "a movement . . . is by definition an unorganized group, a 'social collective,' as Tonnies calls those groups which are large enough to persist and retain their identity in spite of turnover in membership and yet are lacking designated organs, being held together by sentiments and common interests rather than by institutionalized social controls" (1949:351–352). Social movements, however, are distinct from other social formations. We consider a social movement as the "the point of intersection between personal and social change" (Gerlach and Hine, 1970:xvi). Furthermore, all movements are "to some degree spontaneous, self-directing and autonomous" (Wilkinson, 1971:28). The role of conscious volition and personal transformation are central. Social movements are formed when individuals determine that their lot in life is not simply their own personal failure, but reflects in large part group discrimination that has resulted in their disadvantaged status. These are their defining characteristics, not their recourse to nontraditional or even violent means of expressing political demands.

Social movements are strongly linked to social classes—although no longer limited to the "proletarian movement." "If political, economic, and ethnic cleavages coincide, it is difficult to prevent specific grievances and interests from generalizing, thus giving protest a more diffuse character" (Smelser, 1963:279).[6] The middle- and upper-class groups in society need not form a social movement to obtain their goals—they can act directly in politics through the pressure system. This is why social movements result in an increase in ideology in the political debate (or, in E. E. Schattschneider's [1960] terms, promote the socialization of conflict). According to sociologist Heberle, a social movement is "a particular kind of social group" that possesses a "comprehensiveness in aim, of orientation towards a new social order, and of intensity of we-feeling" (1949:349–350). This results in group conflict over the distribution of resources. "A genuine social movement is an attempt of certain groups to bring about fundamental changes in the social order, especially in the basic institutions of property and labor relationships" (Heberle, 1949:348–349). Thus, social movements are "purposive in direction," involve "a critical amount of group consciousness," are based in a voluntary commitment, and result in "both personal and institutional changes" (Freeman, 1975:47; see also, Wilkinson, 1971).

Social movements are necessary because the participants have no other avenue of redress for their grievances—they are essentially outside of the political system. A social movement is based in lifestyle and values at the personal level (and hence, dependent on a group consciousness), and organized to demand change at the social and political level. By this definition, a social movement (e.g., the civil, women's, and gay rights movements) is distinct from what political scientists term *public-interest groups* (e.g., Common Cause, Ralph Nader's Public Citizen Foundation, National Consumer

Union) and *single-issue groups* (e.g., Handgun Control, Inc., Mothers Against Drunk Driving, and nuclear freeze groups).[7]

Political Movements: Middle-Class Politics of the "Haves"

Political movements possess only political goals and are directed toward the public sphere, not the private sphere. It has often been noted that political movements tend to arise from the middle class—(McFarland, 1983; Parkin, 1968), a group that already has representation in both the pressure group and the party system. Yet, it is important to recognize that the opponents of these groups are also drawn from the middle class and that many of these political movements are supported by a relatively small group of "public contributors" among the middle class. Andrew McFarland notes that, "there seem to be 100,000 households in the country that contribute at least $75 a year to three or more of the following: Common Cause, Nader's Public Citizen, LWV [League of Women Voters], ACLU [American Civil Liberties Union], public television/radio, and environmentalist lobbies" (1984:45). About one-half of those contributing to Ralph Nader's Public Citizen Foundation also give to Common Cause, and many Common Cause members are also members of the LWV and the ACLU (McFarland, 1984:45).

Examples of political movements include the new right, antinuclear power, nuclear freeze, pro-life, environmental, and public-interest movements. Political movements may be either liberal (e.g., environmental, public-interest, and nuclear freeze movements) or conservative (e.g., new right and pro-life movements). While public interest and other political movement groups may indeed reflect the values (or world view) of a particular social class, expression of these values in politics do not have the effect of socializing conflict, nor do they require a personal change among the participants.[8] Groups such as those urging a nuclear freeze or penalties against drunk drivers do not wish to expand the scope of government action to restrict the influence of private interests—the socialization of conflict (Schattschneider, 1960). These groups merely wish to alter the direction of an already existing public policy—and were the law to be changed, the group would lose its *raison d'être*.

Those groups considered as public interest groups represent a distinct subcategory of political movements. David Vogel defines the "public-interest movement" as consisting of a "wide variety of law firms, research centers, lobbying groups, membership associations, and community organizations committed to public policies that attempted to reduce the power and privileges of business" (1980:607). Similarly, the activities of public-interest groups such as Common Cause are in line with one tradition of the Progressive Era in the period 1880–1920: that of the corporate and bureaucratic progressive reformers (McFarland, 1984; Vogel, 1980).[9] This political phenomenon, developing in the late 1960s, is not to be confused with either the classic model of the social movement (McCarthy and Zald, 1973), or with political movements organized around issues (Tesh, 1984).

While public interest groups present themselves as representing a "citizen's," a "people's," or a "consumer's" movement, they do not represent an identifiable social group, but, rather, reflect an abstract economic or political category. In practice, these groups focus on procedural issues, not partisan ones; are comprised of elite professional organizers; and, therefore, lack a true grass-roots base (Vogel, 1980; McCarthy and Zald, 1973). The hypertrophy of these professional organizers is reflected in the recent increase in "staff organizations" among what political scientists classify as citizen or voluntary groups (G. Wilson, 1981; Berry, 1984). Staff organizations lack both a mass membership and an elected board of directors. Jack Walker found sponsorship by government agencies and private foundations to comprise a significant component of the initial start-up costs of citizens groups: 89 percent of these groups had received outside financial assistance compared to only 34 percent of the occupationally based groups from the profit sector. A 1977 survey of public-interest lobbies found that fully 30 percent of the groups surveyed had no membership (Berry, 1984). The lack of a grass-roots support that these figures indicate suggests, in part, the difficulty in organizing for purposive incentives (Olson, 1965); also, these groups strain credulity in their claim to represent the public interest.

This defining characteristic (i.e., narrow political goals) is reflected in the truncated organization of political movements: among political movements, one finds either a single organization with a self-selected leader (e.g., Jerry Falwell's Moral Majority [now known as the Liberty Federation] or a small number of groups focused on a single issue [e.g., STOP-ERA, Life Amendment PAC [LA-PAC]). In point of fact, these political movements are quite explicable through a "theory of minority faction" that McFarland (1983) synthesized from such interest-group theorists as Olson, Schattschneider, Grant McConnell, Theodore Lowi (and others). By contrast, social movements constitute an important potential countervailing power to minority faction interests (McFarland, 1983). This reflects the autonomous and spontaneous nature of social movements (Wilkinson, 1971). Unlike political movements, the organized groups of social movements are not limited by the willingness of elites to act as entrepreneurs (Salisbury, 1969) or to provide financial sponsorship of social activism (McCarthy and Zald, 1973). Their organizational structure consists of multiple groups, with leaders recruited—and deposed—from within (Gerlach and Hine, 1970). These manifold differences between political and social movements—in goals, organization, and the source of their membership—have structured their success and failure within the party system. We turn now to a brief history and analysis of "movement politics" within the parties.

AN OVERVIEW OF PARTY REFORM

The history of party reform—particularly in the Democratic party—is a complex one. Our goal in the remainder of this chapter is to provide an overview of the reform process as it relates to social movements. In Table 3.1, we summarize the relevant reform commissions in both parties and their treatment of women, minorities, and youth. The Democratic party has treated these groups differently. The initial McGovern–Fraser Commission provided quotas for each of these three groups, while the Mikulski Commission opted for a looser standard of affirmative action. For women, a quota was reintroduced for the 1980 convention, while other demographic groups remained under the affirmative action guidelines alone. For youth, their 1980 target level was artificially set at 10 percent, well below their presence in the electorate.

The Republican party also has authorized several reform commissions paralleling the Democrats: their treatment of demographic groups is also included in Table 3.1. In no case did the Republicans institute a quota, nor did they provide for any uniform standards for the representation of these groups at their conventions. In this context, the unreformed Republican party serves as a baseline comparison group.

In Figures 3.1 to 3.3, we compare the proportional representation of women, blacks, and youth by party, from the prereform era (1968) through the most recent nominating conventions (1984). These figures indicate the relative difference between the representation of each group between the parties. The representation of each appears to be a function of the reform rules specific to each convention. The proportion of women, blacks, and youth at the 1976 Democratic Convention dropped considerably, approaching the proportion of each at the 1976 Republican Convention. In 1976, the Mikulski Commission eliminated quotas for all groups. With the reinstitution of quotas for women in 1980, we find the proportion of women sharply increasing. By contrast, the proportion of youth steadily declined, while the proportion of blacks increased steadily, but without the sharp increase evidenced by the representation of women.

Social Movements and Democratic Party Reform

Democratic party reforms occurred in response to an internal party crisis. The precursor to Democratic party reform occurred in 1964 when the Democratic party was forced to address the problem of racial discrimination in the delegate selection process. Slavery and the caste of racial discrimination has provided one of the more divisive moral, political, and partisan dilemmas of American politics (Myrdahl et al., 1944). Racism shut blacks out of pressure group politics and influence in the party system. "The overt expressions of this discrimination have made it almost impossible for Negroes to use the

Table 3.1
Demographic Groups Targeted by Party Reforms

ELECTION YEAR AFFECTED	REFORM COMMISSION	GROUPS TARGETED FOR ANTI-DISCRIMINATION OR AFFIRMATIVE ACTION INITIATIVES	GROUPS FOR WHICH PROPORTIONAL REPRESENTATION REQUIRED
DEMOCRATIC COMMISSIONS			
1968	HUGHES	BLACKS	NONE
1972	MCGOVERN-FRASER	MINORITIES	BLACKS WOMEN YOUTH
1976	MIKULSKI	WOMEN MINORITIES	NONE
1980	WINOGRAD	MINORITIES	WOMEN
1984	HUNT	MINORITIES	WOMEN
REPUBLICAN COMMISSIONS			
1972	DO COMMITTEE	MINORITIES WOMEN	NONE
1976	RULE 29 COMMITTEE	MINORITIES WOMEN	NONE

We use the popular names of the various reform commissions. For a more extensive discussion of these commissions, the reader is referred to Price (1983:145–187) and Crotty and Jackson (1985:27–54).

Figure 3.1
Proportion of Women Delegates at National Nominating Conventions, by Party, 1968–1984

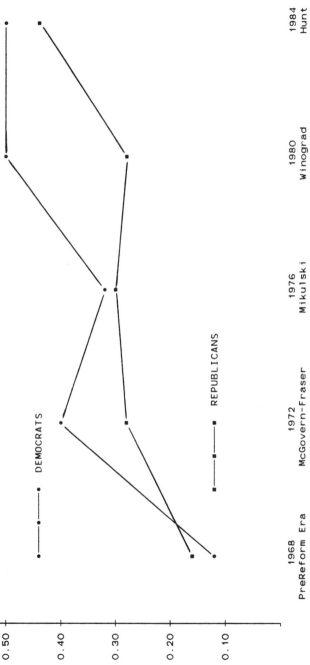

Figure 3.2
**Proportion of Black Delegates at National Nominating Conventions, by Party,
1968–1984**

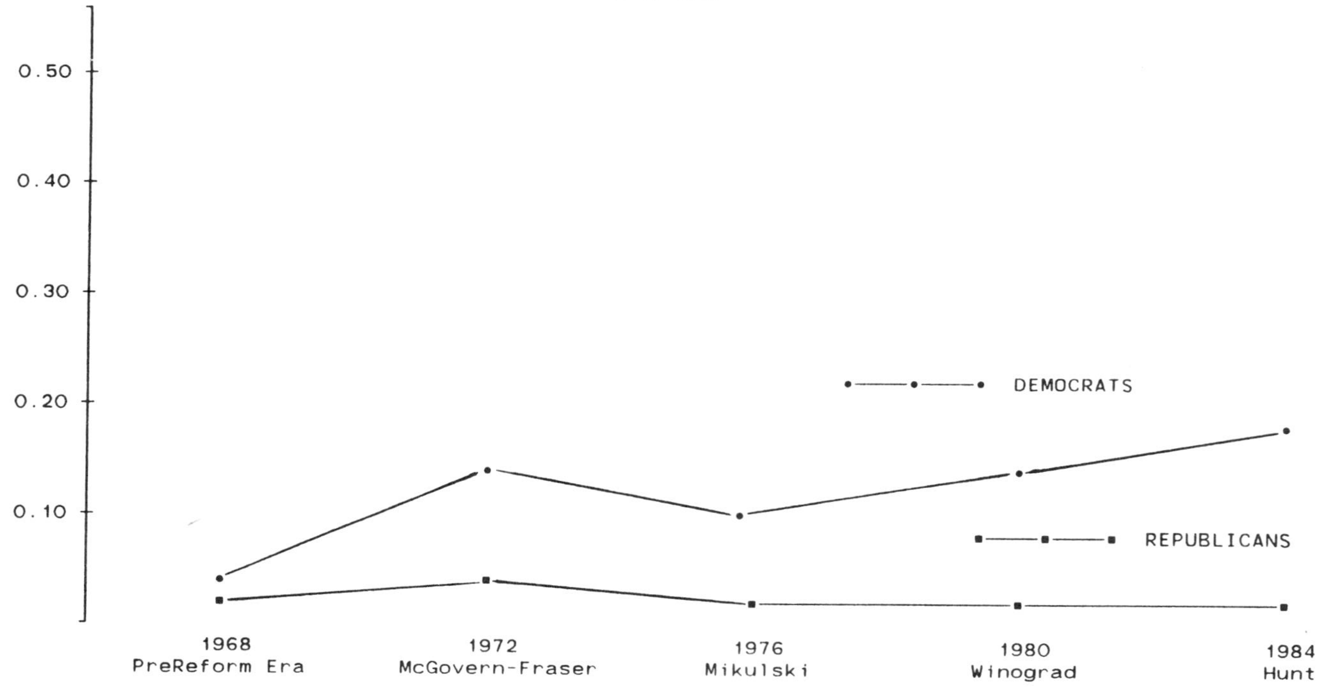

Figure 3.3

Proportion of Delegates Under Thirty Years of Age at National Nominating Conventions, by Party, 1968–1984

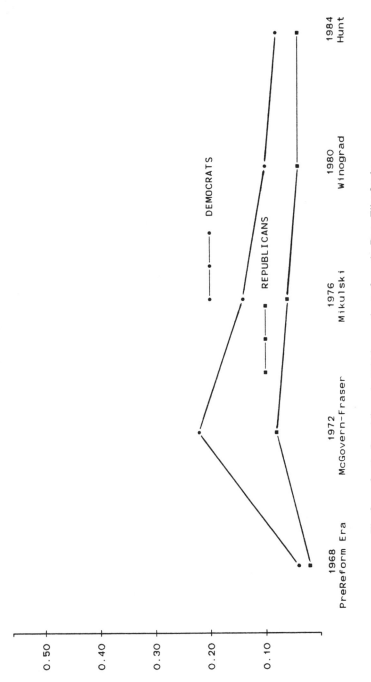

The figure for the Republicans in 1984 is an estimate from the Party Elite Study.

normal political channels in the South—or anywhere in the country, for that matter—for meaningful change" (Walton, 1972:37). The result of discrimination in the party system—despite the fact that blacks have comprised a major part of the Democratic party coalition since the 1932 New Deal realignment—has meant the development of numerous state-level black third political parties (Walton, 1972) and posed a serious internal party conflict for the Democrats by exposing the incongruity of southern whites and southern blacks supporting the same party. Crotty indicates that Democratic party discrimination was nearly total in the South. "In 1964, prior to reform of any kind, two-thirds of the state party delegations to the national convention contained no blacks whatsoever; only one southern state had any black representation, and of the total 671 chosen in the South, one-half of one percent were black" (1983:120).

The civil rights movement presented the first challenge to the Democratic elite oligarchy. A second social movement important in the evolution of Democratic party reform is the contemporary women's rights movement. While the civil rights movement began in the mid–1950s, the women's rights movement began about a decade later. The largest national-level feminist organization—the National Organization for Women (NOW) was organized in 1966. Other groups, unrelated to and unaware of NOW, formed exclusively at the local level. For example, in 1967, Jo Freeman (1983a:20) reports that "at least five groups in five different cities (Chicago, Toronto, Detroit, Seattle, and Gainesville, Florida) formed spontaneously, independently of each other."

In contrast to blacks, women apparently achieved representation in the pressure and party system almost half a century earlier. Both parties established separate women's divisions located within the national committees— the Democrats in 1916 and the Republicans in 1919 (Cotter and Hennessy, 1964:150–51). Following ratification of the Nineteenth Amendment granting the franchise to women, both parties moved to ensure the representation of women via the Fifty-Fifty Rule, which provided for a co-chair of the opposite sex (in practice, almost always a women) for nearly all positions in the party hierarchy (e.g., national, state, and county chairs) and the practice of appointing a national committee*man* and a national committee*woman* from each of the state parties. This appears to give women considerable influence within the party system. Political scientists during this era noted that women active in politics tended to engage in reformist politics. Feminist scholars, however, have suggested that the party system itself discriminates against women (Jaquette, 1974:xxxvi. n. 72).

Strong evidence supporting Jane Jaquette's conclusion is found in a study of the members of the Democratic and Republican National Committees from 1948 to 1963 (Cotter and Hennessy, 1964). Cornelius Cotter and Bernard Hennessy found a sharp contrast between the influence of men and women in the national parties. While the national committee*men* were judged to be important figures in their respective state parties, nearly one-third of Republican women and one-half of the Democratic women were rated as quite unimportant. Cotter and Hennessy conclude that, "if *these* women have little influence, then *no women have much influence in state political parties.* The national committeewomen are as important as any women in the parties, but of very little importance at all by comparison with the male party leaders. In most states, at most levels of party organization, women have *equal representation* with men; there is no evidence that they have ever had *equal influence*" (1964:58; emphasis in original). Thus, the political goal of ending sexism required a frontal attack on the sexism within the parties. The women's rights movement, organized in the mid–1960s, became more self-consciously directed toward the party system with the formation of the National Women's Political Caucus in 1971.

In 1964, a convention challenge to the seating of the official all-white Mississippi delegation was made by the integrated Mississippi Freedom Democratic Party (MFDP). The MFDP reflected the increasing politicization of the civil rights movement, represented by such groups as the National Association for the Advancement of Colored People (NAACP), the Congress for Racial Equality (CORE), the Southern Christian Leadership Conference (SCLC), and the Student Nonviolent Coordinating Committee (SNCC).[10] The MFDP was a "SNCC-founded and SNCC-backed organization" (Stoper, 1983:324). This convention challenge was resolved through a compromise seating of two of the MFDP delegates and the passing of resolutions outlawing racial discrimination in the delegate selection process. The resulting Special Equal Rights Committee, chaired by Governor Richard Hughes of New Jersey, proposed six rules banning racial discrimination at all public meetings of the party that were subsequently adopted by the Democratic National Committee in January 1968. These guidelines provided the foundation for the subsequent party reforms (Crotty and Jackson, 1985).

The year 1968 was a watershed year for the Democrats. Racial tensions continued. In April, Dr. Martin Luther King, head of the SCLC, was assassinated, which was followed by urban unrest and riots in more than 120 cities. Further, the prohibitions against racial discrimination proved to be insufficient in increasing black representation at the convention. "By 1968, and *after* the implementation of the new bans on socially discriminatory practices by the Democrats' Special Committee and the 1968 national convention, the southern states had advanced to the stage of token black representation: All southern states now had some black delegates, but blacks could claim only 10 percent of the region's total (as opposed to 25% of its population)" (Crotty, 1983:120).

The Johnson administration faced increasing protest against its conduct of the Vietnam War—an opposition that was galvanized by the January Tet offensive—that demonstrated a widening "credibility gap" between public perceptions and administration pronouncements. While the Republicans were able to conduct an orderly nominating convention (culminating in the selection of Richard Nixon), the Democratic nomination process was rife with conflict. With the surprise decision of President Lyndon Johnson not to seek re-election in March, the primary field was left open to antiwar critics. Johnson's vice president Hubert Humphrey sought the nomination, but chose not to enter a single primary. On June 5, 1968, following his California primary victory, Robert Kennedy was assassinated. With the elimination of his chief rival, Humphrey easily received the Democratic party nomination in August—but with protesters in the Chicago streets outside the convention hall being beaten by police during one of the bloodiest conventions in the history of the party.

While Humphrey easily won the nomination with 67 percent of the vote, these conflicts split the convention delegates as well. "The convention hall was the scene of dramatic confrontations, as supporters of McCarthy and Kennedy, who opposed the Vietnam War, challenged both the control of the convention by party regulars and the candidacy of Humphrey" (Crotty and Jackson, 1985:30–31). A blue-ribbon *ad hoc* commission put together by disgruntled McCarthy supporters earlier in the spring released its report, *The Democratic Choice*, on the eve of the convention. Chaired by Governor Harold Hughes of Iowa, the commission recommended that an official party commission be appointed to examine problems in delegate selection, concluding that "state systems for selecting delegates to the national convention and the procedures of the convention itself display considerably less fidelity to basic democratic principles than a nation which claims to govern itself can safely tolerate" (quoted in Polsby, 1983a:28). Accordingly, the 1968 Democratic Convention authorized the creation of two reform commissions: the Commission on Party Structure and Delegate Selection (later known as the McGovern–Fraser Commission), and the Commission on Rules (known as the O'Hara Commission) to reconsider national convention procedures.

The defeat of the Democratic nominee by Nixon provided strong incentives for the Democrats to reconsider their nomination process. The McGovern-Fraser Commission reported to the Democratic National Committee in April 1970. Its report, *Mandate for Reform*, provided the basis for a transformation of the presidential nominating process. The commission's report, included in the call to the 1972 convention, recommended wide-ranging changes: rules requiring the timeliness of delegate selection (within the same calendar year as the election), public notice of meeting and due process procedures, the prohibition of *ex officio* delegates, and abolition of the unit rule and provision for proportional representation of mass preferences into delegate seats. The most important rule changes for our purposes were those prohibiting discrimination against minorities and requiring representation of women, blacks, and youth in "reasonable relationship to the group's presence in the population of the state" (quoted in Crotty and Jackson, 1985:33).

The activity of the civil rights and the women's rights movements did not end with the creation of the *Mandate for Reform*. The pressure continued through the implementation stage of the new reforms (i.e., 1970 to 1972) and at the 1972 convention. The newly formed National Women's Political Caucus (in the summer of 1971) was a major actor in the push to interpret the McGovern-Fraser guidelines as a numerical quota, not merely as affirmative action measures. To a lesser extent, black public officials also acted to support this new stronger interpretation (Shafer, 1983:460–491). One political movement conspicuously absent from these negotiations was the student movement (Shafer, 1983:490).

The NWPC continued its pressure through the convention, encouraging women at the state and local levels to run as delegates and setting up a convention headquarters in Miami in their successful quest to gain inclusion of their fifteen-point Rights of Women plank in the party platform (Abzug and Kelber, 1984:36). The women's rights movement and the NWPC received considerable support from the women delegates to the 1972 convention. Virginia Sapiro and Barbara Farah (1980:31) report that 81 percent of the women delegates were sympathetic toward the NWPC and 68 percent were supporters of the "Women's Liberation movement."

One reform goal was left unfinished on the eve of the 1972 convention: the drafting of a party charter. Both the McGovern-Fraser and the O'Hara commissions claimed the authority to draft the charter, but both commissions were preoccupied with their other areas of concern. Just prior to the convention, Donald Fraser and James O'Hara collaborated on a draft charter that they presented in May 1972. The 1972 convention did not debate the document, instead, authorizing a Party Charter Commission, headed by then Duke University President Terry Sanford (now Senator Sanford, D-NC). The successor to the McGovern-Fraser Commission—the Mikulski Commission (the Commission on Delegate Selection and Party Structure)—was also authorized by the 1972 convention. The Mikulski Commission, chaired by then Baltimore city-council member Barbara Mikulski (now Senator Mikulski, D-MD), completed its work first. In contrast to the McGovern-Fraser Commission, the Mikulski Commission was only authorized to propose revision of the delegate selection rules, responsibility for implementation of the guidelines, when approved by the DNC, was assigned to a new group, termed the Compliance Review Commission (1974–1976).

The Mikulski Commission provided a battleground between party regulars and the party reformers. Following the humiliating defeat of George McGovern in 1972, "the party regulars were furious. They were out for blood and their intention was to scuttle the McGovern–Fraser Commission's guidelines" (Crotty, 1983:63). The regulars were aided in their battle by the formation of a new group—the Coalition for a Democratic Majority (CDM)— that opposed the McGovern–Fraser reforms (Crotty, 1978:226–231). The group, organized by Ben J. Wattenberg (1972 campaign manager for Senator Henry Jackson [D-WA] and coauthor, with Richard Scammon of *The Real*

Majority [1970]), sought to return the Democratic party to the New Deal–Fair Deal alliance of groups (labor, ethnics and small farmers) and issues (economics and defense). The group soon affiliated itself with a number of academics (e.g., Austin Ranney and Jeane J. Kirkpatrick) who provided trenchant scholarly critiques of party reform (Ranney, 1975; Kirkpatrick, 1976; 1979). However, as Crotty notes, "in general, the coalition was supportive of the balance of the guidelines" (1978:229)—in particular, the procedural reforms. The major McGovern-Fraser innovation attacked by the group were the quotas—which it considered "arbitrary biological categories" (quoted in Crotty, 1978:228), while supporting the increased presence of party regulars.

The CDM succeeded in achieving its proposed changes. The most significant Mikulski Commission change involved the omission of mandatory quotas, while the state parties were permitted to "select up to 25 percent of a national convention delegation in order to better represent party and public officeholders *and* minorities" (Crotty, 1983:71; emphasis in original). The McGovern-Fraser ban against *ex officio* delegates was retained, while mandatory demographic quotas were specifically banned in favor of the implementation by states of affirmative action programs. The Mikulski guidelines specifically stated that "a State Party which has adopted and implemented an affirmative action plan may not be challenged solely on the basis of delegation composition or primary results" (quoted in Crotty, 1983:71). Thus, for the 1976 convention, no groups were guaranteed a specific proportion of the delegate seats; moreover, challenges were made more difficult. While the brunt of the Mikulski Commission guidelines were considered to provide an endorsement of the reform process, this resulted in a setback for blacks, women, and youth. For each of these groups, their convention representation was sharply reduced in 1976 (see Figs. 3.1 to 3.3).

Given the Party Charter Commission mandate to consider national party reform, the deliberations of this group provided another arena for blacks and women to pursue stronger affirmative action measures. Having lost to the CDM, labor groups such as the AFL-CIO, and the party regulars in the Mikulski Commission, blacks and women redoubled their efforts to ensure the preservation of reforms in the party charter that was to be adopted at the first Democratic midterm conference held in December 1974. The controversy centered around the provisions required for Article 10, which provided for "Full Participation" in the party "at all levels." The stakes were high: the charter provided for a supreme party law that could only be amended by a two-thirds vote of the DNC, or a majority vote of the national convention. Reform opponents sought charter language comparable to the Mikulski Commission guidelines, while supporters of reform sought stronger provisions. The Sanford Commission proposed a version of Article 10 with the weakened Mikulski guidelines that banned mandatory quotas and placed the burden of proof on the challenger to a delegation, not the party that sponsored the delegation. At the midterm convention, following a threatened walkout by blacks and organized efforts by caucuses of women, blacks, and Latinos, the performance of a party unit in meeting affirmative action was made evidence (although not the sole evidence) indicating violation of full participation. While mandatory quotas were banned in section 5, women delegates were able to achieve the addition of the following section 7: "Notwithstanding section 5 above, equal division at any level of delegate or committee positions between delegate men and delegate women or committeeman or committeewoman shall not constitute a violation of any provision above" (reproduced in *Congressional Quarterly*, 1974). While the party charter did not supersede the Mikulski guidelines for the 1976 convention, this proviso provided a loophole for women for the 1980 convention. The 1976 convention endorsed the promotion of equal division—an idea that was clearly gaining support within the party.

Beginning with the 1980 Democratic National Convention, two groups did receive an allotted number of seats. The relevant reform bodies were the Commission on Presidential Nomination and Party Structure—the Winograd Commission (chaired by Morley Winograd)—in effect for the 1980 convention and the Commission on Presidential Nomination—the Hunt Commission (chaired by James B. Hunt, Jr.)—in effect for the 1984 convention. The Winograd Commission provided for a 10 percent "add-on" of pledged delegate seats reserved for state party officials and public officeholders (to be appointed by the state party committees). Affirmative action programs with "specific goals and timetables" were required for women, blacks, Hispanics, and Native Americans (quoted in Price, 1984:153). In contrast to the strengthened requirement for these groups, the Compliance Review Commission that implemented the Winograd guidelines permitted the state parties to uniformly set a goal of 10 percent for youth—well below the approximately 27 percent of Democratic identifiers who comprised this category in the electorate (Crotty, 1983)."[11] Crotty adds that "no one seemed to know (or care) whether the informal objective had been—or in the future would be—reached" (1983:90). While the Winograd Commission rejected a proposal to require an equal division of delegate seats by sex, the Democratic National Committee, under pressure from women, overturned the Winograd Commission on this point. On the eve of the 1978 Democratic midterm conference and nearly a year after the Winograd Commission made its report, the DNC mandated that the state parties "promote" an equal division in its call to the 1980 convention (Crotty, 1983:79).

With little debate, the Hunt Commission affirmed the equal division rule for the 1984 convention, along with the affirmative action guidelines for minorities (Price, 1984:163–166). Opponents to the rule for the 1980 convention were, by 1981, either supporters of equal division, or else, "were maintaining a prudent silence," as the "National Organization for Women and the National Women's Political Caucus testified at every hearing, did their homework, and communicated effectively with commission and DNC members" (Price, 1984:164). More controversial was the "superdelegate" provision. The Hunt Commission added unpledged delegates to the 1984 convention, which resulted in approximately a 17 percent party leader and elected official "add-on" for the state-based delegations, for a total of 14.4 percent unpledged delegates—the superdelegates (Price, 1984:166–171). The superdelegates included 164 Democratic members of the U.S. House of Representatives and 27 Democratic Senators (Crotty and Jackson, 1985:35).

Since 1972, party reform has become a quadrennial phenomenon for the Democrats. The original targeted groups have all fared differently in their treatment by the various delegate reform commissions (see Table 3.1). Representation of the groups is a zero sum game, with trade-offs for one group being a victory for another. "The big winners in the battle over representation appear to be women and party officeholders. Women are guaranteed one-half of the total Democratic seats at national conventions and officeholders between one-fourth and one-fifth (although, of course, their numbers may far exceed this designated share). The big losers are blacks and other minorities and youths" (Crotty, 1983:137). Blacks have greatly increased their delegate representation since 1964. From 2 percent of the delegates to the 1964 convention, blacks comprised 7 percent of the 1968 convention delegates, and averaged about 14 percent of the first three postreform conventions—a figure that approximates their presence in the population, but that still under-represents their contribution to the Democratic party coalition.[12] The 1984 convention represents a "high-water mark for black convention delegates"—about 18 percent of the delegates were black. However, this was primarily because of the candidacy of Jesse Jackson "whose delegate count stood at 375, or almost 10 percent of the total, and a large percentage of Jackson's delegates were black," not because of any change in party rules (Crotty and Jackson, 1985:108). Women now comprise 50 percent of Democratic conventions, up from 13 percent in 1968. Youth (those under thirty), comprising only 3 percent of the delegates in 1968, rose to 22 percent in 1972 and have decreased steadily since then (dropping to 8 percent in 1984) (Crotty and Jackson, 1985:108).

Why have these groups fared so differently? According to Crotty, the evolution of reform reflects the "realities of political power" (1983:137). In a zero sum situation, groups required strong organization to build on the initial commitment—and the resulting representation mirrors its organizational strength vis-à-vis the other groups. All observers agree that the youth or student "movement," while of some political importance from 1968 until 1972, never constituted a viable force or constituency in internal party politics (Shafer, 1983:490; Crotty, 1983:137; Crotty and Jackson, 1985:109). The loss of blacks is ironic as "the civil rights movement was one of the generating forces that led to party reform" (Crotty, 1983:137). While the representation of blacks has substantially increased, it remains less than their contribution to the Democratic party coalition. Byron Shafer argues that blacks were not as active as feminists in the implementation stage of the McGovern-Fraser guidelines because "they were already a recognized major part of the orthodox Democratic coalition" (1983:490). However, after the retrenchment of the Mikulski Commission, blacks were unable to maintain the necessary organization and aggressive leadership to maintain the original party commitment (Crotty, 1983; see also Price, 1984:163). The women's movement and the party regulars, in contrast to the other groups, were able to organize and defend their gains. Thus, the social and political movements of the 1960s have had differential degrees of success with the Democratic party.

Whether the reform consequences have been good or ill is a matter of controversy (e.g., compare Polsby [1983a] with Crotty [1983]), However, most would agree that the direct result has been to open up a formerly closed party system: expanding participation, and greatly, albeit differentially, increasing the elite participation of women, blacks, and other minorities in the Democratic party.

Political Movements and the Republican Party Nonreforms

Democratic party reform was based on the national leadership asserting its national leadership and preeminence over diverse state and local practices. In this context, the Republican party remains "unreformed" in its commitment to state and local autonomy (Polsby, 1983a; Price, 1984; Crotty, 1983; Crotty and Jackson, 1985). The Republican party did, of course, authorize and appoint two reform commissions (the Delegates and Organizations ("DO") Committee authorized by the 1968 convention, and the Rule 29 Committee (named after the party bylaw under which it was established), authorized by the 1972 convention. With the appointment of two reform bodies paralleling the first two Democratic reform commissions that institutionalized Democratic reform, why did the two parties diverge in their approach to reform?

First, the Republicans had little incentive to reform. While the party's electoral base during this era had been eroding (with a steady decline in Republican party identifiers) and the Democrats remained the majority party in terms of identifiers and in dominance of the state houses and the U.S. Congress, the Republicans had won the presidency in 1968 and in 1972. "During 1968, the Republicans had no Chicago convention, no riots, no cries of police state rule, no divisive war to rationalize, no mass demonstrations to counter, no searing party breaches to mend, no raw emotions to placate, and no president to reject" (Crotty, 1983:206). The Republican party's main concern was not any internal party divisiveness, but rather, a public relations problem with a declining group of Republican party supporters and a need to appeal to those sympathetic to the Democratic party—and the Democratic reforms (i.e., independents and Democratic identifiers).

Second, the Republicans also had much less to reform. Democratic reforms encompassed a whole range of due process requirements that were necessary because of its reliance on a "common law" approach to convention procedures and delegate selection. By contrast, the Republicans had "evolved an orderly set of written rules to guide their deliberations" (Crotty, 1983:207). The unit rule—which had raised such conflict among the Democrats—had been banned by the Republicans in 1880 (Crotty, 1978:288–89 n. 51). Many Republicans agreed with then RNC chairperson, Senator Robert Dole, who declared in 1971 that "we're still about forty years ahead of the Democrats as far as reform is concerned" while the opposition was "just catching up!" (quoted in Crotty, 1983:208).

Third, reform of Republican party law is a lengthy and complex process, requiring at least two national conventions for full implementation. A Republican reform committee authorized by one national convention has no independent authority to implement reforms—unlike the Democrats. Instead, its role is to present its conclusions and proposals to the next national convention. Prior to final convention consideration, the reform proposals are presented in turn to the Rules Committee of the national committee, the full RNC, and the Rules Committee of the next convention. Thus, "the party regulars and the party leadership acting through the national committee and the convention retained uncontested power over what if any change would be instituted" (Crotty, 1983:216–17).

These factors, along with the 1973–1975 campaign finance scandal (part of the Watergate scandal), all structured the Republican consideration of reform. The DO Committee (authorized by the 1968 convention) was appointed in June 1969, with the mandate to "review and study the Rules adopted by the 1968 Republican National Convention" and to "report with recommendations to the next Republican National Convention" (Crotty, 1983:221). In particular, the DO Committee was to study Rule 32 of the bylaws, "which provides that participation in a Republican primary, caucus, any meeting or convention held for the purpose of selecting Delegates for a County, State or National Convention shall in no way be abridged for reasons of race, religion, color or national origin . . . " (quoted in Crotty, 1983:221).

The resulting review was entirely "in-house." The DO Committee's membership of seventeen was comprised entirely of members of the RNC. It had no independent staff, and it was chaired by the National Committeewoman from Missouri, Rosemary Ginn, who "had no national reputation or constituency to mobilize on behalf of reform (if she had wanted to). She was unknown politically and had never served in elective political office" (Crotty, 1983:222). This contrasts sharply with the independent organization and outside political leadership of the Democratic commissions. The DO Committee's recommendations were primarily procedural: meetings were to be opened, proxy voting was banned, *ex officio* delegates were prohibited, fees and assessments for delegates were banned, secret voting by convention committees was prohibited, and a new delegate allocation formula was enacted.

The central reforms of concern to the present study, however, were not procedural—just how did the Republicans respond to the demands for representation of the contemporary social movements? Since the civil rights legislation of the 1960s, the allegiance of blacks to the Democratic party coalition was complete. Black voters are solidly Democratic—but comprise an extremely insignificant part of the Republican party coalition. Therefore, one would not expect blacks to comprise a major constituency group within the Republican party.

Women, however, are quite a different story. During the 1950s, *The American Voter* reported that women were 3 to 5 percent more Republican than men, although this has been attributed to demographic differences—secular, rather than political factors (Campbell et al., 1960). Furthermore, the Republican party historically has provided greater levels of support for women at elite party levels. In 1940, the Republican party endorsed the Equal Rights Amendment (first proposed in Congress in 1920); the Democrats followed suit four years later. In a study of Democratic and Republican national committee members serving office in the prereform era (1948–1963), Republican committeewomen were judged to be somewhat more influential in the GOP than were Democratic women in their party (Cotter and Hennessy, 1964:58). And, until quite recently, the majority of women serving in state legislatures and in Congress have been Republican, not Democratic (Sapiro and Farah, 1980; Diamond, 1977; Lynn, 1979). Until 1986 (with the election of Barbara Mikulski [D-MD]), no Democratic woman had been elected in her own right to the U.S. Senate, whereas two Republican women served: Paula Hawkins (R-FL) and Nancy Kassebaum (R-KS) in the Ninety-ninth Congress. The National Federation of Republican Women (NFRW) is a well-organized and well-funded organization that was founded in 1938 to bind together local Republican women's clubs. Headquartered in the RNC, the GFRW is distinct from the women's divisions and has no counterpart among the Democrats (Cotter and Hennessy, 1964:151). Thus, one might expect elite Republican women to comprise a powerful constituent group for reform.

The National Women's Political Caucus was a central actor in the 1972 Democratic party reforms. According to the then NWPC Democratic cochair Bella Abzug, this reflected "the fact that most caucus members were pro-Democratic" (Abzug and Kelber, 1984:37). However, the NWPC also attempted to increase the representation of women at the Republican conventions. At the same time that they contacted DNC chair Lawrence O'Brien (November 1971), the NWPC co-chairs wrote RNC chair Dole urging that women be fairly represented at the 1972 convention. The letter was subsequently released to the press (Shafer, 1983:267–268). One would expect this to produce some pressure on the party, although the DO Committee had completed its report in the preceding summer.

The DO Committee proposed an extension of Rule 32, which was approved by the 1972 convention. The amended Rule 32 provided that the RNC and the state committees "take positive action" to endeavor the "broadest possible participation," "including such participation by women, young people, minority and heritage [ethnic] groups and senior citizens in the delegate selection process" (quoted in Crotty, 1983:213–214). However, this stronger language did not have the force of party law. Crotty stresses that the "provisions amounted to nothing more than recommendations that the state parties were free to adopt, reject, modify, or implement as they saw fit" (1983:217). Thus, these changes, along with a new Rule 29—which authorized a "broadly representative" (the Rule 29) committee to work with the state parties— provided the basis for the first real consideration of the underrepresentation of demographic groups in Republican conventions.

The Rule 29 Committee was chaired by the late congressman William A. Steiger (R-WI), who supported substantial reform to ensure the "open door" policy of the Republican party. The membership was more diversified: its fifty-eight members included elected Republican party officials and state party leaders, as well national committee members (Crotty, 1983:228–230). There was, moreover, a developing constituency for reform among elite Republican women. In 1972, Abzug reports that a "small, informal group of Republican feminists and legislators" supported passage of the strengthened Rule 32 (1984:37). Following the convention, Republican party feminists organized a "formal task force that affiliated with the NWPC and worked more effectively at the 1976 convention" (Abzug and Kelber, 1984:37). The increasing efforts of party feminists were reflected in the amendment sponsored by Congresswoman Margaret Heckler (R-MA). Heckler, along with Steiger, Governor Christopher Bond (R-MO) and Senator Pete Domenici (R-NM), sought to amend Rule 32 to require state action and to require RNC and Rules Committee review and approval for the seating of delegates. Provisions were also proposed providing for bonus delegates for those states complying with Rule 29 suggestions for outreach programs (Crotty, 1977). The opportunity for significant Republican party reform, however, was lost. This amendment was greatly diluted by conservatives when reviewed by the RNC: the party would only "urge," not require, and state parties need not submit the plan itself, only "examples." Finally, the proposals were emphatically not "any type of a quota system," and were specifically not "binding upon any state organization" (quoted in Crotty, 1983:281). Following this evisceration of any enforceable party reform, the Rules Committee of the 1976 Convention refused to reauthorize the Rule 29 Committee. Instead, study of the bylaws was assigned to a Rules Review Committee for the 1980 convention and to a Technical Amendments Subcommittee for the 1984 convention (Price, 1984:158). Both of these groups were contained within the RNC— thus, "ensuring once again a captive group totally unlikely to embarrass the party" (Crotty, 1983:231).

These two committees comprised the apex of national-level Republican reform efforts. By 1977, the reform era was over, with no concrete gains for Republican women. Given previous research (e.g., Sapiro and Farah, 1980;

Cotter and Hennessy, 1964), one might argue that Republican women did not need reform because they already possessed influence in the party. However, the record of the past ten years indicates that this simply is not the case. The Republican party has not only avoided formulating uniform standards for representation of women and minorities but, following the 1976 convention, has alienated the mainstream of Republican women by reversing its historic support for women's rights issues. The representation of women at the convention and the policy issues became linked in 1976. If Republican women did have the influence they are reputed to have, then they would most certainly have avoided the setbacks they suffered at the hands of the new right since 1976.

The Republican Women's Task Force of the NWPC reported on the 1976 convention—speaking of the Republican party's

distressing inclination to turn its back on a history of consistent advances for women. Women held fewer important posts at the 1976 convention than they had in some past conventions; only a letter from task force chair Patricia Goldman, shortly before the convention, resulted in the inclusion of a few more women speakers in the program. Any hope of strengthening Rule 32 was abandoned as task force members fought to avoid diluting what had proved to be an already leaky commitment to expanding women's participation in the conventions. (quoted in Abzug and Kelber, 1984:52)

The major efforts of the Republican feminists were concentrated in a narrow victory retaining the GOP's endorsement of the ERA and in narrowly reversing on the floor the Platform Committee's endorsement of a constitutional ban on abortion (Abzug and Kelber, 1984:51).

In 1980, the party then took a decisive step away from the women's rights movement by its reversal of its forty-year commitment to the ERA in the Republican party platform. This policy change was a direct result of the nomination of Ronald Reagan. The Republican Women's Task Force of the NWPC sent a questionnaire to the presidential candidates (Ronald Reagan, John Anderson, Howard Baker, George Bush, and John Connolly). All—with the exception of Reagan—supported the ERA and opposed a constitutional ban on abortion (Abzug, 1984:81–82). Because Reagan (the apparent nominee) had the delegates, the draft report of the Platform Committee that incorporated planks endorsing a constitutional ban on abortion and one that affirmed support for "equal rights and equality for women" without endorsing the ERA was nearly a *fait accompli*. Elite Republican women were bitterly opposed to this turn of events. "On July 14, the day the convention opened, ten thousand women marched through downtown Detroit to the GOP meeting place in a demonstration of support for the ERA; leading Republican women and the nine pro-ERA Platform Committee members were visibly up front" (Abzug and Kelber, 1984:82). At the conclusion of the 1980 convention vote on the platform, RNC co-chair Mary Crisp resigned her position, sharply and publicly criticizing the platform positions on ERA and abortion (Malbin, 1981:112).

The Reagan campaign attempted to defuse the potentially volatile issue. Crisp was succeeded by Betty Heitman, then president of the NFRW. Historically, the NFRW was regarded as a conservative influence in the party (Cotter and Hennessy, 1964:154). Under Heitman's leadership, the NFRW had been moving toward a more active role in women's issues, and Heitman had been instrumental in forming an advisory council of Republican women (including public officeholders) that presented a list of specific legislative and administrative proposals to the platform subcommittee on human resources, after gaining Reagan's support. The nominee-apparent had agreed with the federation plank, "asking only that language be added pledging enforcement of statutes already on the books and repeal of statutes that promote discrimination against women" (Malbin, 1981:109). While this specific language was inadvertently left out of the final platform draft, this compromise was the basis for the "Fifty States Project," which was Reagan's plan to work for equal rights without a constitutional amendment. This plan was presented to the prominent ERA supporters among the delegates just prior to the convention vote on the platform.[13] The Fifty States Project underwent a quick *denouement* in 1983 when Barbara Honegger publicly resigned from her position as project director of the Attorney General's Gender Discrimination Agency Review and denounced the project as a sham (Abzug and Kelber, 1981:141).

In the 1984 campaign, the Republican convention affirmed a platform that opposed ratification of the Equal Rights Amendment. The Reagan campaign, increasingly sensitive to the political issue of the gender gap, sought to reduce perceptions that the Republican party was antiwoman by increasing the proportion of women among the delegates and the visibility of female delegates on the podium. This superficial attempt to appeal to women was quietly boycotted by Kassebaum (R-KS), who appeared at the convention only to make her keynote speech, claiming that she did not wish to be "window dressing." Meanwhile, former party chair Mary Louise Smith (and others) held press conferences criticizing the direction that the party had taken (MacPherson, 1984). Smith, chair of the Reagan-Bush Women's Policy Board, had been removed as a member of the Civil Rights Commission. At an off-the-record meeting of high-ranking Republican women in early 1984, Judy Mann (1984) reports one Republican woman as asserting "it was loyalty to Mary Louise that kept a lot of people in line in 1980 and there isn't a single Republican woman in the nation who doesn't know what they've done to her." Thus, the new policy commitments of the Republican party, strongly supported by the new right, were opposed by women at the highest reaches of the party.

We discussed the 1980 Republican convention in some detail to indicate that the Republican party indeed does possess a constituent group that has lobbied for internal party reform. However, the recent history of the Republican party indicates that the party has turned away from the reform and policy interests of these women toward representation of the new right, while ironically increasing the proportion of women at the 1984 convention as a public relations move.

What is the new right? Is it a newly developing social movement that simply has been more successful than the women's rights movement? We argue that the answer is no. The new right is a political movement, formed as a strategic alliance between conservative Republican elites and several prominent televangelists. The significance of the new right is that it crosscuts the New Deal coalition and allows the Republican party to successfully appeal to the Democratic South without an overt use of the sensitive race issue.

We make this argument for four reasons. First, activists on the Republican right sought an alliance with televangelists and a link to the conservative social issues of abortion and the ERA because it was politically useful. The factional fight between the Republican right wing and Republican moderates intensified in 1974–1975, with Republican voter identification reaching its nadir in mid–1974 following the resignation of Nixon and Gerald Ford's assumption of the presidency.

What, conservatives asked themselves, had over six years of Republican governance accomplished? South Vietnam had gone under, Red China had been recognized, detente had become the entrenched foreign policy, and the military balance of power was shifting in the Soviets' favor. More school children were being bused than ever before, and a Republican administration had even established racial quotas. One Republican president had declared himself a Keynesian and surrendered to wage and price controls, while his successor had proposed huge budgets with huge deficits. All the while, Great Society programs survived and grew. (Reinhard, 1983:229)

As Barbara Ehrenreich (1984:155) notes, right wing interest in feminist issues increased because the old issues of anticommunism "were not selling as well as they once had." While certainly not an unprincipled move (feminism had always been viewed as a threat to national security) from a tactical perspective, the controversy over women's rights permitted a group widely regarded on the fringe of Republican party politics to enter the mainstream. With the election of Jimmy Carter in 1976, the apparent beneficiary of the evangelical vote—a large socially conservative group—the Republican right wing "saw a new constituency for the New Right" (Hershey, 1984:16). According to Gary Jarmin (of the American Conservative Union), "the beauty of it is that we don't have to organize these voters. They already have their own television networks, publications, schools, meeting places, and respected leaders who are sympathetic to our goals" (quoted in Guth, 1983:69).

Second, the organization of major new right groups is both new and derives from a recent alliance between secular conservatives and televangelists. James

Guth (1983) dates the origins of the new right from 1979, with the formation of the Moral Majority, shortly followed by the Christian Voice, the Religious Roundtable, and the National Christian Action Coalition. Jerry Cardwell stresses, in his study of televangelism, that the "Moral Majority is a political organization, not a religious one. The men who came up with the idea for a Christian political movement were not preachers; they were, in fact, political professionals" (1984:158). These political professionals included secular political strategists Paul Weyrich (Committee for the Survival of a Free Congress), Howard Phillips (Conservative Caucus), Jarmin (American Conservative Union), and Richard Viguerie and Terry Dolan (National Conservative Political Action Committee). On realizing the potential of the alliance in late 1978,

New Right leaders set about recruiting the evangelicals. Viguerie provided his mass-mailing expertise, Robert Billings joined Falwell to set up Moral Majority, Gary Jarmin moved to Christian Voice, and Conservative Caucus field organizer Edward McAteer created the Religious Roundtable.... Congressional conservatives were equally helpful, as New Right heroes such as Sens. Orrin Hatch, R-UT; James McClure, R-ID; Roger Jepsen, R-IA; and Gordon Humphrey, R-NH; joined House members Larry McDonald, D-GA; Daniel Crane, R-IL; and Robert Dornan, R-CA, on the "advisory board" of Christian Voice. But the key figure in showing the Christian Right the political ropes was Republican Sen. Jesse Helms of North Carolina, a Southern Baptist. Helms introduced their lobbyists to his colleagues, advised Moral Majority on organization strategy, and assisted in fund-raising efforts. (Guth, 1983:69)

Third, the appeal to Christian fundamentalists and the new social issues of abortion and the ERA provided issues that crosscut the New Deal coalition of the Democratic party. In the northeast, Catholics and ethnics comprise a core group of the New Deal coalition. Yet, it was among these social groups that local pro-life activists were drawn from the state-by-state battles over the liberalization of abortion laws (Luker, 1984). In 1973, the *Roe v. Wade* Supreme Court decision nationalized the abortion controversy and divided the Democratic party. Ellen McCormick, the Long Island housewife who ran for President of the United States in 1976 as the Right to Life candidate, gained her start in politics lobbying against liberalization of the New York state abortion law and entered the 1976 Democratic party primaries after *Roe v. Wade*.

The abortion controversy detracted from Democratic support in the South, where evangelical strength is concentrated (Wald, 1987:201). More important for the new right strategists, this controversy overlapped the increasingly sensitive issue of race. The Democratic party was losing support among southern whites who opposed integration; yet an overt Republican appeal to these elements on the basis of race (e.g., Nixon's "southern strategy") was considered too risky. The "Republican preference [among evangelicals] was established *before* the Christian Right organizations began their mobilizing efforts" (Wald, 1987:202, 186; emphasis in original). At most, conservative social issues permitted a direct appeal to those already sympathetic to the Republican party.

And fourth, the development of the new right is closely linked to the increasing community of interest between the Republican party right wing and the politically active business community. The elections of 1976 and 1978 provided an important turning point, resulting in an increase in conservative members of Congress. Prior to the mid–1970s, the right had viewed business as a "fair-weather ally," while business, for its part, considered the right as "a fringe group, treacherously unsophisticated, and, as such, a political liability in Washington" (Edsall, 1984:73–74). The gains in congressional representation provided a block of votes in Congress that transformed the right from an insignificant fringe group, while the shifting pattern of campaign contributions increased the political importance of the South in the Republican party coalition. Within the politically active business community, "the growth . . . was toward the sunbelt, as the most active, aggressive, and conservative of the corporate leaders were the entrepreneurs and oilmen of the South, Southwest, and West" (Edsall, 1984:75). The interests of the Republican right wing and political contributors to the Republican party converged in the mid–1970s. What was lacking was a mass level constituency—and this was precisely what the electronic church of the televangelists promised.

We have thus explained why the new right has succeeded in electing a President and in apparently "taking over" the Republican party. Yet, the critical issue is whether or not the constituency of the new right comprises a social movement. Preceding the rise of the new right in 1979 (Guth, 1983), we find an upsurge in evangelical revivalism. Revivals are, of course, an episodic phenomenon in American religious culture (McLoughlin, 1978). Fundamentalist churches had been in a period of growth, while the mainstream churches were experiencing a drop-off in their membership. In 1983, George Gallup estimated that approximately 20 percent of American adults were evangelicals. As Benson and Williams point out, "it has been widely assumed that these two movements are necessarily linked; many outside the evangelical camp believe that evangelicals are, almost without exception, politically conservative and supportive of the New Christian Right" (1982:173).

To what extent are the two movements linked? One piece of evidence is voting behavior. Yet, among standard political science analyses, the status of evangelical or "born-again" is rarely used as a category of social group (e.g., see Nelson, 1985). It should be noted that about one-quarter of evangelicals are black and about 10 to 15 percent are Catholic (Wald, 1987:201). Exit polls conducted by the network news programs found that evangelicals did vote at higher rate for Reagan, but that result is confounded with other factors (e.g., southern whites). One study of the 1980 election concluded that "the Christian Right had virtually no influence at all . . . the most important issue was inflation and those who picked it voted for Reagan 2 to 1" (Johnson and Tamney, 1982:128). In fact, those evangelicals first entering the electorate in 1980 were more supportive of the Democratic candidate, compared to both nonevangelicals and evangelicals who had voted prior to 1980. And in 1982, many of the 1980 Reagan evangelical voters voted Democratic (Wald, 1987:202).

Public opinion surveys of evangelicals indicate majority support for approved school prayer, support for Israel, and tuition tax credits. However, the majority of evangelicals also supported the distribution of birth control information in the schools and passage of the Equal Rights Amendment and disagreed "that acquired immune deficiency syndrome (AIDS) is a form of divine retribution for homosexuality." The Reverend Jerry Falwell "was actually less popular among respondents than was the National Organization for Women." Among the general public, support for profamily agenda of the New Right has declined over the course of the 1970s and 1980s (Wald, 1987:1192–1193). These facts have not been lost on New Right leaders. Following the 1984 election, Falwell felt compelled to merge the Moral Majority within a new umbrella organization, the Liberty Federation, principally because of the substantial negatives attached to the original name.

Perhaps it is the case that evangelicals simply do not have enough "group consciousness." Therefore, it is pertinent to examine political elites, who are usually attuned to social and political changes in advance of the masses and who are generally more consistent ideologically. Benson and Williams interviewed evangelical members of Congress at length to determine their religious and political views. They find that "the heaviest concentrations of evangelicals are at the extreme ends of the political continua" (1982:175). Using an Americans for Democratic Action measure, 22 percent of their sample was solidly liberal; using the Christian Voice index of the new right, 40 percent of their sample was solidly liberal. Moreover, the new right has been criticized by prominent evangelical groups and theologians (Wald, 1987:198).

It is also important to recognize that the televangelists, who comprise the leadership of the new right, are not a disadvantaged economic or social group. Guth (1983:64) cites research indicating that from 1960 to 1976, the lower status position of evangelicals had almost pulled even with mainline Protestants. This socioeconomic transformation has increased the wealth and activities of the churches. No longer protected by the claim of immunity under the free exercise clause, the private provision of social services by these "corporate" churches brought them under increasing government regulation. This provides a strong economic incentive to oppose government regulation (Wald, 1987:208–209).

Yet regulation does not necessarily mean a disadvantage. Peter Horsfield points out that due to rulings of the Federal Communications Commission (FCC), the broadcasting of the paid-time audience-supported programs of such shows as Jerry Falwell's "Old Time Gospel Hour" and Marion Robertson's "700 Club" has been advantaged over the station-supported sustaining-time programs of the mainstream churches. Horsfield indicates that television is now dominated by these paid-time syndicated programs, even though they are not necessarily more popular in show ratings or audience size. Due to the FCC's rulings that religious programming comprises a category of "public interest" and that the fairness doctrine need not apply in determining which faiths are to be broadcast, television stations have followed the most profitable alternative: the steady replacement of sustaining-time programs with the syndicated audience-supported shows of the televangelists.

If the evangelical movement does not circumscribe the new right, to what extent does the audience of the electronic church? It is important to recognize that the audience sizes for these programs (as a group) "reached a plateau around the year 1977." In actuality, the electronic church represents a *"specialized programming service for a specialized audience"* (Horsfield, 1984:165; emphasis in original). Research indicates that the "typical viewer of TV religion is an older female, not as well educated as a member of the middle class, and more than likely resides in the Southern region of the United States" (Cardwell, 1984:79). However, the majority of evangelicals do not watch (Horsfield, 1984:117). Among those who do, it is unlikely that they have much effect in political mobilization. Research indicates that televangelism has very little effect even in religious conversion. As concerns the call to the station announcing a religious conversion, studies indicate that most were previous Christians who had religious experience. Horsfield concludes that "the call to the station appears to have been an expression of this earlier decision or a confirmation of it" (1984:135–136). The evidence indicates that most do not follow up a television conversion with church attendance—there is little overlap between the evangelical movement and the viewers of the electronic church. Of those who do go on to attend church, a large of group already had a personal relationship with a church member, e.g., a fiancé (Horsfield, 1984:143–144).

It is our conclusion that the evangelicals comprise a religious movement, not a political or a social movement. John Hammond, in his historical study of the relationship of revival religion and voting behavior, stresses the limited impact that religious values can have, *except* "when their issues become identified with major economic or political interests. Slavery was a symbolic issue for the revivalists, for its continued existence symbolized the state of sin in which the country lay. For others, it came to be the focus of intersectional economic and political conflict. . . . Prohibition, on the other hand, never came to be identified with a fundamental conflict of political interests" (Hammond, 1979:34). And this is precisely what happened with the rise of the new right.

There simply is no identifiable *social* group that comprises the new right; it reflects instead the elite organization of multiple single issues. The largest political organization of the new right—the Moral Majority (or Liberty Federation)—for example, includes members of diverse social backgrounds: Jews and Catholics, as well as Protestants. In the short term, this has benefited the Republicans in the electoral arena by allowing Republican candidates to appeal to disaffected Democrats. The attempt to exploit submerged conflicts within the opposing party's coalition is the "heart of political strategy" (Adamany, 1975: xxv). But we find no evidence that these groups comprise a grass-roots constituency within the Republican party coalition. On the contrary, there is evidence to support our view that the new right comprises a political movement. First, in a recent assessment of the status of the "Reagan Revolution," one of the most prominent new right figures, Paul Weyrich (1987:50–53), concludes that the revolution has failed *precisely because* it lacked a grass-roots constituency. And second, Warren Miller and M. Kent Jennings (1986) found some systematic differences among those newly mobilized to elite party activity among the 1980 convention delegates they surveyed that support this point. Those who were newly mobilized among the Democrats, when compared to those delegates who were disengaged from campaign activity, were closer to their rank-and-file party identifiers; while the newly mobilized among the Republican delegates were "more *distant* from the 1980 rank and file than were the disengaged. . . . On balance, the replacement process of presidential campaign activists had the net effect of bringing the Democratic elite more in line with its base while driving the GOP elite further out of line with the Republican mass base" (Miller and Jennings, 1986:214; emphasis in original). This is precisely as we would predict the case to be if the Republican party's turn to the right was not predicated on a social movement. While the Democratic party's mobilization was indeed based on social movements with a true grass-roots constituency, the appeal to Christian fundamentalists has been one made by a long-time Republican party faction (the Republican right) to a group outside of the party. Therefore, we conclude that the loss of influence by Republican women has not been at the hands of a new social movement, but rather, from party regulars.

CONCLUSIONS

In the preceding chapters, we noted the observation of Stephen and Barbara Salmore that the Democrats have engaged in "expressive" reforms while the Republicans have focused on "competitive" reforms. We argue that the parties must be judged on their ability to develop or respond to the formation of new elites. In doing so, we recognize the fundamental difference in political culture between the parties (Freeman, 1986). As Crotty argued, "the two national parties are distinctively different entities, each with its own traditions, social roots, and organizational and personal values" (1983:206). The parties reflect different social formations, with different philosophies of government—both in terms of the polity and in internal party politics. The key to understanding Republican party nonreforms lies in these differences, and the litmus test for assessing the democratic responsiveness of Republican party elite cadres lies in how responsive they have been to groups within their own coalition—not those within the Democratic party coalition. For the Republicans, this includes women and, more recently, the new right. The Republicans have made a turn toward the new right, which has meant a turn away from the traditional Republican women already active in the party who favor women's rights issues. Women comprise an identifiable social group within the Republican party, while we have argued that the new right comprises no such identifiable constituency. We conclude that to the extent that they have not responded to the group interests of Republican women, they have submerged a potentially serious internal party conflict.

NOTES

1. Others (e.g., Simons and Mechling, 1981:418) term what we have called a trend an historical movement. We prefer to reserve the term movement for social groups exhibiting organized collective action.

2. Examples of quasi-movements include *mass actions* (e.g., short-lived group actions including a wildcat strike, a race riot, a mass migration, a gold rush, or a *coup d' état*), *followings* (a "collectivity united in its attention to and admiration of a public individual"), and *cults* (a group, e.g., a religious cult, which "makes demands only on the behavior of its members") (Turner and Killian, 1972:246–247; see also Heberle, 1949).

3. Religious institutions are separate from political institutions, and we distinguish between religious movements, which seek to change the faith or practices of individuals, and social movements, which seek to change society (whose ideology encompasses change in the behavior of nonparticipants or nonbelievers, e.g., a nonsexist society requires radical changes in the behavior of men, and not only among women). Gerlach and Hine (1970) and Wilkinson (1971) view religious movements as social movements. In making a distinction between the (public) political sphere and the (private) religious sphere (becausee this is not a theocracy), we distinguish religious movements (without political aims) from social movements (with social and political aims). Of course, religious movements may engender political cleavages that culminate in new social or political movements (e.g., the new right).

4. In this context, it is important to recall that Olson (1965) not only predicted that latent groups among the mass public were unlikely, but also that the national-level Chamber of Commerce also comprised a large latent group facing similar difficulties in organization. Not only have ideologically oriented social movements appeared in national politics, but so, too, has the Chamber of Commerce (Edsall, 1984).

5. Jack Nagel (1987:131), for example, classifies the Student Nonviolent Coordinating Committee (SNCC) as an example of an organization characterized by moral incentives and a deficit of "incentive balance"; while organizations as diverse as Common Cause, the American Civil Liberties Union (ACLU), the Moral Majority, and the National Association for the Advancement of Colored People (NAACP) are

examples of the same type of organization—one exhibiting a "modest deficit" in the "incentive balance." While it is certainly true that SNCC demanded relatively more of its members than did other civil rights organizations (Stoper, 1983), we regard Nagel's typology as ignoring the forest for the trees. We will argue that there is an important difference between political (e.g., the public interest movement as represented by Common Cause and Ralph Nader's organizations) and social movements (e.g., the women's and civil rights movements).

6. Our delineation of social movements corresponds in some respects to Neil Smelser's (1963) concept of "value-oriented" movements. However, our distinction differs considerably from Smelser's typology of norm- versus value-oriented movements. His theory of collective behavior was developed prior to the expansion of the civil rights movement and the development of the contemporary women's rights movement, which results in an indeterminateness in his classification of cases. He classifies both labor and "feminism" as "general social movements" that "provide a backdrop from which many specific norm-oriented movements emanate" (1963:273). Norm-oriented movements, for Smelser, are those that focus on limited goals (norms), without a restructuring of values (ideology), and result in "normative innovations— a new law, custom, bureau, association, or segment of a political party" (1963:270). Feminism, for Smelser, remains a political movement, distinct from the social movement of women that we address. Examples of value-oriented movements include those stressing religious (e.g., Seventh Day Adventist, Shaker, Christian Science) and secular (e.g., nationalism, communism, socialism, anarchism, syndicalism) values. His typology illuminates little of interest to political scientists (democracy, public versus nonpublic spheres, etc.).

7. This distinction may be more precise in the abstract than in reality. For example, one of the larger of the national nuclear freeze groups, Critical Mass, is "affiliated with Ralph Nader's environmental and political investigation network, the Public Interest Research Groups. . . . Ralph Nader is the group's leader" (Dwyer, 1983:150).

8. The point we wish to make is to distinguish between those who participate either out of a sense of "class" responsibilities or consciousness (i.e., a sense of noblesse oblige or the voluntary tradition among middle- and upper-class housewives [Gold, 1971]; the participation of "mothers" in the civil rights movement [Blumberg, 1980]) or out of a sense of "social" consciousness (e.g., white college students active in the civil rights movement, men active in the feminist movement) and those who are themselves members of the disadvantaged group and participate out of group consciousness. The key distinction between groups is whether they require a personal change (based on group consciousness) as well as making political demands for social and political change. Certainly, a group consciousness may evolve out of the participation in the social movement of another group. Sara Evans (1980) provides an excellent description of the development of a feminist consciousness among women active in the early civil rights movement (see McGlen and O'Connor, 1983). A group that demands a personal change, but makes no effort to promote societal acceptance of the group (i.e., by political demands) remains a cult, not a social movement (Turner and Killian, 1972:247).

9. While one group of reformers (the anticorporate and democratic progressives) sought to limit corporate political influence by supporting reforms instituting the primary, the recall, the initiative and the referendum, the direct election of Senators

and decentralization (e.g., home rule), the corporate reformers "emphasized the desirability of infusing more values, methods and personnel from the business community into traditional political practices. Its reforms promoted such basic corporate values as efficiency, production, planning, centralization, nonpartisanship, hierarchy, administration, expertise, *and stability against prevailing practices that exalted partisanship, majority rule, decentralized power, legislation, and voter participation—particularly participation by poorer voters*" (Thelen, 1981:38; emphasis added).

10. Douglas McAdam (1983:302) terms the NAACP, CORE, SCLC, and SNCC the Big Four of the civil rights movement. He excludes the National Urban League because despite its visibility among the "liberal establishment," "few protest activities or movement campaigns involved the Urban League" (1983:302 n).

11. There have been two Compliance Review Commissions appointed: the first to monitor the Mikulski Commission guidelines and the second to monitor the Winograd Commission guidelines.

12. David Price estimates that in 1980, blacks comprised 20.5 percent of Democratic party identifiers and 22 percent of the Carter vote (1984:192).

13. Present at the meeting were:

Mary Louise Smith, the chairman of the RNC before Brock; Helen Milliken, president of ERAmerica and wife of the governor of Michigan; Betty Southard Murphy, former chairman of the National Labor Relations Board; Carla Hills, former secretary of housing and urban development; Senator Nancy Kassebaum of Kansas; Representative Margaret Heckler; Maureen Reagan, the nominee's daughter and an active campaigner for the amendment; Betty Heitman, Pamela Curtis [representing the NWPC's Republican Women's Task Force]; Lorelei Kinder [a Reagan campaign aide tracking ERA on the platform committee]; and seven others. (Malbin, 1981:115)

4

Elite Cadres, Intermediation, and Social Movements

INTRODUCTION

In this chapter, we outline our theoretical framework—the central elements of which include a conceptualization of political parties as composed of *elite cadres* and an argument that both political parties and social movements are fundamental to democratic politics and governance. Political parties have long been recognized as essential for democracy. This is because parties *accumulate power*, yet remain *permeable* to political movements. But elite cadres also tend toward *oligarchy*. Because of the exclusion of some groups from political influence, *social movements arise* as a periodic phenomenon *that* like political parties, *promote democracy by developing new elites.*

Elite status is furthered by *information*, and a closer link between elites and masses is forged when *political participation* is informed. Thus, *voting* is a necessary, but insufficient, condition for democracy. Also essential for the democratic representation of interests are social movements, which arise from social out-groups, while entrenched interests may achieve representation through the pressure group system and political movements. At the juncture of these elements is interest *intermediation*. It is the organizational function of the party elite cadres to intermediate between partisan support groups in the electorate and the party-in-office.

The concept of intermediation does not have an unequivocal meaning in party scholarship. This is surprising and significant because the assumed decline in party intermediation is a critical concept in the debate over party reform. Reform critics incorporate a distinct interpretation of intermediation (derived from pluralist and mass society theory): party elites "intermediate" by linking elites and the mass through their group memberships. In doing so, they leave unacknowledged the different meanings offered in the literature. One opposing view that is acknowledged is the responsible party system (discussed in Chapter 2). This view assumes a direct link between the voter and the party-in-office, based on support for the party's success in implementing the party platform. This view, denigrated by critics of party reform, bypasses the role of group identity and membership. There are other theories, as well, that, like pluralism, focus on group membership and the party system.

A PARTY ELITE THEORY OF DEMOCRACY

Our theoretical formulation, based in large part on social movement theory, provides a concept of interest intermediation consonant with plurist theory. We accept the pluralist assumption that enduring political attitudes are formed in concrete, face-to-face groups, but argue that preexisting groups often reflect the dominant status hierarchy. We incorporate a comprehensive assessment of a range of theories that address the group role in elite-mass linkage and include in it an extended comparison of the mass society critique of party reform (and other changes in the party system) with competing interpretations from social movement theory. We now turn to our definition of democracy.

Elites and Democracy

There are two critical aspects to any consideration of the role of political elites: their defining features and their role in the political system—in this case a democratic political system. We define elites as those who exercise power; they are in juxtaposition to a mass public (the non-elites), which does not. Furthermore, "the mentality of leaders is never identical with that of the masses even if the leaders are of the same social composition as the masses. In fact, whatever may be their origins, leaders tend to draw closer together and to constitute naturally a leader class. The idea of scientific representation is an illusion: all power is oligarchic" (Michels, 1962:189). This is a fundamental insight to be found in most works on group behavior whether one understands this elite group as David Truman's "active minority" (1958), Robert Michels's "oligarchy" (1962), or Gaetano Mosca's "ruling class" (1939). Maurice Duverger, who laid great stress on the importance of "government by the people *by an elite sprung from the people*" (1954:425, emphasis in original), nonetheless endorsed this notion of a psychological transformation among party leaders of working-class origins.

It is a fundamental sociological truism that organized elites tend toward oligarchy (Michels, 1962). The application of this insight for political parties is immediately evident in the exclusiveness of the party elite cadres historically and in the reluctance of the two major parties to expand suffrage. As we indicated in Chapter 2, prior to party reform, Democratic and Republican elite cadres were predominantly older, white male professionals. And these elites have acted to compartmentalize and limit the influence of female and minority elites—a pervasive group-level discrimination that, as we saw in

Chapter 3, ended only with organized pressure focusing on reform of the party system.

The expansion of suffrage is closely linked to the democratization of elite recruitment. The influence of social out-groups in the party system is only achieved when their group members have access to the vote. Suffrage, which, for many, comprises the only form of participation, has only been extended in the United States in response to external pressure—the result of social movements (e.g., the women's and civil rights movements) and political movements (e.g., the student and anti-Vietnam War movements) (Crotty, 1978). We conclude that mass-level movements constitute a necessary, albeit episodic, challenge to elite cadre oligarchy.

Parties, distinct from bureaucratic organizations, are also permeable. Leadership positions in the parties are usually restricted to those recruited from within the party. Yet, this does not mean that the parties are institutionalized in the same fashion as bureaucracies (Eldersveld, 1964). As Michels noted, electoral competition and the party's need to outbid its opponents results in the loss of "political virginity," "by entering into promiscuous relationships with the most heterogeneous political elements" (1962:341). Competition between subcoalitions of the parties may result in upward recruitment for some leaders (promotion) and in a loss of position for others (demotion) (Eldersveld, 1964:144).[1] Attaining and retaining an elite party position is related to conflicts between candidate factions and the support of interest groups within the party subcoalitions (Jewell and Olson, 1978:65–76). The position of the state party chair, in particular, appears to suffer extremely high turnover due to the "factional fights which rack so many state parties every two or four years" (Cotter and Hennessy 1964:59; see also Jewell and Olson, 1978:70–71).[2] Thus, parties are permeable—but only to those groups already possessing representation within the pressure group system.

In contrast to Harold Lasswell and others, we define elites not as those who *receive* "the most of what there is to get" (Lasswell, 1958:13), but those who *determine* "who gets what, when, [and] how." Thus, our definition of elites is a leadership group, although we do not mean this as a categorical distinction—influence, after all, is a matter of degree. This definition includes those individuals who occupy leadership positions in the parties; in government; in interest groups; and in major economic, educational, and social institutions. Within the parties, these leadership positions would include elite cadres (Duverger, 1954:64) at all levels of the party—county and state chairs, national committee members and national convention delegates.

We diverge from Duverger and Lasswell in our conceptualization of the basis of elite influence. Duverger articulated the concept of the cadre party as based "in the grouping of notabilities" (1954:64). Organized as they are around elections and the conduct of campaigns, cadre parties are "decentralized and weakly knit" (1954:67). We use the term cadre to signify the membership of the decentralized (and federal) structure of the American party system, but argue that these cadres are increasingly comprised of full-time party leaders whose organization persists from one election to the next. The increasing organizational coherence is evident at all levels of party—local, state and national party cadres (Cotter et al., 1984). Moreover, state and national parties are increasingly interdependent—a "two-way pattern of interaction" (Huckshorn et al., 1986:978) that differs markedly from the reciprocal deference found in a stratarchical system (Eldersveld, 1964).

Lasswell's concern was with elites whose power was an extension of property rights. However, there are many persons with substantial property rights and yet little or no political influence—and such persons are rightly classified as part of the mass. Moreover, property (or economic notability) is no longer a prerequisite of elite status. In our view, contemporary elites in the United States obtain their positions primarily through a mastery of information. However, we intend the term information differently than Lasswell does in his discussion of the use of "symbols of the common destiny." "Such symbols are the 'ideology' of the established order, the 'utopia' of counter-elites" (Lasswell, 1958:31). Lasswell examined the use of language as well as ideas, but his primary concern was the promulgation of propaganda.

We hold that information represents a marshaling of the "facts" so as to result in a better, i.e., managerial, understanding of the "true" state of public affairs and politics. Information in this sense is essential to effective political action. Voting is only one form of political participation. By itself, voting communicates very little information to political elites. We consider those people who only vote to be engaging in symbolic participation (Milbrath and Goel, 1977). While the results of an election may be important in the aggregate, at the individual level, the act of voting requires very little information or initiative (Verba and Nie, 1972:48–52). Thus, the essential indicator for democratic participation is the degree of participation by groups in parties, pressure groups, and political and social movements.

The act of voting is weakly related to these more demanding forms of participation; thus we do not consider voting, per se, "as a valid indicator of mass mobilization" (Milbrath and Goel, 1977:13). Electoral mandates are not created by an election, but rather, through group subcoalitions within the winning party coalition. This more demanding notion of participation does come with a certain information cost: one does not vote for a party out of habit, but out of conviction, and one does not place pressure on elites without some knowledge of politics and policy. The information cost may result in some decline in voter turnout. As Anthony Downs (1957) indicated, from a rational perspective, the amount of pressure placed on political elites from a single vote is not counterbalanced by the information cost of an informed vote. We recognize and accept this unknown decrement in voter turnout as the price of transition from a party system based on a psychological identification to one based on a substantive commitment. (We return to the question of the magnitude of this cost at the end of the chapter.)

In an electorally based democracy, all elites are susceptible to pressure. While propertied elites may buy or procure "experts" to provide the needed information, it is not their exclusive province. Information is potentially available to all with the requisite level of education and wit; it is not restricted to those who control the organs of mass communication. Information facilitates persuasion and enables interests to place their demands before political elites in a credible way. This is to be distinguished from the use of propaganda or symbols to beguile the uninformed (mass) public so as to prevent their recognizing their grievances. Lastly, an elite based on information as opposed to property is one that is fundamentally more permeable.

An elite stratum is an inevitable part of any political system. More important still is the permeability of that stratum. While we personally favor a high level of political participation, any polity of large size must depend on some delegation of decision making. Carol Pateman (1970) argued most persuasively that a high level of political participation is unlikely without a fully developed sense of efficacy derived through true participation in other and more immediate spheres of social life—the family, the schools, the workplace and other primary groups. However, even if society provided such avenues of widespread participation (which is another issue), we find this an impractical solution, if for no other reason than because group decision making is an incredibly time-consuming process. In modern society, we are all enmeshed in so many spheres of activity that some delegation to others—the "leaders" or "elites" is inevitable and practical.[3] We do not regard the category of "mass" as a pejorative classification. It is a distinction between those who exercise delegated authority and those who do not. This distinction, however, does have other, quite different implications *if certain individuals are systematically excluded from elite leadership positions in all spheres of society*, i.e., a group or caste disadvantage.

This is important for our definition of democracy: the masses, per se, are not excluded from power, but different groups may be. Following Duverger, we define true democracy as liberty for all groups in society; "not only liberty for those privileged by birth, fortune, position, or education, but real liberty for all, and this implies a certain standard of living, a certain basic education, some kind of social equality, some kind of political equilibrium" (1954:424). Duverger goes on to conclude that "liberty and the party system coincide" when it is no longer the case that "economic and financial powers alone disposed of the Press, of techniques of information and propaganda, and of a means of organizing the electorate" (1954:424–425). Given the basis of elite power in the preparty era in property, the distinctive contribution of parties historically is that "they provided the necessary framework enabling the masses to recruit from among themselves their own elites" (Duverger, 1954:426). Therefore, like Duverger, we believe that parties promote democracy by encouraging the development of new elites.

Other party scholars have, of course, based their work on alternate definitions of democracy. Both V. O. Key and E. E. Schattschneider, whose work we have relied on extensively, stressed the role of party competition in a two-party system. We wish to consider each party system on its merits, rather than defining democracy as a mechanism: whether a system is democratic depends on whether it produces liberty for all groups and whether elites are recruited from all groups—a substantive result. We agree with Michels that "democracy is a treasure which no one will ever discover by deliberate search" (1962:368). However important organized competition is, defining democracy to be the product of competition alone ignores both the examples of the temporary one-party state (e.g., Kemal's Turkey [Duverger, 1954]) that *promoted* liberty, and of the two-party system (e.g., the realignment of 1896 [Schattschneider, 1960]) that *undermined* liberty. While "a regime without parties is of necessity a conservative one" (Duverger, 1954:426), the critical issue for democracy is not whether parties exist (they may indeed be present in a totalitarian or fascist form) or whether there is only one or two or more parties in a party system, but whether the party system functions to incorporate new elites as recruited through their *own* groups (i.e., groups that they control). Essentially, our definition of democracy demands that all social groups—and not merely the dominant class— engage in the "honor of participating in government recruiting" (Michels, 1962:355). After all, as Duverger pointed out, when "a man of the people" is recruited through the institutions of the governing oligarchy, "he must also work his way up the ladder of middle-class education and lose contact with the class in which he was born" (1954:426). Our definition of democracy focuses on the party system as a crucial agency for promoting democracy by promoting more active forms of participation and, in doing so, by developing new political elites.

Social Movements and Political Parties

Duverger's theory of parties was based on the assumption that the mass-membership party was a more modern form of political party than the cadre party. This particular assumption was not held by many American party scholars (e.g., Epstein, 1967). However, this assumption—which we now examine—was based on an important insight: the new mass-membership parties were important not only in promoting democracy, but in the creation of an alternative elite recruitment structure for the lower classes. For the European working classes, Duverger reminds us that "freedom was a collective conquest" (1954:170). Thus, the first parties to organize at the mass level were the socialist parties. "Historically speaking parties were born when the masses of the people really made their entrance into political life" (1954:426). The limitation of Duverger's focus on the working classes in the American context is that class consciousness has never comprised a major cleavage in American culture (Hartz, 1955) and that labor has been declining in influence since the mid–1950s (Edwards and Podgursky, 1986).

What Duverger did not consider is that the birth of parties (in the period 1830–1848) occurred alongside the birth of social movements. According to the historian Charles Tilly, "the rise of the meeting, the rise of the association, and the rise of electoral politics occurred in tandem" (1979:150). Tilly (1979; 1983) divides mass political actions into two "repertoires": the old regime and the new regime. "The social movement, as we know it, came into being with the new regime" (1983:466).

What was the difference? Broadly speaking, the repertoire of the seventeenth to nineteenth centuries held to a *parochial* scope: It addressed local actors or the local representatives of national actors. It also relied heavily on *patronage*—appealing to immediately available power holders to convey grievances or settle disputes. . . . The repertoire that crystallized in the nineteenth century and prevails today is, in general, more *national* in scope: Although available for local issues and enemies, it lends itself easily to coordination among many localities. As compared with the older repertoire, its actions are relatively *autonomous*: instead of staying within the shadow of existing power holders, users of the new repertoire tend to initiate their own statements of grievances and demands. (Tilly, 1983:465–466)

An example of the earlier repertoire would be the *turnout* (in which workers in a given craft would march through town and send a delegation to the local employers with their grievances) versus the *strike* (which covers a whole town, industry, or country, and the statement of grievances occurs independently from conversations with the immediate employers).

Social movements are distinctively modern avenues of collective action. With the decline of public mockings at authorized celebrations (e.g., parades and festivals), the burning of effigies, unplanned assemblies, and turnouts, the emerging repertoire of political participation included strikes, planned public meetings, the development of special purpose associations, election rallies, and social movements.

In Chapter 3, we defined political movements as possessing only political goals, while social movements are based in a personal transformation and encompass both social and political aims. The point of our distinction between political and social movements is to illuminate the distinctive and historic role of social movements in democratic systems. The simultaneous appearance of parties and social movements was not a coincidence. As Leon Epstein points out, many of the early democratic party organizations *began* as social movements. "Those which began as working class 'movements' in nineteenth century Europe did not at first seek votes so much as advocate a cause by propaganda or economic pressure, simultaneously organizing trade unionists and socialists" (1967:99). The working-class movements and the labor movements of nineteenth century Europe and the United States were genuine social movements because they rested on a definable social characteristic (the working-class in Europe, and the working and immigrant class in the United States). In Europe, however, these working class movements became political parties. "They were electoral machines only secondarily, or they subsequently became electoral in response to a delayed popular franchise. Then socialists sought votes as well as members" (Epstein, 1967:99). The cadre parties typical of American political parties developed in an entirely different context. Universal (white) manhood suffrage was extended by about 1830, while the United States remained predominantly an agrarian society. The American parties that developed during this era did so prior to the early labor movements. They thus differed in their historical development by an exclusive concern with "primarily and almost entirely electoral functions" (1967:99).

Social movements do have a life cycle—although this does not follow any predetermined sociological law. Each is distinct, and their success or failure in achieving their goals depends on a "complex interplay of external and internal factors" (Marx, 1979:94). At some point, a social movement may be so successful that it becomes an institutionalized interest group: a movement ceases to be when it no longer seeks change (Wilkinson, 1971:30). While social movements develop new elites, "the defining characteristic of . . . pressure group organizations is that group leaders and members are already integrated into full participation in the political system and such groups have full and recognized rights of access to executive and legislative organs of government" (Wilkinson, 1971:116). This, we suggest, has happened to the original American labor movement (Edwards and Podgursky, 1986).[4] The transition from a social movement to an interest group may be a slow and painful one, as Anne Costain (1982) indicates is the case with the women's rights movement. Insofar as movements utilize unorthodox means to obtain their objectives, there may be a "pressure not to lobby" (Costain, 1982:22). Thus, some movements may combine traditional pressure group structure and tactics and yet remain a social movement committed to change.

Thus far, we have concluded that the first social movements were those of the working classes (and reflected a class consciousness) and that cadre parties were not based on a preexisting social movement. Because American parties began as an extension of the legislative caucus and then evolved into cadre parties, does this mean that social movements are irrelevant in the American context? We would argue that the answer is no. The same phenomenon—the expression and organization of demands for representation by an out-group in society—is readily apparent. It appears, however, under a different conceptual framework: the role of third parties in promoting partisan realignment. As Key argued, both the realignment of 1896 and that of 1932 were preceded by the rise and fall of a third party.[5]

Political parties and social movements are intimately connected. They both arose in the same crucible of expanding political participation. Rudolf Heberle points out that a social movement may be represented in a number of parties (e.g., the proletarian movement in both socialist and communist parties) and that a "party can be part of a broader social movement, like the Socialist labor parties which form one of the branches of the labor movement" (1949:352). In the multiparty context, social movements may comprise a single party (Epstein, 1967). In the two-party context, social movements historically have appeared as third or minor parties due to the oligarchy of power in the two major parties. As Key concluded, "the occurrence of great episodes of third-party activity depends on the rise of movements or bursts of sentiment which cannot work themselves out through a major party" (1964:281). The electoral system has provided an opportunity for affecting the party system despite the oligarchy of the extant major party leaders. "The minor party accomplishes this end in part by demonstrating the existence of a block of voters for whose support a major party may bid. To woo this support the major party must take a stand on the new issues insistently raised by the minor party. Thus the minor party may serve as a bridge for the movement of people from party to party and in the process each party may lose some of its dissident elements to the other" (Key, 1964:258). Third parties not only facilitate voter realignment, but are based in the conflict of "factions within major parties" (Key, 1964:280).

In Schattschneider's (1975) terms, party competition is dynamic as the parties continually seek to displace and substitute conflict. This facet of American party politics is endemic in a two-party system—no party can win control of government without mobilizing a majority; yet the resulting alignments cannot "satisfy all interests equally" (1975:73). As the Democratic and Republican labels have become institutionalized (Epstein, 1986), the advent of the third party has ended in American politics. The rise of social movements has enlarged the scope of party competition between the Democratic and Republican parties.

Democracy and the Formation of New Elites within the Parties

Both political parties and social movements are vehicles of group representation apart from the pressure group system. Our party elite theory of democracy bases its definition of democracy in the formation of new elites. As party elite cadres tend toward oligarchy, social out-group elites may resort to social movements to force recognition by the parties. Thus, party reform has served as an antidote to elite party oligarchy.

The Democratic party, in reforming its rules, has encouraged the participation of these new elites, while the Republican party has not. The Republican party has promulgated no national guidelines that require the state and local parties to include any targeted groups, nor has it formally monitored compliance with urgings of "affirmative action." In fact, those efforts that have been made by the Republicans (e.g., 44 percent of the delegates at the 1984 Republican National Convention were women) were responses to the threat of electoral competitiveness by the Democrats rather than responses to internal demands for expanded representation. Thus, in our view, the Democratic party reforms have fostered democracy. Recall that the expanded role of primaries in the nominating process was *not* an internal Democratic party reform but a concomitant state-level development. Our arguments conflict however with the pluralist/mass society critique of party reform that we have sketched in earlier chapters and to which we now return.

THE MASS SOCIETY CRITIQUE OF PARTY REFORM

Those political party scholars who have studied the effects of party reform have been nearly unanimous in their criticism of Democratic party reform. They argue that reform has been a major (if not the primary) factor in causing party decline. Nelson Polsby concludes that due to reform, "the gate keeping functions of party leaders and party organizations were permitted to atrophy (1980:55). Byron Shafer terms the story of Democratic party reform a "puzzle of [elite] self-liquidation" (1983:527). "At bottom, the result of all these reforms was *the diminution, the constriction, at times the elimination, of the regular party in the politics of presidential selection*" (Shafer, 1983:525; emphasis in the original). We term this position the *reform hypothesis*. This view has been the dominant one among many party scholars, although as we saw in earlier chapters, scholars do not agree that parties remain in decline—or indeed ever declined.[6]

Reform Critics and the Problem of Analyzing Party Reform

Major proponents of the reform hypothesis include Edward Banfield (1980a; 1980b), James Ceaser (1982), Jeane Kirkpatrick (1976; 1979), Everett Carll Ladd, Jr. (1977; 1981), Polsby (1980; 1983a; 1983b), Austin Ranney (1975; 1978), and Shafer (1983). These scholars generally view party reform much as Edmund Burke viewed the French revolution—all reform is bad, and therefore individual reforms are indistinguishable. Banfield typified this view when he concluded that "a political system is an accident, and that to meddle with one that works well is the greatest foolishness of which men are capable" (1980a:20). Banfield argues that the recent reforms were the culmination of "more than a century of effort" (1980a:30). With a similar grand sweep of history, Ceaser (1980:97) lumps the reformers of the Progressive Era, the intellectual position staked out by the APSA Committee on Political Parties for a more responsible party system, and the "proponents of an open presidential selection process" together as indicators of the same phenomenon—despite their differences.[7]

The reform hypothesis has also received considerable currency in Democratic party affairs. As discussed in Chapter 2, several prominent reform critics have been active in an interest group (the CDM) opposing party reform. Ranney served on both the McGovern-Fraser and the Winograd Commissions; Kirkpatrick served on the Winograd Commission. We are less concerned here with any possible partisan bias than we are with the intellectual underpinnings of the reform hypothesis. The intellectual bias against political reform revealed here erects a fundamental barrier to analysis. Ladd, for example, considers the reforms undertaken by the Democratic and Republican parties to be quite similar in their effects. Ladd is also unable to distinguish between the different reform provisions implemented by the Democratic party after 1972. Writing in 1977, he argues that not only did the Mikulski Commission *not* compromise away the McGovern–Fraser reforms, but that the "Winograd Commission seems likely to be remembered primarily for reconfirming the victory won by McGovern reformers six years earlier" (1977:54–55). Shafer's recent critique of the quiet revolution (1983) in Democratic party politics is based entirely on an extended history of the evolution of the McGovern–Fraser reforms, as is Polsby's analysis, *Consequences of Party Reform* (1983a).

This indiscriminate lumping together of all reforms ignores the differential treatment of groups that we discussed earlier. These reform provisions have had differential effects on the representation of the original targeted groups. As seen in Chapter 3, contrary to the assumptions of reform critics, the representation of women, blacks, and youth was a function of the reform rules specific to each convention. The changing representation of these groups indicates, at minimum, that the proportional representation of these groups is quite sensitive to the specific reform rules—and is not a gross response to the epiphenomenon of the 1972 McGovern–Fraser reforms. These data indicate that without nationally set party goals, the local parties are impermeable to participation by women. In this context, we are in agreement with the assessment by reform critic Ladd. "If the formal mechanisms of party had not been so abruptly dismantled, they might have provided some *barrier* to the excessive intrusion of activists . . . " (1977:66; emphasis added). Our argument here is that reform, per se, is neither good nor bad; all reform must be judged on its merits. The normative question we pose is whether the reforms result in the recognition of new elite groups. For reform critics, the normative question is quite different: has political intermediation declined so as to diminish accountability?

Reform critics argue that the answer is yes; contemporary developments in the interest group structure have raised concerns that we are evolving toward a mass society. "Staff organizations," those small interest groups with members having only a "checkbook affiliation," are, as Michael Hayes suggests, the "quintessential 'mass organizations' " (1983:111, 122). As indicated in Chapter 3, we agree with Hayes that they only offer the "illusion of participation" while offering few opportunities for face-to-face contact and group influence (1983:119).[8] We further argue that these groups fail democracy by not creating new elites among those groups they purport to represent, while representing the political interests of the middle- and upper class elites who staff and fund them. We conclude, however, that social movements constitute an important exception to this trend.

For reform critics, this gradual evolution toward a mass society encompasses *all* of the new citizens groups and raises severe problems for democracy. "Ultimately, the stage is set for disillusionment and a crisis of confidence in public authority. The salience of national politics is increasing while the capacity of political institutions to manage conflict has been significantly eroded" (Hayes, 1983:124). Parties might serve as an antidote to this dangerous trend. However, according to the reform hypothesis, rather than a locus of activity at the state and local level, "recent reforms have moved the two major parties closer to becoming mass organizations themselves" (Hayes, 1983:122). Indeed, Polsby raises the specter of governing entirely without parties. "The idea of a political party as a coalition of interests and groups bound together by many sorts of ties, including the hope of electing a president, is fast becoming an anachronism" (1983a:132). Polsby argues that party reform has had wider consequences: party mediation through traditional intermediary groups has nearly disappeared, supplanted by the mass media. Banfield tells us that intermediate authorities (such as state and local party leaders) have "become fewer and less influential now" (1980a:26). According to what Polsby terms conventional notions, "intermediary groups are supposed to interpret the desires of ordinary people to leaders and to inform publics of alternatives available to them, thus tutoring their expectations about the activities of government" (1983a:138). Conventional notions aside, these assessments raise more questions than they answer. What is meant by the term mass organizations? What is the distinctive contribution of the party? And who are the "traditional" agents of political intermediation? The answers are by no means obvious. After all, political linkage between elites and masses can occur through a wide variety of mechanisms (e.g., rational informed voters, pressure group system, belief sharing or socialization, elite representational roles, and government manipulation of opinion), of which parties constitute only one option (Luttbeg, 1981; Weissberg, 1976). Moreover, apart from those scholars expounding the reform hypothesis, there is no agreement among party scholars over how political parties provide linkage (Lawson, 1980) or whether parties indeed do anything unique (Ranney, 1975; Epstein, 1967). Finally, the evidence indicates that state and local parties never declined (Cotter et al., 1984). The reform hypothesis, in sum, is based on a specific theoretical concept of partisan linkage and cannot be evaluated apart from a consideration of its theoretical underpinnings. Therefore, to answer these questions, we now turn to an examination of mass society theory and the theory on which it is based—pluralism.

Pluralism and the Mass Society Critique

Both pluralist and mass society theories developed in response to a distinct set of historically circumscribed concerns following World War II: the seeming instability of some electoral democracies during periods of rapid electoral change. Writing at the beginning of that intellectual cycle, Heberle concluded that,

the experience of two world wars, the revolutions in Russia and Germany thirty years ago, the rise and fall of Mussolini and Hitler, the Civil War in China, the expansion of the Soviet sphere of influence into the very heart of Europe and the ensuing tensions between the partisans of capitalism, socialism and communism have aroused an intensified interest in the study of those forces and factors which have contributed to the present crisis of Western society. (1949:347)

This concern was heightened by the scholarship of a number of émigré scholars in both sociology and political science (Pateman, 1970). Major theorists of mass society include Hannah Arendt (1954), Erich Fromm (1945), Karl Mannheim (1940), Robert Nisbet (1953), and Phillip Selznick (1952). William Kornhauser's *The Politics of Mass Society* (1959) provides a comprehensive synthesis of both elite and democratic theories of mass society. This perspective, drawn from early political sociology, has had such pervasive effects on theories of democracy in political science that the original sources are rarely cited (for an exception, see Hayes, 1983). We first examine the underpinnings of the reform hypothesis in mass society theory and then turn to the underlying theory of pluralism.

Party Reform and the Decline of Intermediation. The emphasis of mass society theorists on crisis and social disintegration is also found in most elaborations of the reform hypothesis. For reform critics, the reforms were instituted in a crisis situation. Polsby, for example, rather than discussing the individual impact of the changing reforms after 1972, stresses that the "wave of reform" emerged in a specific context, one "rather inhospitable to reasoned reflection of any sort: the turmoil of 1968 and its aftermath, and the trauma of Watergate and the impeachment crisis" (1983a:132). For reform critics, the focus on the crisis atmosphere accentuates the assumed irrationality and *ad hoc* nature of the reform response by Democratic party elites.

To return to mass society theory: mass society theory assumes that the "mass" is a concrete group found only in "mass society." Mass society is created under situations of social disorganization; intermediary groups are disorganized and individuals become socially atomized. Thus, mass society is characterized by a social atomization among the masses in electoral democracies such that *"elites are readily accessible to influence by nonelites and nonelites are readily available for mobilization by elites"* (Kornhauser, 1959:39, emphasis in the original).

Similarly, the reform critics do not argue that the "transformation of the nomination process from an elite to a mass phenomenon" (Polsby, 1980:59) results in the disappearance of elites. On the contrary, the result is the rise of a new elite, one "skilled in currying favor with reporters and news media

gatekeepers" (Polsby, 1980:65). Ladd (1970:275-281) argues that a new political class is now in ascendency: the professional and managerial stratum
comprised of "brain workers" (including the research scientist, the acade-
mician, and the corporate official). J. Kirkpatrick (1976) concludes that the
effect of party reforms has been to open up the parties to these new "symbol
specialists," thereby resulting in a "new presidential elite."

Mass society theory argues that this relationship between elites and masses
has political implications: the masses are typified by homogeneous, but extremely unstable, attitudes and behavior that render traditional social categories (e.g., family, class, community or region, and ethnic identity) obsolete.
This development undermines democracy. As summarized by Joseph R.
Gusfield,

the socially alienated individual is not only politically alienated; he is also more likely
to become the extremist activist than is the member of a structured interest group.
He is no longer limited in his attack on rivals by the controls of a structured pluralist
society. His resentments against opposing groups and against the existing institutions
need not be confined to the calculative, instrumental style of democratic politics. The
mass man is a passionate supporter of democracy. (1962:24)

This, too, has a parallel in the reform hypothesis: according to reform
critics, the effect of instrumentally oriented interest groups is to "reduce
greatly the intensity of ideological conflict and to make political life more
stable and conservative" (Banfield, 1980b:139). Polsby characterizes the
"mass" as nondeliberative (1980:60) and argues that the effect of reform is
to transform party nominations from an elite to a mass phenomenon
(1980:54). The result of reform (along with other social trends) is to erode
the "tyranny of geographical propinquity in determining the options that
people have in adopting one or more organizations as their political intermediaries of choice" (1983a:138). Traditional intermediation agents include
the nuclear and extended family, "school, primary communal groups such
as exist in a work place or church or neighborhood, or a voluntary association
organized for the purpose of promoting some shared interest" (1983a:138).

Both pluralist and mass society theory focus on the role of voluntary groups
that are intermediate between the nuclear family and the large modern political state. However, the two theories diverge on the formation of these
groups. Mass society theory, with its concern about the degeneration of
pluralist society, views the formation of new groups with national-level concerns with alarm. The "best society," according to the mass society thesis,
is a pragmatic one dominated by local groups with economic or instrumental
political interests. Mass society theorists thus view intermediary groups narrowly in their socialization role of promoting "proper" citizenship values.

Similarly, for reform critics, intermediary groups do not directly engage
the individual in politics. Like mass society theorists, reform critics distin-

guish between the diversity of (nonpolitical) associations at the mass level and the instrumental calculation of economic interest groups at the national— and elite—level (Banfield, 1980a). Under the old party system, Polsby and Aaron Wildavsky distinguished between the "electoral" and the "governing" coalitions. Under the electoral coalition, intermediation occurs as,

the two political parties ... act as transmission belts for policy preferences in the general population. ... In order to win the great prize of the Presidency, [the partisans] must gather support from a variety of groups in the electorate, and to the organized groups which represent its various interests. By giving this support at the polls to party winners, interest groups gain opportunities to participate in party and governmental decision-making. (1971:297)

The electoral coalition does not give rise to an electoral mandate or a responsible party system. Interest-group support for the winning candidate only gains an opportunity to participate in the governing coalition. The governing coalition is broader (including not only the two parties, but the president and Congress, bureaucrats, all "variously situated") and is developed on an issue-by-issue basis (Polsby and Wildavsky, 1971:312).

For reform critics, there is thus no direct link between the intermediary groups and the pressure groups. Polsby argues that "there are opportunities here as well as dangers": while making the party leaders beholden to leaders of organized interests, the inclusion of traditional intermediaries (labor leaders in the Democratic coalition) "constitutes a long term strategy for enlisting that portion of public opinion subject to their influence" (1983a:137). Thus, critics conclude that the omission of labor—until recently, the only organized Democratic constituent group—from Democratic party reforms alienated the Democratic party from its base while advantaging certain other interest groups (e.g., Common Cause, Ralph Nader's organizations, and "those speaking for interests widely perceived as historically disadvantaged such as black, Hispanic-American, and militant women's groups" (1983a:133; see also Shafer, 1983). These new interest groups are organized differently, being the "creatures of the mass media," rather than organizing "around the economic or status needs of their clientele" (Polsby 1983a:133–134).

The role of intermediary groups, according to the mass society thesis, is considered critical in promoting proper citizenship values in electoral based democracies. The danger under politically egalitarian societies is the development of the "mass"—large aggregates of individuals who are not attached to the larger institutions and norms. Elites are accessible to influence by nonelites in electoral-based pluralist democracies. But pluralism functions to increase political support and to insulate the mass from elite mobilization. While individuals at the mass level participate in approved ways (e.g., by voting), they are relatively uninvolved politically. Thus, pluralist societies do produce the necessary minimal consensus for democratic government, but it is a consensus forged out of political apathy.

In "mass society," the atomization and normlessness of the "mass" renders the masses vulnerable to demagogic movements. Thus, the mass is potentially manipulable with such mass organizations as the mass media and large bureaucratic institutions in control, but this results in unstable attitudes. Mass behavior is focused on political objects remote and distant from everyday life. According to this view, "institutions functioning under conditions of mass society do not touch the character and the personal values of those exposed to them" (Gusfield, 1962:21). This results in a contrast between the institutions of cultural uniformity (the mass media and large, national-level or bureaucratic organizations) versus those of cultural diversity (i.e., locally based intermediate groups). The inability of mass organizations to structure the electorate in any fundamental way results in the twin phenomena of mass apathy punctuated by episodes of mass activism. And in societies where elites are not accessible, this social atomization may result in totalitarianism (Kornhauser, 1959).

Reform critics likewise stress the power of the media to fashion opinions. What are the implications? Polsby (1980:64–66) indicates that the political consequences are to increase the intensity of short-term opinion ("crazes or manias"), the social contagion of ideas ("fads"), the typecasting of political celebrities ("heros and bums"), to reduce elite accountability, and to resuscitate mass ideology. This results in both reduced voter turnout (1983a) and in elite "fights for control over the attention of publics" (1980:65). "This does not imply that the media are reaching directly into the homes of totally atomized voters. Rather, political leaders are broadcasting to publics mobilized and organized around certain principles of attentiveness and inattention, and this has implications for interest groups and their success in politics" (Polsby, 1983a:134).

Polsby argues that this also has implications for the ability of parties to forge coalitions: under the new system, "rather than build coalitions, they must mobilize factions" (1983a:65). In making this distinction, Polsby is using the term faction in the opposite sense of Key (1950). Key reserved the term faction to mean a fleeting group without a label that was organized around a single individual or clique. A faction, such as operated in the southern states he studied, was undemocratic in not allowing voters even a minimal level of choice. However, Polsby means faction as "a group acting through a political party in pursuit of a common interest"; when acting outside the party, it is an interest group. Polsby uses the term faction to reflect enduring interests, whereas Key used it to mean short-lived coteries of elites. Polsby concludes, as did Key, that "where party organizations are strong, coalition-building flourishes; where they are weak, the politics of factional rivalry prevails" (1983a:66). Quite frankly, we have no difficulty with Polsby's assessment here, but wish to disassociate the normative opprobrium usually attached to Key's use of the term from Polsby's quite distinct use. Political interests, or Polsby's "factions," are, after all, a normal part of the party system and essential to coalitional politics. Polsby argues that coalitions ensue from interests required to act strategically and through instrumental calculation because of "consensus-forcing institutions" (1983a:66). Thus, coalitions for the reform critics rest on a temporary strategic *ad hoc* consensus, not an enduring, substantive one.

Reform critics as well distinguish between local versus national-level groups. Banfield concludes that "as the power of these other [intermediate] authorities declines, that of the central one must increase" (1980a:26). Polsby argues that groups that organize on a communal or face-to-face basis have lost ground, "in particular the groups traditionally served by city machines, geographically compact and ethnically homogeneous neighborhood groups" (1983a:154). This results in a strained distinction between political parties and social movements. "Women with a history of activism in political parties may be at a disadvantage compared with women with a history of activism in the women's movement" (1983a:154). Polsby is implicitly arguing that it is the socially atomized who participate in the women's movement (i.e., those not involved in communal groups), while other women have already achieved representation in communal groups. Polsby does acknowledge that blacks have been discriminated by local parties in the South, but rejects any centralized solutions.

The reform hypothesis is thus based on the concept of mass society, and "mass society" possesses a number of characteristics that raise concerns about the future of "democracy." Thus, any actions taken by elites that render "mass society" more likely (e.g., party reforms) are reprehensible. Yet, the mass society view assumes a certain level of apathy, and participation for most is limited to the vote. It is important, however, to distinguish mass society theory from pluralism: mass society theory is drawn from pluralism; yet, pluralism possesses a more general applicability. In point of fact, some of the more trenchant critiques of pluralism (e.g., Bachrach, 1966), are in reality critiques of the derivative theory of mass society.

Pluralism and Group Formation. Pluralist theory diverges from mass society theory by not distinguishing between economic and noneconomic groups. As such, pluralism is entirely consonant with our conceptualization of democracy. As Seymour Lipset, Martin Trow, and James Coleman (1956) found in their study of the American Typographical Union, (pluralist) democracy is furthered by the presence of competing centers of power distinct from the central governing authority. As we indicated earlier was the case for social movements, these locally organized groups allow for the possibility of new elite formation apart from the national party oligarchy.

The strongest exposition of pluralism focuses on the broadest functions of groups (e.g., Truman, 1958), rather than on the narrowly political sphere of public decision making (e.g., Dahl, 1961b). Thus, pluralism broadly conceived emphasizes the adjustive aspects of groups and the formation of attitudes in groups (Truman, 1958). Groups form because of economic and social disruption due to the "continual frustration of established expectations consequent upon rapid changes" (Truman, 1958:57). Because of the complex interrelationship of groups, group formation tends to occur in waves. Moreover, "so closely do these developments follow, in fact, that the rate of association formation may be used as an index of the stability of a society, and their number may be used as an index of its complexity" (Truman, 1958:57).

While the mass society thesis requires pluralist theory, pluralism as a theory is not so limited. The particular strength of Truman's basing of pluralism in social psychological theory is that it provides an explanation of political change. The process through which voters are informed about politics is not through individual rational analysis, but through their group ties. Political attitudes are formed in concrete, face-to-face groups. This occurs because of the adjustive function of groups: groups aid the individual's adjustment to social change. Individuals may respond to a disturbance in the pattern of their group equilibrium pathologically (e.g., acting out through deviance or depression), or they may create a new group.

This provides a broader perspective of the process of political change, particularly as Truman acknowledges the wave formation of groups following periods of rapid social change. In the era that Truman was discussing, the most common were "those stemming from economic institutions." Truman goes on to note what we regard as the essential flaw of the mass society critique. "So common have these groups become and so involved has government activity been with economic policy, that many writers have fallen into the error of treating economic groups as the only important interest groups" (Truman, 1958:61). The formation and relative importance of groups is a function of "technological and cultural changes of all kinds" (Truman, 1958:64). We agree with Truman that "classifications that neglect such emerging trends or that underemphasize the processes by which they take place are a serious handicap to understanding" (1958:64). Therefore, Truman's theory is quite compatible with the formation of social movements, while the more historically circumscribed mass society theory is not.

Assessing the Mass Society Critique of Reform

If the mass society theory of the reform critics and our alternative one relying on social movement theory are both consonant with pluralism, the issue then becomes one of empirical validity: which one best describes the current state of affairs? As discussed in Chapter 2, one key assumption of the reform critics is clearly contradictory: the state and local party organizations have gradually increased in strength (Cotter et al., 1984). While the national parties have indeed increased in strength as well (Herrnson, 1986), the relation of the strength of the federal party units appears to be consonant, not zero sum.

Critics of Cotter and his associates' position on party transformation have stressed that the increase in state and local party organizations was essentially bureaucratic in nature; a renaissance fueled by the new campaign technology that A. James Reichley argues "can be marketed more efficiently through national party structures than through party organizations based on state-houses, county courthouses or city halls" (1985:199). Hence, Reichley identifies the rise of a "national party machine." Reichley acknowledges that state parties may have augmented their "bureaucracies," but argues that "these expansions hardly made up for the continuing decay of patronage-fed grass-roots organizations in the towns and precincts. . . . The direction in most states and cities was away from political competition built primarily around parties and toward a politics driven by movement enthusiasms" (1985:181). This conclusion is strongly refuted by the research of Dwayne Marvick (1986) in Los Angeles and Samuel Eldersveld (1986) in Detroit, whose work provides the only longitudinal comparative data available spanning both prereform and postreform local parties. Summarizing the longitudinal data in both cities, Eldersveld concludes (contrary to Reichley) that the local parties as rival (local) groups continue to compete as effectively as before. "While never highly efficient systems, they clearly have not declined in the enthusiasm with which people enter party work, in their desire to stay in party work, in their performance of critical campaign tasks" (1986:118).

If state and local parties have not declined, then what about the increase in activism outside of the party system (Reichley's "movement politics")? Reform critics, drawing on mass society theory, have provided an apparently powerful explanation for these new groups: it is the socially atomized who engage in "extremist" politics of "mass movements." Actually, the assumption has undergone considerable empirical investigation, particularly among sociologists and psychologists.

One of the strongest findings is that there appears to be very little linkage between social atomization and participation in social movements. One of the most thorough examinations of mass society theory is provided by Maurice Pinard's (1971) study of the rise of the extremist Social Credit Party in Quebec in 1962. Pinard found that the party was most supported not by the socially atomized, but by those more strongly integrated into local community groups. He explains this finding as follows. "Not all components of the intermediate structure are fit to work toward the redress of a given set of grievances (think of the primary groups, the community social networks, leisure and religious associations in a modern society facing an economic depression), while potentially all can act as communication and mobilization centers for a new movement" (Pinard, 1971:192). One of the most persuasive pieces of evidence supporting this point is the study of the Watts riot by David Sears and John McConahay (1973). Sears and McConahay found that riot participants were not the socially atomized, the "criminal element," an economic ghetto underclass, products of broken families, or southern newcomers (to Los Angeles). In fact, native, long-time residents and "those who attended church most often were most likely to have participated in the upheaval" (Sears and McConahay, 1973:21).

Research by psychologists provides suggestive evidence that the role of social atomization is to stimulate participation in religious cults (e.g., the People's Temple of Jonestown) rather than in politics. Glendon Schubert summarizes the characteristics of these cults as

(1) self-appointed messiahs, who have (2) charismatic, domineering personalities; (3) only two motives, to recruit and to raise money; (4) the group purports to be both innovative and exclusive; (5) the leader is venerated personally; (6) a double ethical standard, positive toward insiders but negative toward outsiders; (7) an authoritarian power structure; and hence (8) member behavior is subject to the total control of the organization. Recruits as a class have no special characteristics *except* for their shared experience of temporary instability (due to loss of a lover, a job, parents and a home, etc.) which makes them particularly vulnerable at the time of their recruitment. (1985:226)

Reform critics assume that local community groups are indeed open to participation. In doing so, they have ignored the function of these groups in status allocation with the rise of industrialism in the twentieth century. While municipal reformers of the Progressive Era sought to limit the local party machine and the scope of politics in city government, economic and social elites shifted their activity from government to voluntary groups. "The functions of status allocation and recognition had once been fulfilled by public officeholding, in the 'golden age' when patricians dominated city affairs. In the industrial city, new ways of fulfilling those functions had to be devised. Beginning about the turn of the century, there was a proliferation of private institutions that served to enhance the influence of the upper class" (Judd, 1984:111). Social welfare (e.g., the American Red Cross, family welfare, and charity) and cultural functions (symphony, museums, and libraries) were all the purview of local community groups. Research among a number of large cities, according to Dennis Judd (1984:112) indicates that these groups served as social-screening devices for those with the proper credentials—including race, "wealth, occupational status, family and religion."

The party—in particular the party machine—could theoretically serve as an alternative recruitment device. Thus, reform critics have stressed that the party machine was a more democratic recruitment vehicle than the postreform party system (e.g., J. Kirkpatrick, 1979). But the prereform party system did discriminate against women and blacks. As discussed in Chapter 3, despite the Fifty-Fifty Rule providing for national committee members of both sexes, the national committeewomen did not have the influence of the committeemen (Cotter and Hennessy, 1964). Eldersveld (1964) found in his study of local parties in Wayne County, Michigan, that there was a group of nonmobile, yet continuously active aspirers to higher office among precinct leaders. In both parties, the nonmobile included the older activists, those with lower income and educational attainment, and those with blue-collar (i.e., nonprofessional) occupations. "There were also certain interesting concentrations for each party. Republican women (35% of this Republican group) and Catholics (48%) had particular difficulty rising in the hierarchy. There was also a large concentration of labor union actives (75%) among this Democractic group of nonmobiles" (Eldersveld, 1964:149). Half of these "aspiring but perpetual precinct captains" were recruited by party leaders (compared to 29 percent of all precinct leaders)—a fact that "raise[s] serious questions about the so-called phenomenon of oligarchy" (1964:149–150).

More recent evidence of the oligarchical nature of machine politics comes from one of the most successful local party machines—the Daley machine of Chicago. One study of the Daley machine concluded that "we discovered that the Chicago Democratic machine has always utilized a a few women . . . the characteristics of the handful of women whom it sponsors have varied but little. Either their backgrounds, interests, assigned tasks and attitudes toward political power present a composite picture of a *womanly* woman who restricts herself to women's work, and/or these women are useful to the organization because they are women" (Porter and Matasar, 1974:85–86). Furthermore, "while women have a role in the Daley organization, they have no status, never have had status, and will not attain status" (Porter and Matasar, 1974:87). The delegation that the Daley machine slated for the 1972 convention severely underrepresented targeted groups. "To satisfy the McGovern-Fraser criteria, twenty-one delegates would have had to be black, six Latin Americans, twenty-nine women, and eighteen youths. In turn, the 'Daley 59,' as the press called them, included twelve blacks, one Latino, six women, and eight young people" (Crotty, 1983:162). The Daley delegation was challenged on grounds of "gross and deliberate" violations of the reforms; the 1972 convention voted to seat the delegation put together by Jesse Jackson and William Singer. During the contentious deliberations of the Credentials Committee, one of the attorneys for the Daley delegation noted that "some of the delegates would not be adverse to letting women on the delegation, perhaps their wives" (quoted in Crotty, 1983:195).

The Daley machine has changed: in 1979, Jane Byrne, a woman, was elected mayor and in 1983, Harold Washington, a black, was elected mayor. But elite oligarchy has not changed. A 1981 survey of ward and township committee members in Chicago and Cook County found that the party organization—"the continuing base of political power—is controlled by men" (74% list their spouses' occupation as housewife) with "black 'plantation wards' . . . bought off, and at a relatively cheap price" (Crotty, 1986:158, 192). Crotty found blacks to comprise the major potential political problem for the machine. Michael Preston concludes that Washington, the first viable black candidate, was a symbolic figure for many blacks. The increase in black participation that resulted in Washington's victory was due to the group consciousness of blacks and their own individual and group-based "selfishness" (e.g., "fear of losing jobs"), the "long history of machine exploitation," and "the amazing amount of racism that surfaced among white ethnics" (Preston, 1987:145–46).

The history of state and local parties and voluntary associations is one of discrimination against specific out-groups and a relatively closed oligarchy. Yet, the state and local parties have always been open and permeable to political movements. David Price (1984:156) notes that among the Republicans, and prior to reform in either party, "insurgent elements in the party did not find the [party] rules a barrier to working their will in the 1964 convention."

The reform critique has also faulted reform for merely creating another elite. This misses the mark: of course it did. This charge ignores the essential role of elites in all groups and the fact that the very function of social movements is to develop new elites. Therefore, one cannot criticize party reform just because the "new" elites are just as different from the "masses" as the old elites. Party reform did not create the stratum of political elites, it merely allowed the representation of "elites sprung from the masses."

There is one final charge implicit in the reform critique that we must consider: that social movements do not possess a grass-roots base (e.g., Polsby, 1983a:133) and, therefore, may be described as mass organizations. The characteristics of mass organizations are manifold: mass politics are unstable and irrational, and reflect demagogic leadership and the impact of the mass media. Mass organizations also cannot touch the values of those who are members. To respond to these characterizations, we must now turn to social movement theory and research, and examine the process by which social movements arise.

SOCIAL MOVEMENTS AND PARTY REFORM:
AN ANTIDOTE TO PARTY OLIGARCHY

The central characteristic of social movements is their basis in a personal and social transformation. As we saw in Chapter 3, this is in sharp contrast to political movements. Social movements do not merely reflect values, but are transformative. As James Q. Wilson (1973:64) points out, the function of movement groups is to effect a transformation which renders the lower class participant "middle class"—or in other words, politically active. For example, Sidney Verba and Norman Nie (1972) demonstrated that black group consciousness among blacks can overcome the deficit of their generally lower socioeconomic status. Similarly, Claire Knoche Fulenwider (1980) found feminist consciousness to increase political activity among women.

Social movements are based on an ideology which explains their disadvantaged group status both politically and socially. This ideology has ramifications for all social and political institutions. As such, social movements are characterized by a multiplicity of social movement groups (e.g., among blacks, the National Association for the Advancement of Colored People (NAACP), the Southern Christian Leadership Conference (SCLC), the Congress for Racial Equality (CORE), Student Nonviolent Coordinating Committee (SNCC). This includes not only organizations at the national level (e.g., NAACP), but major institutions (e.g., the Black Caucus in the U.S. Congress) and the traditional interest sector (the Black Caucus in the APSA).

The recent literature on social movements (e.g., Freeman, 1983 a and 1983b) considers any trend which involves group or collective action as a movement. Hence, religious cults (e.g., the "Unification movement" [Bromley and Shupe, 1983]) or any action taken on what is regarded as a social problem—occupational health issues (e.g., the "brown and black lung movements" [Judkins, 1983]) and poor housing conditions (e.g., the "tenant movement" [R. Lawson, 1983])—have been described as social movements. We would describe them quite differently: *either* as a religious conversion (i.e., a change of belief potentially available to all nonbelievers and not limited to group members) giving rise either to a separatist cult or a *religious movement* within the established faiths (such as Methodism), or, when they possess only political goals, as a *political movement*, such as the nuclear freeze movement (Dwyer, 1983).

The fundamental problem with the indiscriminate combining of all movement-style groups as expressions of the same phenomenon is that this does not separate the social movement groups which produce their own elites from within the group from other movement-style groups which are organized by professional, trained organizers. Saul Alinsky (1969; 1972) is probably the most well known proponent of the efficacy of outside community organizers.

Despite the best intentions of social reformers, there are inherent problems in organizing the poor. This has been meticulously analyzed by Frances Fox Piven and Richard A. Cloward (1971; 1977). They dispute the notion that the poor possess the necessary resources (e.g., education and money) or the institutional positions which provide regular interaction or the leverage to press for redress of their grievances. In their view, the poor are located in marginal institutions (e.g., the welfare office) which do not facilitate organization. Piven and Cloward maintain that "political influence by the poor is mobilized, not organized" (1977:284). One can be poor due to widely disparate reasons, and organizing the poor is hampered by the difficulty in locating a common denominator. It is "not clear how activists could, as a practical day-to-day matter of organizing, mount an attack on poverty by attacking its main cause—underemployment and unemployment" (1977:277). Piven and Cloward (and also Roberta "Ash" Garner, 1977) hold to a model of class conflict in which the "have nots" make advances only at the expense of the "haves."

The level of poverty is in large part a function of economic moderniza-tion, but *who* experiences poverty in any given society is a social decision. Genuine social movement groups, according to the "classical model" (McCarthy and Zald, 1973), are able to mobilize the poor because they define disadvantage not in terms of poverty, but in terms of group dis-crimination, which often results in poverty. The rise of staff organiza-tions, operative only at the elite level, are a perversion of the concept of social movements. Social movements provide an alternative avenue of elite recruitment—but one which is controlled by the out-group itself. *It is for this reason that social movements further democracy.* Groups which are orga-nized by middle-class outside organizers can only serve as vehicles for as-similation, not alternative structures.

Our theoretical formulation is therefore distinct from the resource mobi-lization theory of John McCarthy and Mayer Zald (1973). This view devel-oped in opposition to the dominant view found in early political sociology—the mass society thesis, which focused on the social psychology (or pathology) of individual movement participants.[9] While there are a number of different theorists who together are considered in opposition to this earlier view (see Perrow, 1977), there are important distinctions between our own formulation based in the "classical approach" to social movement formation (e.g., Gam-son, 1975; Oberschall, 1973), and McCarthy and Zald's (1973) emphasis on the role of professional reformers in resource mobilization for disadvantaged groups.[10] While both the classical and the resource mobilization approach share a rejection of the earlier emphasis on the psychological stress of the participants or the influence of crowd psychology (e.g., LeBon, 1879; Turner and Killian, 1972), they diverge from each other the internal dynamics of movement organization.

For McCarthy and Zald, the critical characteristic of these new (social movement) groups is the separation of the membership base from the external funding and leadership. In their view, we have not produced a larger pool of active middle-class participants; the increase in these social movement-style groups is instead linked to a larger pool of college students and profes-sionals with the discretionary time to devote to socio-political activities. This (in conjunction with the changed funding patterns of charitable trusts, foun-dations, churches and the government) has created a "massive social move-ment industry" (1973:27). However, because this industry was created by elites, McCarthy and Zald conclude that "some portion of the increase in professional social movement activity could quite rapidly be reversed if the political elite were determined to bring about such a change" (1973:27). For McCarthy and Zald, social movements are increasingly an extension of elite-level support and conflict.

Normally, social movements are multi-generational, although youth do tend to comprise a significant core of many social—and political—move-ments. Age is a temporary component of life and generally not a political cleavage. Hence, while the continuation of "youth as a stage" (Keniston, 1968) and the demographic phenomenon of the retired elderly have increased the significance of the social categories of age, we regard groups such as various student groups (e.g., draft resistance movements) and the Gray Panthers as political movements, not as social movements. Moreover, the focus of these groups was not on group status, per se, (e.g., student or retired), but upon particular issues, such as Social Security or draft eligibility.[11]

Historically, the lower or working classes constituted a definable social characteristic. This is no longer so clearly the case. One of the more salient changes of the contemporary era is a decline in the traditional cleavage of class: the lower classes no longer vote "left" with such unanimity. Ronald Inglehart explained this phenomenon by proposing the increasing salience of a new cleavage based on what he terms postmaterialist values, which has neutralized the cleavage of social class (1971). According to Inglehart, postmaterialist values are formed during early socialization in an environment of "economic and physical security" (1986:27). It therefore represents an intergenerational cleavage, being more prevalent among the postwar generation than earlier cohorts—and an inversion of social class. Furthermore, "when postmaterialist issues (such as environmentalism, the women's movement, unilateral disarmament, opposition to nuclear power) become central, they may stimulate a materialist reaction in which much of the working class sides with the right to reaffirm the traditional materialist emphasis on economic growth, military security, and domestic law and order" (Inglehart, 1986:28). A decade after he identified the prevalence of postmaterialist values among students, Inglehart (1981) concludes that the postmaterialists now predominate among thirty- to forty- year-olds in jobs leading to top civil service and management posts. Thus, the change of social values from materialist to postmaterialist, while based in differential socialization, occurs through the mechanism of generational replacement. As such, Inglehart's theory bears similarities to Key's (1959) theory of secular realignment.

While we agree with Inglehart that the working class is less often allied with the left, we would argue that this is due to the changing nature of the structure of employment. Unions are not only declining in all major industrialized nations (which constitute Inglehart's focus), but unions which are increasing in size tend to be middle-class, white-collar unions, e.g., American Federation of State, County and Municipal Employees (Edwards and Podgursky, 1986). Moreover, a focus on the changing intergenerational and class conflict ignores the fact that social movements are multigenerational, ignores the critical distinction between the (middle-class) public interest and political groups, and ignores the social movements which represent disadvantaged social classes. Inglehart (1979) found that those with postmaterialist values are more likely to be politically active than those with materialist values. Thus, we believe that Inglehart's research provides a better explanation for the recent increase in political movements, but not social movements.

Women, after all, constitute a group which has suffered economically from their ascribed status, as have blacks. For this reason, the women's rights and the civil rights movements have concrete material goals, as well as status concerns. Inglehart's analysis, while highlighting the generational impact of demographic change, ignores the actual conflicts between women's rights groups, civil rights groups, and new right groups. Women's rights groups and civil rights groups share an intimate, yet often conflictual history dating from the Civil War (Stimpson, 1971). In addition to the political conflicts between organized women's rights and civil rights movements, women and blacks have had quite distinct economic and social roles, *and* different socialization experiences. The dramatic demographic changes among women since the 1950s, with the decline of the traditional family (Di Bianchi and Spaine, 1983), has resulted in delays in household formation, smaller families and the rise of the two-earner family (with sharing of child care responsibilities), an increase in the proportion of women who head single-parent households, and, with the persistence of employment and wage discrimination, the "feminization of poverty." The recent rise of the gender gap—the greater support of women since 1980 for the Democratic party and for more liberal social policies—reflects these phenomena (Baxter and Lansing, 1984; Klein, 1984). The gender gap in public opinion reflects the changing demographic position of women, indicating a secular realignment (Key, 1959). While the women's rights movement is also based on demographic changes, the two phenomena are conceptually distinct: one describes mass-level opinion, wheras the other describes a collectivity organized for social change (which appeared two decades earlier).

We now turn to a formal explanation of how social movements arise. Following the analysis of Nancy McGlen and Karen O'Connor (1983), we view the rise of social movements as occurring under certain specific circumstances. First is an economic modernization that results in economic and social dislocation (or structural strain). Second, potential leaders of the movement, through their elite positions within the out-group, are most aware of the group-level implications. Third, these leaders engage in the groundwork that prepares the way for a true grass-roots movement. Fourth, the social movement develops when a critical mobilizing event galvanizes out-group members at the mass level. This occurs through the fifth factor, group consciousness (defined here as a felt sense of common oppression and need for a common solution). This development is reflected in formation of new social movement organizations and in the activation of preexisting, and often nonpolitical, organizations (the traditional interest groups) in support of movement goals.

The Role of Leaders

The mass society theory holds that mass movements occur when individuals are atomized and isolated from intermediate groups. The rational choice theory outlined by Mancur Olson (1965) points out that due to the "free rider" problem, there are not sufficient incentives for large latent groups to organize solely for purposive or collective goods. We have argued that leaders (or elites) comprise a normal part of any political activity, including social movements. While arising from disadvantaged groups at the mass level, potential leaders communicate through a preexisting communications network and share a quasi-privileged status, which makes them particularly sensitive to group discrimination.

The Communications Network. Research on social movements found, contrary to the mass society critique, that the leaders who comprise the core of social movements are not isolated and socially atomized individuals, but on the contrary, join together to form the basis of a movement precisely because of preexisting communication networks (Pinard, 1971). The civil rights movement found its basis in the regular exchange of ideas among black civil rights lawyers, who, incidentally, shared a common law-school experience at Howard University law school (Vose, 1972). Jo Freeman (1975) documented how the "older" branch of the women's rights movement developed out of the communication networks built among women active on the federal and state Commissions on the Status of Women, and the "younger" branch developed out of the communication networks built through the "radical community" of the student and civil rights protest groups. Both the older and younger branches of the women's rights movement were peopled with politically active individuals.

Social movements do not originate from the mass media, but from internally controlled alternative communication networks. Social (and political) movements do attempt to use the media to communicate their group aims (Molotch, 1977). This communication, however, is directed toward nongroup members. Social movements, after all, comprise a minority and require access to the media to help place their group demands on the public agenda of the majority. Yet, social movements do not communicate with participants and group members through the mass media—or any other centralized source. Communication is closely linked to recruitment. Not only is recruitment to a social movement face-to-face, but it "flows along lines of pre-existing, significant social relationships of positive-affect" (Gerlach and Hine, 1970:97). The extensive nature of these personal and social ties is facilitated by the fact that this recruitment is "largely initiated by lay members of cell groups at the grass roots level rather than by noted leaders" (Gerlach and Hine, 1970:97). These personal links between participants result in a "grapevine" of "interlocking personal and group networks" through which intragroup communication occurs (Gerlach and Hine, 1970:62).

Leaders as Quasi-Privileged. Movement leaders are not only strongly integrated into the community, but possess political and economic resources. McGlen and O'Connor point out that "the presence of such persons transforms the group from Olson's large latent group to a quasi-privileged group" (1983:7). Social movements arise first among the middle-class leadership because it is this stratum in any social outgroup who suffer the disparity between achieved status and ascribed status most. It is this that can give rise to Truman's "continual frustration of established expectations" (1958:57).

This process has been described as creating conditions of marginality and relative deprivation among middle-class members of an out-group. According to Tedd Gurr, "relative deprivation is a condition where there is a perceived discrepancy between men's value expectations and their value capabilities. Value expectations are goods and conditions of life to which people believe they are rightfully entitled. Value capabilities are the goods and conditions they think they are capable of attaining or maintaining, given the social means available to them" (1970:29). This "perceived discrepancy" may occur from an inconsistency between statuses, rising value expectations, or from downward mobility or declining perceptions of value capabilities (Gurr, 1969).

Not only do middle-class members tend to have a higher sense of "relative deprivation," but potential leaders experience "marginality" through their professional activities and social position. The concept of marginality refers to the difficulties of assimilating between two groups with conflicting value demands. Marianne Githens and Jewell Prestage describe the marginal woman:

Like the marginal man, the woman in politics is intensively involved with two groups, women and politicians. Each group represents a way of life; at the same time, each provides an identity and strong social ties. Women who seek to enter the male-dominated political elite reject, whether they want to or not, at least some of the values and norms of most women. . . . The political woman no longer feels comfortable with nonpolitical women; she has problems engaging in informal conversation and in acknowledging other women's evaluations as criteria for her own self-esteem. On the other hand, the politician group, where she wishes to establish contact, displays reticence in accepting her. The woman in politics thus finds herself isolated from both groups. (1977:7)

Scholars describing the idiographic causation of specific movements (e.g., Matthews and Prothro, 1966:422–423; Oberschall, 1973:209–214, in terms of the civil rights movement; Freeman, 1975:28–32; Chafe, 1977; Klein, 1984, in terms of the women's rights movement) have stressed the pervasive impact of perceptions of deprivation (relative to in-group members of the same achieved status) and feelings of isolation from both reference groups (marginality). Yet, it is critical to acknowledge that these do not simply describe a generalized psychological affect; but, rather, indignities and humiliations arising continuously from everyday life. These daily reminders are particularly crucial for potential leaders. The Reverend Martin Luther King, Jr., for example, held a doctorate from Boston University and was the son of the pastor of Atlanta's Ebenezer Baptist Church, an elite position in one of the most elite institutions in the black community. King may have led the Montgomery bus boycott, but he, himself, did not ride the buses. Despite his elite status within the black community, he regularly suffered from racial distinctions when traveling that resulted in his going hungry, waiting in rear waiting rooms, or being unable to obtain accommodations for his family while on vacation (Garrow, 1986:79–80). Similarly, Dorothy Osler, a Republican state representative in the Connecticut legislature, found herself turned down for a loan to purchase a car to drive to the state capitol. "Even though she had just been elected to the state legislature, where she drew a salary of $5,000 a year, the local bank refused her a loan without the co-signature of her husband. This happened despite her personal friendship with the bank president and the fact that she had banked there for the last twenty-five years" (Tolchin and Tolchin, 1974:111). Hence, for potential leaders, regularizing that "marginal" status is a bread-and-butter issue, not some distant or abstract symbolic goal as the mass society hypothesis would indicate.

The role of a professional stake in the early organizational efforts of elites in social movements is another relevant factor. This is reflected in the origins of NOW on June 30, 1966. NOW was formed after the newly created Equal Employment Opportunity Commission refused to enforce the "sex" provision of the 1964 Civil Rights Act. Freeman points out that "not everyone within the EEOC was opposed to the 'sex' provision. There was a 'pro-woman' coterie which argued that 'sex' would be taken more seriously if there were 'some sort of NAACP for women' to put pressure on the government. As government employees they could not organize such a group, but they spoke privately with those whom they thought could do so" (1975:54). Thus, the formation of NOW was a direct result of action from those with a professional stake. Movement leaders (i.e., the out-group elites) are essential to the development of a social movement. These leaders are indeed different from participants at the mass level. Yet, they are not opportunistic elites. They share the group-level material economic and social disadvantages of the fellow group members—as well as the benefits of organizing for social change.

Organizational Base and Structure

Social movements are a distinct phenomena—neither simply an interest group nor as unstructured as a "collective action" of the same sort as a riot, crowds, or panics (Freeman, 1975:44–47). Yet, to be successful, social movements require organization. This organization is facilitated by extragroup inputs or a preexisting social movement (McGlen and O'Connor, 1983:8–9). It is critical to distinguish this facilitation from the rise of "staff organizations"—those without a mass membership or an elected board of directors. All social movement groups possess a mass base and are organized either solely at the local level (e.g., many of the gay rights groups and the younger branch of the women's rights movement), or organized at the national level, with local affiliates (e.g., the civil rights groups and the older branch of the women's rights movement). While the initial events that signal the development of an active social movement may indeed emanate from a small number of organizations, social movement activity is autonomous and spontaneous, not under centralized direction. While the "Big Four" of the civil rights movement (NAACP, SCLC, CORE, and SNCC) initiated 85 percent of the "events" of the movement, "between 1968 and 1970 'other movement organizations' accounted for nearly half (47 percent) of all events initiated by formal movement groups" (McAdam, 1983:304).

In organizational form, social movements are neither centralized nor are the political actions taken on behalf of a movement entirely random. Luther Gerlach and Virginia Hine describe the organization of social movements as a distinct third type: characterized by decentralization, segmentation, and reticulation. Social movements are *decentralized* because the leaders disagree, are unaware of all the groups active in the movement, and do not have regulatory power over the movement. No leader speaks for the movement as a whole, nor are there "card-carrying" members. Gerlach and Hine point out that participants "recognize each other on the basis of criteria born of a common experience, not because a leader announces that so-and-so is a participant in the movement" (1970:37). Movements are *segmented* due to the competition among leaders, the differentiation of groups along preexisting personal and social cleavages, ideological splits among group factions, and the personal access to power based on out-group experiences, not from any organizational position. Social movements are *reticulate* not hierarchical: this term describes "an organization in which the cells, or nodes, are tied together, not through any central point, but rather through intersecting sets of personal relationships and other intergroup linkages" (Gerlach and Hines, 1970:55). These linkages include personal relationships between leaders and among members of local groups, extragroup linkages, unifying events, and ideology, not some distant bureaucratic organization. In contrast to public interest groups or other political movements, social movements are not engendered by entrepreneurs.[12]

While social movements do rely heavily on extragroup inputs for their organizational success, the primary groups that provide this support *are those institutions controlled by the disenfranchised group*. In this context, Anthony Oberschall (1973) stresses the importance of the black churches and the black clergy and Freeman (1983a) points to the black colleges in providing an organized structure and a leadership group not controlled by the white power structure. Similarly, McGlen and O'Connor identify three separate women's rights movements in American history, each of which has been facilitated by an organizational base and extragroup inputs. For example, the second movement (which culminated in ratification of the Nineteenth Amendment granting women suffrage in 1920) built on the preexisting suffrage organization (the National American Woman Suffrage Association), the Women's Christian Temperance Union (founded in 1874), the Federation of Women's Clubs (formed in 1890), the settlement house movement, the National Consumers' and Trade Union leagues, and the Progressive movement—each of which women either controlled or played a major organizational role.

Sense of Collective Oppression and Need for Common Solution

We indicated the pervasive nature of race and sex discrimination in the party system in Chapter 3. This disadvantaged status has resulted in a group consciousness that has been shown to increase political participation among both blacks (e.g., Verba and Nie, 1972) and women (Fulenwider, 1980). Earlier, we indicated that movement leaders may be motivated by selective incentives because of their quasi-privileged status. We now consider how these selective incentives may also exist for the mass-level members of (or adherents to) a social movement. In their analysis of the American Agriculture Movement, Allan Cigler and John Mark Hansen (1983:96–100) point out that selective benefits need not be material. Expressive benefits (Salisbury, 1969:16) are those "where the action involved gives expression to the interests or values of a person or group rather than instrumentally pursuing interests or values." That is, participation in a group may affirm one's identity or values—a selective benefit not to be shared with nongroup participants—rather than being calculated in terms of collective benefits or purposive goals. However, in contrast to Robert Salisbury's formulation, for those who participate in genuine social movements, these values are *central*, not peripheral to the participants' lives.

The Critical Mobilizing Event

According to both mass society and rational choice theories, mass movements are irrational psychological events. By contrast, social movement theory emphasizes the rational purposiveness through the critical mobilizing event. The mobilizing event for a group desiring change tends to consist of a signal that group mobilization is likely to be successful. As we indicated above, group consciousness and an affirmation of group/individual values provide a crucial solidarity for the movement. This in-group/out-group perspective is continuous, yet active social movements are episodic. It is the critical mobilizing event that transforms a quasi-movement into an active social movement.

Social movements form on the heels of partial successes. The catalyst for the civil rights movement, for example, was the 1954 Supreme Court decision desegregating public schools, *Brown v. Board of Education of Topeka*. Similarly, the mobilizing events for the rise of the contemporary women's rights movement (the older branch) was the 1961 establishment of the President's Commission on the Status of Women, passage of the 1963 Equal Pay Act, and the 1964 Civil Rights Act, alongside the refusal of the Equal Employment Opportunity Commission to enforce provisions of the Civil Rights Act prohibiting sex discrimination in employment (McGlen and O'Connor, 1983:28–29). In both cases, the critical mobilizing event was the result of extensive effort on the part of out-group elites.[13] Social movements may be considered irrational if they have no chance of success. A critical mobilizing event, however, indicates that, if organized, the movement may achieve success.

Elite Cadres and the Significance of Social Movements

Social movements are not only a normal part of social adjustment, they are rational mechanisms by which social groups adversely affected by social change adapt. We argued that elite cadres tend toward oligarchy. If this is true, then all elite leadership groups have a limited capacity to respond to change. Social movements comprise an episodic, albeit normal, part of party realignment, and the alternative methods of political action they employ (strikes, marches, demonstrations, etc.) are part of a continuum of political participation. We joined social movement theory with traditional party theory (pluralism, critical and secular realignments), and with extant explanations of contemporary American politics (e.g., Inglehart's [1986] "postmaterialist culture"). Our treatment of these theories is summarized in Table 4.1.

Not all party elites are derived from social movements. This represents a crucial divergence of our theoretical perspective from the mass society hyopothesis of reform critics. Reform critics argue that *all* of society has changed, all party elites are reformed. Our theory accounts for the diversity of party elite motivations—both those drawn from contemporary social movements and those recruited through more mainstream political interest groups. Our theory predicts that while the social movement's affinity for ideology (Schattschneider's socialization of conflict) has moved the party system in a more ideological direction, it remains pragmatic as well. Our theory is an advance on the organizational redefinition we discussed in Chapter 2. We need not remove the mass from theoretical consideration in order to fashion an empirical theory of the party system that can explain the increase in

Table 4.1

Major Explanations of the Changing Pressure System

FUNDAMENTAL CAUSE	THEORY	SCHOLARS	MECHANISM OF CHANGE	COMMENT
MASS LEVEL SECULAR CHANGE	SECULAR REALIGNMENT	Key, 1959	Demographic Change	Explains Gender Gap
	SOCIALIZATION	Inglehart, 1971; 1981; 1986	Generational Replacement	Explains Change, but Ignores Group Conflict
EXTENSION OF ELITE LEVEL CONFLICT	LOGIC OF COLLECTIVE ACTION	Olson, 1965 Walker, 1983	External Group Sponsorship	Explains Difficulties of Social Movements, Not Their Successes
	RESOURCE MOBILIZATION	McCarthy & Zald, 1973 Salisbury, 1969	Professionalization of Reform and Political Entrepreneurs	Explains Public Interest Groups
MASS & ELITE LEVELS: STRUCTURAL CHANGE AND DISLOCATION [CONSENSUS CONFLICT]	RELATIVE DEPRIVATION	Gurr, 1970	Value Discrepancies	Explains One Important Precondition to Change, But Only One
	PLURALISM	Truman, 1958	Equilibrium Disturbance	
	MASS SOCIETY	Kornhauser, 1959	Social Disorganization	Counterfactual -- Socially Atomized Individuals Do Not Participate
	CLASS CONFLICT	Ash Garner, 1977 Piven & Cloward, 1977	Lower Class Revolt	Class Consciousness Declining
	SOCIAL GROUP CONFLICT	Tilly, 1973 Oberschall, 1973 Gamson, 1973	Social Movement	Explains Civil Rights and Women's Rights Movements
	CRITICAL REALIGNMENT	Key, 1955	Third Parties	Third Parties Are Difficult and Unlikely

ideology. Our theoretical reformulation of traditional party theory has broadened its scope, while maintaining the capacity for normative criticism that was the distinctive contribution of the reform critics.

The critical issue, then, is what happens when society changes. Anthropologists who study developing societies argue that social movements may be "acculturative." "These movements are seen as mechanisms with which whole groups adapt to changed conditions. By means of such mechanisms new types of leadership are developed, new social structures created, and new values accepted and internalized" (Gerlach and Hine, 1970:xiv). We argue that this is what has happened with the contemporary social movements (e.g., the women's rights and the civil rights movements). The result of these new movements has produced a group conflict over how our society is to deal with the consequences of economic change. Americans have maintained their economic status by women entering the work force, with the rise of two-earner families. This means that one of the most salient conflicts turns around the role of women. How the parties respond to what is commonly understood only as a "social" issue will determine in no small part the basis of the partisan cleavage between Republicans and Democrats for the 1980s and beyond.

MOVEMENTS, DEMOCRACY AND THE INFORMATION COSTS OF PARTICIPATION

Our definition of democracy rests on liberty for all groups in society and is based on the process of elite formation. Participation is a key element in not only developing citizen character, but in this process of elite formation. We have thus placed greater emphasis on the more demanding forms of political participation, and not merely voting.

Voting is important because, for many Americans, it comprises the only form of participation. "If people do not vote, they are not likely at all to engage in any of the other forms of political activity" (Crotty and Jacobson, 1984:10). Voting represents a minimal act of participation—and all thoughtful observers are understandably concerned about the decline in voter turnout, evident in presidential elections since 1964 (Hill and Luttbeg, 1983:98). The vote may comprise a political resource especially important for social out-groups—it is the only resource that out-groups have in abundance. The civil rights movement focused on the vote as a political resource; the Reverend Martin Luther King, Jr., believed that "the chief weapon in our fight for civil rights is the vote" (Garrow, 1986:77; see also Williams, 1987). Yet, voting should not be overestimated. Blacks in the South were denied the vote, yet they were not doomed to political impotence. Donald Matthews and James Prothro (1966:37–58) found that voting was an inadequate index of black participation in the South, particularly when community factors were considered. Their study

(1966:52) also indicated that southern blacks were *more* active than southern whites in their membership in political organizations and associations.
This is as our theory would predict: nonelites act independently and are
not limited to the altruism of political elites (in this case, southern
whites); hence, elite and mass are interdependent.[14]

It is worth noting that the decline in voter turnout developed eight
years prior to the first election following Democratic party reform. Moreover, the decline in voter participation is not paralleled by other forms of
political participation. Measures of participation in political campaigns
(e.g., persuading others, attending political meetings, working for a party
or candidate, donating money, and writing to public officials) have either
remained the same or increased somewhat over the same time period
(Conway, 1985:5–8).[15] "The most common of these other forms is trying
to persuade others how to vote; since 1952, the proportion of the electorate reporting that they have engaged in that activity has ranged from 28
to 37 percent in presidential years and from 17 to 27 percent in midterm
years" (Conway, 1985:5). Other indicators of participation in politics indicate not a decline, but increased activity. A wave of interest groups
formed in the past two decades, and interest groups are more active in national politics. There are new ideological groups formed both on the right
and on the left, public interest groups, movement groups, and increased
business activity (Berry, 1984:18–41).

The puzzle of participation is that vote turnout provides the only measure
of decline, and yet education—a factor strongly linked to voter turnout—has
increased, and barriers to registration have been reduced with voting rights
legislation banning race discrimination and setting a maximum residency
requirement of 30 days for presidential elections. These data require an
explanation specific to voting, which also accounts for the increase of voter
participation among blacks and women, and in the South (Conway, 1985:24–
29; Hill and Luttbeg, 1983:89–101). Reform critics have inferred that the
mainstream of voters have become alienated. We propose a simpler explanation and suggest that following the principle of Occam's razor, it best
explains the paradox.

First, it is important to recognize that voter turnout is based on both
psychological and structural factors. These two sets of factors are related:
voting is a habit that is learned, as is partisanship. Keeping voters out of the
polling booth not only reduces the opportunities for learning about the political system, but it may also increase alienation. Therefore, we argue, as
does Carol Pateman (1970), that one cannot examine the psychological causes
of the vote until one has examined the structural causes of the vote.

Steven Rosenstone and Raymond Wolfinger (1984) found that registration
requirements greatly increase the costs of turnout. Turnout among the states
varies with the ease of voter registration. They conclude that "if every state
had had registration laws in 1972 as permissive as those in the most permissive

states, turnout would have been about nine percentage points higher in the presidential election" (1984:75). Evidence indicating that the ease of registration is a factor separable from voter turnout is the finding that voter turnout has declined only in terms of the *potential* electorate, not among registered voters. In a study of registration and voting from 1964 to 1980, "one clear-cut finding . . . is that once people register, they overwhelmingly go to the polls and vote. Unlike the overall voting rate, which declined 10 percentage points between 1964 and 1980, turnout among persons who were registered declined slightly from 91 percent in 1968 to 89 percent in 1976 and 1980" (U.S. Bureau of the Census, 1984:2).

While registration requirements have been eased due to federal intervention, the need to reregister after moving remains. While the proportion of the overall population moving has gradually declined, this overall decline is related to the smaller size of families. Moreover, from the period preceding voter turnout decline (1947–1962) to the immediate period following the onset of declining voter participation (1963–1971), this decline is found only among those who move to a different house within the same county. Because voter registration is a local responsibility, it is among this group that the costs of reregistration are minimized. However, the rates of population mobility increased among those making within state (but out-of-county) and interstate moves over this same time frame (Greenwood, 1981:23). In a comparison of population mobility from 1965 to 1970 and from 1970 to 1975, the rate of mobility increased for all three categories of moves (Greenwood, 1981:24). Mobility among young adults (aged 20–24 years) has increased as well (Greenwood, 1981:26).

An examination of the differential structural impact of mobility explains the lower voter turnout of younger voters and among the less educated. On moving to a new community or state, in order to register, one must obtain the essential information about where and how to register to vote. For the better educated, or for older voters who have more experience in registering to vote, the act of registration is easier to accomplish. Moreover, "for someone who is interested in politics, can anticipate the need for registration before the peak excitement of election eve, and can easily locate the registrar's office, registration is a relatively costless act. On the other hand, for someone whose interest is aroused only a few days before the election, has minimal exposure to information, and is less adept at learning things like places and hours of registration, the whole process is a much more difficult hurdle" (Rosenstone and Wolfinger, 1984:71).

We conclude from these data that the decline in voter turnout has very little to do with the change in the party system and a great deal to do with the secular phenomenon of increased mobility among specific groups in the population. We make no argument that voters are more informed than heretofore; voters are, however, more apt to make their vote decision on the basis of issues (Hill and Luttbeg, 1983:104). The significant fact is that one may move, retain active participation in voluntary groups, and participate in political campaigns without being registered to vote. And these more demanding forms of participation show every evidence of becoming more common among the electorate. To return to the issue of the rational Downsian voter who refuses to vote because he or she has discerned that the benefit of voting is not counterbalanced by the information costs: we would argue that such a rational voter already possesses a great deal of information about the political system to engage in the more demanding forms of participation that do provide a profitable payoff. The problem is that the average citizen does not have the information necessary for such a rational calculus and, therefore, reports a lack of participation as a lack of interest.

SOCIAL MOVEMENTS AND PARTY TRANSFORMATION AND RESURGENCE

Critics of party reform have felt confident in concluding that "there is widespread agreement that the parties have been seriously weakened without being made more democratic" as a consequence of the recent party reforms (Banfield, 1980a:32; see also Polsby, 1983a; Shafer, 1983; Kirkpatrick, 1976, 1979; Ladd, 1977, 1981). We argue that critics of reform have widely missed the mark—they have criticized reforms for merely creating another elite. Of course they have; that is precisely the contribution of the reforms. And this is what makes the reforms democratic. The critics have relied on a dated (and historically circumscribed) set of normative concerns—societal instability and the rise of totalitarian movements—based on a theory of mass society that has distorted their views of all social movements. We proposed a theoretical synthesis that is consistent with the history of party realignments in American history and with the distincitve "American mold" of institutionalized parties (Epstein, 1986). Social movements are intimately and structurally related to political parties and comprise a normal part of our political and social development.

It is no accident that the precursors of the party transformation we have identified here *predate* the 1972 Democratic party reforms. In 1971, Gerald Pomper argued that the electorate had fundamentally changed: it was more perceptive of ideological differences between the parties, with an increasing congruence between partisanship and issue position. Elites were also perceiving a partisan difference in the era prior to reform. In an analysis of 1980 caucus-convention delegates in eleven states, one study found that a sizable minority had switched parties; "23.4 percent of the Republican delegates and 12.9 percent of the Democratic delegates had once considered themselves members of the opposite party" (Kweit and Kweit, 1986:209). As this was a study of state level-elites and activists, this indicates a grass-roots and local aspect to the "incipient realignment" that resulted in "liberals moving out of the Republican Party and into the Democratic Party and conservatives making the reverse move." Of those who switched in the 1960s, the liberals "are more liberal than the mainstream of the Democratic party and the conservatives are more conservative than the mainstream of the Republican party" (Kweit and Kweit, 1986:211).

Moreover, the parties are resurgent. The question we must consider is what indicators of party health we are relying on. In organizational terms, the two parties are flourishing. Party identification is undergoing a process of readjustment—from one based on inherited group loyalties to one based on a substantive political consensus. Turnout has declined, but primarily due to the increasing structural costs of participation, not because of a lesser attachment to parties. In fact, all other measures of party participation are up. Issue voting has increased, as well as the activity of interest groups *and* contemporary social movements within the party system, not without. All this expands the base of the party system. The parties are not only stronger, but also undergoing a transformation that has expanded the scope of party competition and forged closer linkages between elites and nonelites.

At the mass level, parties are moving from a patchwork quilt—an amalgam—of local interests to a substantive consensus. But this consensus is not one of (mass) cultural uniformity; on the contrary, it is one of partisan cleavage. These new groups forming at the mass level do differ in their support of the parties—they are not neutral or merely partisan through the happenstance of early socialization. This is surely more democratic than the history of the party machines, which systematically discriminated against certain groups and obtained their support through vote buying and a quid pro quo exchange between the jobless voter and the vote-hungry machine.

At the elite level, the formation of new elites has had significant effects. For the first time, we find the development of a true coalition at the elite level as well as at the mass level. While Polsby and Wildavsky (1971) describe the old party system as resting on a distinction between the electoral and the governing coalitions, the broadening of the elite party cadres has resulted in a blurring of this distinction. With the increasing difficulty of mounting a third party, it is no surprise that contemporary social movements are concentrating on working within the existing party system. These changes are not unrelated. Elites and nonelites differ, each with their own independent sphere of action, yet are linked through groups. While reform critics hold that groups are nonpolitical and that proper representation takes place through formal governing institutions, we argue that a fundamental shift has occurred yielding a new system: politicized groups with political parties as the preeminent representative agencies.

NOTES

1. In his 1956 study, Samuel Eldersveld found that 23% of the Republican and 12% of the Democratic executive board members he surveyed in Wayne County,

Michigan, had suffered "demotion" in that they had previously held more important posts in the party.

2. Cornelius Cotter and Bernard Hennessy (1964:44–45) note that in comparison with the regular RNC members, the state chairs on the RNC exhibited very high turnover. More recently, Cotter (1984:18, and his associates 44) found that the average number of state chairs for each party was seven over a twenty year period, and that the median number of county chairs was about two-and-one-half for an eleven year period.

3. Consider the middle-class two-earner family: to obtain "full" participation, the parents would have to participate in their place of work, in the school(s) which their children attended, in the church, in any specialized schools their children attended (e.g., dance, swimming lessons, summer camp, etc.), and in the family group. This is probably impractical in the ideal case, and is absurd in a single-parent family where there is probably little or no flexibility of income and schedule.

4. While some would argue that labor has acted as a "party within a party" (i.e., the Democrats) (Rehmus and Nesbitt, 1978:432), it is also true that labor has worked more within the pressure group system than it has the party system. Charles Rehmus concludes that, "American labor organizations have engaged in substantial political activities throughout their history. . . . These activities, however, have assumed the pattern of pressure politics—attempts to influence public policy—rather than party politics, *per se*" (Rehmus, 1978:24).

5. The Populist candidacy of General James B. Weaver in 1892 received one of every twelve popular votes and was a major factor in the 1896 realignment. William Jennings Bryan, supported by the insurgent wing, received the Democratic party nomination in 1896. In doing so, Key notes that this resulted in a "strong infusion of Populism within the Democratic Party" which was "accompanied by a desertion by conservative Democrats" (Key, 1964:258). The Progressive candidacy of Robert M. LaFollette in 1924 received one of every six popular votes. LaFollette, a Wisconsin Republican, drew strength from both parties. The result was to sharpen major party differences: in 1928 the Republicans opposed western farm issues while the Democrats endorsed the "remedy advocated by agrarian radicals" (Key, 1964:262).

6. Of those who have written on the topic, only Crotty (1983) and Crotty and J. S. Jackson (1985) clearly favor the reforms; they describe the anti-reform position as the "restoration view."

7. What is viewed as the same phenomenon we would argue consists of two radically different political movements active at the turn of the century (Thelen, 1981), an intellectual position argued by a very small number of political scientists at mid-century and the distinct social and political movements of the contemporary era.

8. Hayes modified his assessment in a revised essay ("The New Group Universe") published in 1986. Hayes makes a distinction between pure staff organizations (funded by outside patrons and sponsors) and mass groups (funded by the membership), both of which provide little opportunity for face-to-face relationships, and solidary groups, which do provide for face-to-face contacts (some of which may be funded by the membership, and others subsidized by outside patrons). In developing this two-fold typology, Hayes provides for the possibility that groups evolve, thereby significantly altering their organizational form. In doing so, Hayes proffers a much less pessimistic assessment of the prospects for representation.

9. Among sociologists, this perspective is known as the "collective behavior"

approach; we refer to these alternatively as the pluralist or mass society approach (theory).

10. "In the classical model the membership base provides money, voluntary manpower, and leadership. Modern movements can increasingly find these resources outside of self-interested memberships concerned with personally held grievances. . . . Early civil rights organizations, for instance, were heavily peopled by whites, while the prime beneficiaries of any successful civil rights actions were black" (McCarthy and Zald, 1973:17–18).

11. Certainly there are those who would argue with our characterization of the youth or student movement of the 1960s (e.g., Wilkinson, 1971:23). We do not intend to erect a strict taxonomy that excludes youth movements, per se, from being classified as a social movement. Relations between generations are complex and depend on a number of factors (e.g., the pace of social and economic change, immigrant status, etc.) (see Eisenstadt, 1965 and Mead, 1978). Movements comprised primarily of youth may be considered a social movement when they are characterized by a group status (based on an identifiable social characteristic); possess group consciousness; are organized; and act to produce personal, social and institutional changes. We do not believe that this was the case in the 1960s and concur with Gary Marx's assessment of the antiwar and student movements of the 1960s. "They were at best heterogeneous and loosely held together by opposition to particular policies that were changed. They did not draw on shared interests growing out of historic or enduring cleavages and a culture of opposition within the society" (Marx, 1979:120).

12. Jack Nagel (1987:127) stresses the individual initiative of Betty Friedan in founding NOW. Friedan was the first president of NOW; however, her role was not that of an entrepreneur as was John Gardiner's role in the formation of Common Cause. One can, for example, discuss the formation of the women's rights movement with very little mention of Friedan (e.g., Freeman, 1975); while one cannot discuss Common Cause without discussing the initiative of John Gardiner and his stake in Common Cause (McFarland, 1984).

13. The NAACP (founded in 1909) and the network of Howard University law school graduates sought, through a legal strategy, to develop a more receptive climate for civil rights—a strategy which culminated in the *Brown* decision. Women were less well organized during this era: many of the women's organizations active during the suffrage movement had all either ceased to exist or were "a pale shadow of their former selves" in the late 1950s (Freeman, 1983:18). Women's colleges, and the 180,000-member Federation of Professional and Business Women's Clubs, while "a good source of adherents" for a feminist movement, "were determined not to be the source of leadership" (Freeman, 1983:18). The vehicle for bringing together potential feminist sympathizers was the establishment, in 1961, of the President's Commission on the Status of Women "at the behest of Esther Peterson, then director of the Women's Bureau" (Freeman, 1983a:18). Shortly thereafter, governors of the fifty states followed suit and established state-level commissions. The research conducted by these commissions, the establishment of a local communications network among potential feminist leaders, the publication of *The Feminine Mystique* by Friedan, and the activity of feminists in Congress (especially Martha Griffiths [D-MI]) were critical in facilitating opposition to the EEOC's refusal to enforce the "sex" provision of the Equal Pay Act.

14. We are indebted to Cornelius P. Cotter for this insight.

15. One measure of campaign participation that has declined is wearing a campaign button or putting a bumper sticker on a car—from a high of 21 percent in 1960 to less than 10 percent since the mid–1970s (Conway, 1985:6–7). This, of course, is a noninteractive and undemanding form of political participation. Moreover, its decline is probably less a function of individual propensities than it is of the budgetary priorities of modern campaigns which are limited in their expenditures and must choose between campaign paraphernalia and media advertising.

PART II

ELITE CADRES AND PARTY ORIENTATIONS

We now turn to an empirical assessment of the various party cadres. Our analyses are based on the 1980 and 1984 versions of the Party Elite Study, comparable data from National Election Study (NES) surveys, and aggregate county-level data assembled from various sources.[1] The elite groups surveyed in the Party Elite Study include national convention delegates, county chairs, national committee members and state chairs from both parties.

In the following chapters, our data analysis will provide support for a number of propositions discussed earlier. In Chapter 5, we find that internal party reforms were clearly in keeping with developing social movements. Using the women's movement, we observe that party rules mandating equal representation for women have not contributed to nonparty supporters having too much influence or stimulated the creation of artificial factions within the party elite cadres; these divisions mirror those found elsewhere in society—including among unreformed party elites. In connection with equal representation rules for women at the 1984 Democratic National Convention, we see clear evidence of a greater level of elite stratum permeability in that women elites who had risen through their *own* elite groups were present among the Democratic ranks.

In Chapter 6, we examine some costs associated with increased party democracy. We assess the consequences of national party rule making on local party elite cadres. We find that for the Democrats (the reformed party), a noteworthy segment of the local party cadres are in fact alienated from the national party. Furthermore, we present evidence suggesting that in 1984, many of these individuals were unwilling to support the national party's presidential nominee—and there was some small (county-level) decline in presidential vote associated with this. However, given that these elite cadres have a history of excluding individuals based on group-level characteristics, we do not find any evidence so compelling as to suggest that the costs of greater party democracy are unaffordable.

In Chapter 7, we assess levels and types of party support among the party elite cadres and find substantial levels of abstract support for party, per se. There is less generalized support for party among national convention delegates than elsewhere, but even here overall levels are high. We examine different types of party supporters and find that there are meaningful divisions among the party elite cadres corresponding to two ideal types described in the party literature—the pragmatic party type associated with indigenous American institutions and the responsible party type from the famous 1950 APSA Committee report. We find little evidence that the various party hierarchies and elite cadres have been infiltrated by antiparty personnel.

In Chapter 8, we analyze the positions of the party cadres in 1980 and 1984—arguably a period of ideological cleavage and significant political change—and find evidence supporting the thesis that the Republican and Democratic parties do represent different groups and philosophies, *but* the evidence also indicates a significant degree of sensibility toward an often shifting mass-level center of gravity.

NOTE

1. These data were made available by the Inter-University Consortium for Political and Social Research (ICPSR).

5

Party Reform or Social Change?

INTRODUCTION

We argued in Part I that party reform was a necessary response to emergent social movements. In this chapter we provide an empirical assessment of that proposition. We compare Democratic and Republican party elites across party, gender, and elite level (i.e., national convention delegates versus county chairs) in order to empirically examine certain criticisms of Democratic party reform—namely, the excess influence of nonparty supporters, the creation of factions, and the undue influence of factions in the nominating process. More specifically, we consider whether the use of quotas for women (this being a major reform issue) is a contributing factor to the problems of faction and excess influence articulated in criticisms of reform. We term this the reform hypothesis. We contrast this with our position, the social movement hypothesis, which is that changes in the Democratic party are reflections of societal changes and adaptations to those changes. In this analysis, we compare convention delegates (reformed and unreformed) and local (unreformed) party elites—county chairs.

Many supporters of the reforms acknowledge that there have been some undesirable and unintended consequences associated with them, and many critics of the reforms acknowledge the significant influence of factors external to the party organization (e.g., rise of new social movements and campaign finance regulation). Nonetheless, the two sides offer very different accounts of the present state of the party system.

THE REFORM AND SOCIAL MOVEMENT HYPOTHESES COMPARED

Democratic party reform commissions since 1968 have initiated a series of wide-ranging changes within the party. Democratic reforms include affirmative action for minorities, equal division of delegates by sex, proportional representation of candidate preference, exclusion (and now inclusion) of *ex officio* delegates, and strictures on the timeliness and procedural fairness of delegate selection (Polsby, 1983a; Price, 1984; Crotty and Jackson, 1985). Concomitant with these reforms has been an increase in the number of states requiring primaries—a change in the overall nominating system that has affected the Republican party as well. Most of the major criticisms lodged against the contemporary system center on the effect of party reforms on the *characteristics* of party activists and interest groups in the nominating process. What is at issue is not just the permeability of the new system, but whether the reformed system overrepresents narrow or special interests (the reform hypothesis). We identify three interrelated claims.

1. The Artificial (i.e., an artifact of party reform) Increase in Influence in Party Affairs by Individuals Who Are Not Party Supporters. Critics distinguish between party regulars and party amateurs (e.g., Ranney, 1975). Jeane Kirkpatrick, for example, argues that reform measures such as the mandated proportional representation of women, minorities, and youth at the Democratic convention (combined with the greater permeability of the parties) have made it possible for political parties to be penetrated by "persons without seasoned and reliable ties" (1979:10). Kirkpatrick further charges that "quotas" reflect "a desired balance of power, not the actual strength of actual social groups" (1979:23). Similarly, former North Carolina governor Terry Sanford questions whether the increased presence of women (and minorities) at Democratic conventions is actually based on an intellectual and political contribution, or whether in reality "their presence [is] merely a sop, a token presence, a possible insult, even a fraud" (1981:92). In essence, then, these critics are suggesting that women and minorities would not be as active in party politics in the absence of party reform. It is because these new participants in party politics are not thought to be representing a previously political neglected interest—as reform supporters assert (Bode and Casey, 1980; Crotty, 1980; Fraser, 1980; Crotty and Jackson, 1985)—that critics can question "the assumption that women cannot adequately represent men and men women" (Polsby, 1983b:696).

2. The Artificial Creation of Factions in Party Activity. Critics argue that the increasing role of amateurs in parties undermines party cohesion and coalition building. Nelson Polsby, for example, cited a decline in traditional interest groups (those organized around economic interests or communal ties) while others such as those "perceived as historically disadvantaged such as black, Hispanic-American, and militant women's groups" have flourished as a consequence of reform (1983a:133). To highlight the narrow appeal of these groups, Polsby describes them as being, "for the most part, erroneously billed as grass-roots organizations" (1983a:133). Kirkpatrick cites this change as being due to the abolition of the unit rule in delegate voting and the requirement of proportional representation of candidate preferences

(1979:22–23). These changes in the Democratic party encourage factionalism by favoring those with "extreme views on issues" (Polsby, 1983a:64–71; Kirkpatrick, 1979:16). By contrast, supporters of reform stress that the result of quotas and affirmative action is to broaden participation and increase the legitimacy of the party—not to "guarantee advantages to any segment of the Democratic electorate" (Bode and Casey, 1980:15).

3. The Disproportionate Influence of These Artificial Groups on the Presidential Nominating Process. The mobilization of intense support during primaries and the narrow interests that these groups are thought to advance, combined with the relatively low level of information and interest among the general public and low primary turnout, have magnified the influence of party factions (Keeter and Zukin, 1983; Lengle, 1981). Hence, while critics raise concerns that increased numbers of women and minorities at Democratic conventions may be reducing the numbers of real party supporters who might attend, they simultaneously propose that the result of party reform has been to overrepresent the intense views of narrow minorities (e.g., note Polsby's reference to "militant women's groups" rather than "women"). This has resulted in the nomination of unelectable candidates nonetheless strongly supported by extreme and narrow party interests. Polsby argues that "if majorities are supposed to win in a democracy, then the American presidential process has not lately been mobilizing them," citing the defeat of the majority Democrats in 1972 and 1980 and Jimmy Carter's one-term presidency as *prima facie* evidence for this conclusion (Polsby, 1983a:87). Reform supporters, on the other hand, view quotas as politically neutral in candidate selection (e.g., Fraser, 1980:122).

The artificial increase in nonparty supporters and factions, and their overrepresentation in presidential nominations and elections present serious criticisms of the reform process—if accurate. Certainly some indirect support is found in studies of the amateur political style. While the amateur style is unrelated to ideology, it *is* related to the more extreme viewpoints in both parties (Soule and Clarke, 1970; Roback, 1975; Baer and Jackson, 1985). A direct causal link between the reforms and declining support for the party system has not been proven, however (Eldersveld, 1982; Nakamura, 1983). We believe that this is the case because most expositions of these criticisms of the reform process rely on macrolevel assessments of such criteria as "electability" and "accountability" as influenced by all party factions acting in concert.

Our analysis will focus on the effects of one reform mechanism: the use of quotas. Certainly, other aspects of reform have been the source of controversy (Bode and Casey, 1980; Price, 1984). However, our concern is with the group-level effects of reform. Critics have criticized quotas because they believe that it encourages the representation of artificial groups—not because of any a priori opposition to the participation of minorities and women.[1] Both reform supporters and critics have deplored the increased prominence of primaries (cf. Fraser, 1980; Polsby, 1983a; Pomper, 1980:98–101). The difference between critics and supporters on the use of primaries lies not simply in heightened media influence in primary nominations, but in the way that critics believe that the media advances the influence of artificial groups (e.g., Polsby, 1983a). Further, the use of quotas is not without its effects on the representation of party regulars (i.e., party and elected public officials)— a group preferred by reform critics (Crotty, 1980; Price, 1984:200–201). It is for these reasons that we believe our focus on quotas addresses one of the more important of the critics' charges.

Robert Nakamura (1983) points out that critics have relied on several unexamined assumptions, in part because of the characteristics attributed to the prereform system. While we cannot retroactively determine the extent to which the prereform system possessed the virtues claimed by critics, we can examine the contemporary system to identify whether the faults attributed to it are present—and can be attributed to the use of quotas for women.[2] This empirical approach necessitates a microlevel analysis, based on the assumption that if party reform has resulted in negative effects, then these effects should be evident among *those groups that have benefited from reform.*

INTRAPARTY AND INTERPARTY COMPARISON GROUPS

Our intent is to test the three tenets of the reform hypothesis as stated here with the social movement position advanced in Chapters 3 and 4. Our analytic strategy is a threefold one in which we (1) compare Democrats with Republicans, (2) compare delegates with county chairs, and (3) focus on the changing participation of women. In doing this, we utilize a data analytic technique appropriate for simultaneously testing these cross-level and cross-party gender differences.

1. Democrats versus Republicans. The critics of reform have focused on internal Democratic reform of the selection process of nominating convention delegates. As Polsby put it, "the Republican Party remains unreformed" with respect to many of the changes undertaken by the Democrats, for example, demographic quotas, affirmative action procedures, monitoring of state delegation procedures, and confederate legal structure of the party. (1983a:53). Supporters of reform have pointed out that the Democratic party was the focus of reform movements because it was the majority party and had a more heterogeneous political and demographic coalition (Crotty and Jackson, 1985). The Republican party has been affected by some of these changes, such as the increase in primaries. However, critics such as Polsby have stressed that the negative aspects of party reform deriving from the increase in primaries have "worked disproportionately to the disadvantage of the majority party, the Democrats, by leading to the nomination of candidates unable to command widespread support within the party" (1983a:86).

We conclude, therefore, that the negative effects of reform should be limited to the Democrats, and not extend to the Republicans—if the reform process itself is the cause of change (the reform hypothesis).

If, on the other hand, the supporters of reform are correct in identifying the primary origins of change in social movements (the social movement hypothesis), then we would expect to find effects in both parties. We are assuming here that mass-based social movements direct their efforts toward change throughout society and do not limit themselves to only one institution (in this case, the Democratic party). Among women (the case being considered here), we base this assumption on (1) the dramatic demographic changes among women over the past twenty-five years in labor force participation, family structure, and lifestyle (di Bianchi and Spaine, 1983); (2) the effects these demographic changes have had on the political activity and expression of women; and (3) the mass-based structure of the contemporary women's rights movement (McGlen and O'Connor, 1983; Sapiro, 1983; Klein, 1984). Thus, the social movement hypothesis predicts that the women's rights movement would find adherents in both parties. Of course we would expect somewhat greater inclusion of these disadvantaged groups (in our analysis, women) among the Democrats. We expect this because the Democrats as the majority party during this era were the focus of reform efforts and because the Democrats made structural changes to ensure representation of these groups.[3]

2. Delegates versus County Chairs. Previous research has sought to examine the effects of Democratic reform by examining the characteristics of delegates, and then comparing these characteristics to the mass public (e.g., Kirkpatrick, 1976). This approach relies on a restrictive notion of representation in assuming that elites do not differ from the masses. In fact, most political science theory and research suggests just the opposite—that elites, as central actors in defining the political agenda, shape public opinion as well as represent it (e.g., Key, 1961; McClosky and Brill, 1983). Our position on this is quite clear. Kenneth Prewitt (1970) described the process of elite recruitment as a "Chinese box puzzle," with successive cuts made among the "eligibles" resulting in successively smaller and more elite groups (i.e., political activists, recruits, political apprentices, and candidates for office). Thus, we know the elites to be unlike the mass public and to differ among themselves as well.

The concern raised by reform critics is that the interests of reformed party elites differ from that of prereform or unreformed party elites. If so, the proper basis of comparison should be the *regular party leadership*, not the mass public or party identifiers. Our sample of county chairs is particularly appropriate for this type of comparison. County chairs are presumably reflective of their local party activists and supporters. Kirkpatrick's (1976) study of 1972 convention delegates found the Democratic delegates to be out of step with their rank and file compared to the Republican delegates; yet a study of county chairs in that same year came to the opposite conclusion—

it was the Democratic county chairs who most closely reflected their rank and file (Montjoy et al., 1980).

More important, county chairs have not been affected by any reform rules in either their selection or tenure. There are no proportional requirements for demographic representation or affirmative action rules governing the selection of county chairs. If party reform has resulted in the elevation of a new class of issue activists, then we expect to find its effects only among the convention delegates and *not* the county chairs of either party.[4]. On the other hand, if supporters of party reform are correct, then the effects of social movements should occur at all levels of the party and not be limited to convention delegates.

3. Focus on Women. Of all the groups targeted by the various reform commissions since 1968, women have benefited more than any other. After all, it is women who have gained a "quota" of half of the Democratic nominating convention slots for the 1980 and 1984 conventions. While proportional representation was mandated by the McGovern–Fraser Commission for the 1972 convention for blacks and youth as well as for women, only women as a group have maintained their privileged position (see Figs. 3.1 to 3.3). Thus, when reform critics writing in the late 1970s and 1980s criticize demographic representation, unless they are understood to refer to the single historical event of the 1972 Democratic National Convention (which is patently not the case), the only reasonable referent is to women.

Women constitute a particularly appropriate group for analysis in the context of the 1984 presidential election. In 1984, approximately 6 percent of the delegates were members of the National Organization for Women (NOW) or the National Women's Political Caucus (NWPC). In sharp contrast to its previously bipartisan stance, the national board of NOW interviewed Democratic candidates Walter Mondale, Gary Hart, and Jesse Jackson before endorsing Mondale's campaign on December 10, 1983. Shortly before the mid-July Democratic convention, Mondale selected U.S. Representative Geraldine Ferraro of New York as his running mate—an historic move that made Ferraro the first woman to run as a major party candidate on a presidential ticket. This also resulted in a ticket headed by two northern liberals, an unbalanced ticket to many conservatives and southerners. Mondale's selection was preceded by NOW's 1984 national conference during which NOW members publicly warned that unless a woman was selected, there would be a "thunderstorm." Thus, it appeared that NOW's early Mondale endorsement and his eventual vice-presidential choice reflected special interest politics, rather than the traditional choice of the most able and experienced candidate whose primary role was to broaden the appeal of the presidential nominee (Orren, 1985:70; Hargrove and Nelson, 1984:205).

The data analytic technique which we use is the difference *of differences* in a means test (a procedure not regularly seen in party research).[5] We selected this test because we assume that the convention delegates will, in general, be relatively more "elite" than the local county chairs, and that male and female elites will, in general, have divergent backgrounds and attitudes. In fact, the importance of opening up the parties to out-group elites is a measure of this divergence. This finding, of course, has been the conclusion of numerous studies of political elites (e.g., Kirkpatrick, 1974, 1976; Jennings and Farah, 1981; Gertzog, 1984). As a shorthand, we will refer to these sex or gender differences as a gender gap.

Our empirical question is whether Republican delegates systematically differ from Democratic delegates and whether each party's delegates differ from their respective county chairs. As we are focusing on women, we wish to determine whether the gender gap among one group is the same size as that of the comparison group. Thus, this test will be used to assess whether the *proportional or average* difference (or gender gap) between men and women delegates is the same as that among each party's respective chairs and between the delegates of the two parties. Our assumption here is that if reform rules have not distorted the recruitment process (even as more elite individuals are recruited upward), the proportional difference among male and female elites should not be altered. Note that we make no assumptions as to the size of any gender gap. Our data analytic strategy merely permits the measurement of any potential divergence between male and female elites. It is the possible overrepresentation of "militant" women's groups among party elites that critics have argued developed with Democratic party reform. Therefore, we wish our data analysis to be sensitive to any proportional sex differences between county chairs and delegates.

A Profile of National Convention Delegates and County Chairs

At this juncture, it is important for us to briefly profile the national convention delegates and county chairs. This is necessary for two reasons. First, while the Democratic county chairs remain unreformed in the *de jure* sense, do they remain unreformed in the *de facto* sense? Second, for our analyses, we assume that the national convention delegates are relatively more elite than the county chairs, and thus, some evidence to support that claim would be desirable (Table 5.1).

There are a number of very striking observations to be made from the data in Table 5.1. First, the Democratic county chairs is a male-dominated group with men outnumbering women three to one. Thus, there is little evidence to support a claim that they have become like the delegates in some indirect sense (diffusion of reform). In fact, the Republican and Democratic county chairs are fairly similar groups in terms of education, gender distribution, employment, and public officeholding. This is further evidence against the diffusion thesis. They are *very* unlike their same-party national convention delegates.

The national convention delegates do appear to be a more elite group,

Table 5.1
A Selective Profile of Men and Women by Party and Elite Level

CRITERIA	DEMOCRATS				REPUBLICANS			
	Delegates		County Chairs		Delegates		County Chairs	
	Men (%)	Women (%)	Men (%)	Women (%)	Men (%)	Women (%)	Men (%)	Women (%)
BACHELOR'S DEGREE	79	69	62	52	76	52	61	49
MARRIED	71	57	86	75	84	81	90	84
FULLY EMPLOYED/ PROFESSIONAL JOB	73	58	55	42	65	29	48	27
PART-TIME/ UNEMPLOYED	9	23	10	30	11	46	8	40
HOUSEWIVES	0	7	0	12	0	26	0	25
RETIRED	3	4	11	10	8	12	11	16
HOLD PUBLIC OFFICE	47	26	43	24	49	28	40	21
TOTALS (N =)	203	264	448	168	292	268	350	118

as we have assumed. They are considerably more educated, located in. professional jobs, and not working part-time (or unemployed). There are fewer retirees among their numbers. They are also more likely to hold public office, albeit only slightly so. These differences hold for both the Republicans and the Democrats. Thus, we would conclude that our assumption is a good one.

There are a few other important observations to be made from Table 5.1 that are salient to our analyses here. The women delegates to the Democratic National Convention are a substantially *less-married* group when compared to all other groups. Only 57 percent responded that they were married. This is almost 25 percentage points less than is seen in some of the other comparison groups. Furthermore, male delegates and women county chairs on the Democratic side are significantly less married than other groups as well, but not to the dramatic degree seen for the Democratic women delegates.

The Democratic women delegates are remarkable for other reasons. They are more educated than any other group of women and more likely to hold a professional job, and they are less likely to be unemployed or underemployed, or to be a housewife than any other women elite cadre. They are more like their male delegate counterparts in both parties than any of the county chairs (male or female) or the Republican women delegates.

The Republican women elites, local and national, are over twice as likely to be a housewife as their Democratic counterparts, and their aggregate characteristics are rather undistinguished insofar as their employment and educational backgrounds are concerned. This suggests that the "competitive" impulses of the Republican party results in recruitment of women without the requisite backgrounds to apparently elite positions. Are these women truly influential (see Cotter and Hennessy, 1964:58) or is this a response to fears of a menacing gender gap?

Do Nonparty Supporters Have Too Much Influence?

We will examine party support through issue positions, ideological extremity, and party professionalism. In each case, our analytical strategy is to identify those instances in which Democratic women selected under reform rules differ more from their male counterparts than do women and men in the unreformed party elites.

Issue Positions and Ideological Extremism. The first set of comparisons focus on contemporary policy issues. Reported gender differences (differences of means) for the party elites on a number of domestic and foreign policy issues are shown in Table 5.2. The Republican elites are generally right of center on these issues with relatively small differences between the delegates and county chairs. The Democrats are generally left of center on these issues but with the county chairs expressing less liberal views—though not greatly so— than their party's convention delegates. We do not think that these findings by themselves indicate any particularly extreme stances on the part of either party's elites.

Among the Democratic elites, we found that on five issues the male-female differences among Democratic delegates were different in magnitude from those among Democratic county chairs (see Table 5.2, Test I). These issues were defense funding, government help for minorities, detente, government job guarantees (i.e., Humphrey–Hawkins), and the Equal Rights Amendment (ERA). In each instance, it was among the Democratic county chairs where the gender gap was greatest. Male and female Democratic delegates were quite homogenous in their issue preferences, while there existed a considerable gender gap among the county chairs. The female Democratic county chairs were consistently more liberal than their male peers. Male and female Democratic delegates expressed much greater agreement than male and female county chairs, and the female delegates were actually more conservative in their expression of opinion on at least two issues. This is contrary to the reform hypothesis: recruitment (via quotas) to the delegate level corresponded with increased *similarity* on issues, not ideological extremism on the part of the Democratic women delegates.

Among the Republicans, we found no difference in the magnitude of gender differences across elite level on any issue (see Table 5.2, Test II). The Republicans at both the county seat and the national convention were quite homogeneous at the group level in their issue positions. The homogeneity of views across gender on these issues among both parties' convention del-

Table 5.2
A Comparison of Men and Women on Selected Foreign and Domestic Policy Issues by Party and Elite Level

ISSUES	DEMOCRATS				REPUBLICANS				TEST					
	Delegates		County Chairs		Delegates		County Chairs		I		II		III	
	(1) Men	(2) Women	(3) Men	(4) Women	(5) Men	(6) Women	(7) Men	(8) Women	t	P(t)	t	P(t)	t	P(t)
DEFENSE FUNDING	2.75	2.57	3.37	2.90	4.74	4.79	4.75	4.81	-1.8	0.04	0.3	0.79	1.3	0.10
DETENTE	2.51	2.33	2.97	2.51	4.44	4.38	4.44	4.29	-2.6	0.01	-0.4	0.67	-0.4	0.34
EQUAL RIGHTS AMENDMENT (% FAVOR)	94	97	76	86	19	25	18	28	-1.8	0.04	-0.7	0.49	-0.8	0.25
GOVERNMENT:														
HELP FOR MINORITIES	3.02	2.99	3.85	3.46	4.96	5.12	5.21	5.32	-1.9	0.03	-0.3	0.76	1.1	0.14
SERVICES & SPENDING	2.73	2.47	3.11	2.77	5.07	4.96	5.00	4.93	-0.5	0.31	0.2	0.83	0.8	0.21
JOB GUARANTEES	2.97	3.20	3.88	3.69	5.88	5.96	5.76	5.98	-2.2	0.02	0.8	0.41	-0.9	0.18
HEALTH PLAN	2.88	2.94	3.48	3.16	5.79	5.82	5.58	5.59	-1.6	0.06	-0.1	0.95	-0.2	0.43
TOTALS (N =)	202	260	444	164	287	260	348	118						

Items used are seven-point Likert types, with low values corresponding to more liberal positions and with 4 being neutral. For this and Table 5.3, Test I is Ho: $\mu_1 - \mu_2 < \mu_3 - \mu_4$ versus Ha: $\mu_1 - \mu_2 \geq \mu_3 - \mu_4$; Test II is Ho: $\mu_5 - \mu_6 = \mu_7 - \mu_8$ versus Ha: $\mu_5 - \mu_6 \neq \mu_7 - \mu_8$; and Test III is Ho: $\mu_1 - \mu_2 > \mu_5 - \mu_6$ versus Ha: $\mu_1 - \mu_2 \leq \mu_5 - \mu_6$. Negative t values indicate a smaller gender gap for the Democratic National Convention delegates than for the relevant comparison group; a negative t value for Test II indicates a smaller gender gap for the Republican National Convention delegates than for the Republican county chairs; positive t values indicate otherwise.

egates in 1984 is reflected in the finding of no differences across party (Test III).

Party Support. We next turn to an analysis of party professionalism. We examined the responses to the statement, "I generally consider myself to be a 'party regular.' "[6] We also analyzed how individuals characterized themselves: as one who "works for the party year after year, win or lose, and whether or not you like the candidate or issues" *or* one who "works for the party only when there is a particularly worthwhile candidate or issue." We did find, as the reform critics charged, less support for party and party professionalism with the Democratic delegates than with any other party elite cadre. Furthermore, women indicated less support for party than men among the Democratic delegate group.

A similar pattern is found in response to both questions, as shown in Table 5.3. With the exception of the Democratic delegates, the trend is for the women to be more "professional," (i.e., a party regular), than was true of the men. The pattern is reversed for the Democratic delegates, with the women significantly less likely to adopt the "professional" position. Not only were the Democratic delegates as a whole less characteristically party regulars than was true of all the other elite groups, but the magnitude of their gender differences was greater than that found among the Democratic county chairs as well.

The magnitude of gender differences was similar across elite levels in the Republican party. The magnitude of gender differences across party delegate groups was, however, statistically significant. The gap between men and women among the Democratic delegates on party support was not only greater than that found among the Republican delegates, but while the Democratic women were *less* party oriented than their male peers, the Republican women were *more* so.

The singularity of the lesser professionalism among female Democratic delegates lends support to the first of the critics' charges (for a similar finding in 1980, see Baer and Jackson, 1985). However, the distinctiveness of female Democratic delegates on this point is not explicable through the causal mechanisms posited by critics. The lesser support for the party among Democratic women delegates is *not* combined with ideological extremism when compared to either county chairs or male delegates. The reform critics argued that the new class of activists were "purist" and less "professional" in their attitudes *because* of their ideological extremism. Our findings on party support corroborate the charge that Democratic women delegates (and men as well) are less party supporters, but insofar as supporting the party reform hypothesis, the findings are mixed. Yet, the consistent finding that female Democratic delegates are more "amateur" while other female party elites tend to be more "professional" does suggest that this lesser professionalism is an artifact of some aspect of the recruitment process—and not inherent in the nature of

Table 5.3
A Comparison of Men and Women on Party and Interest Groups Activity by Party and Elite Level

CRITERIA	DEMOCRATS Delegates (1) Men (%)	(2) Women (%)	County Chairs (3) Men (%)	(4) Women (%)	REPUBLICANS Delegates (5) Men (%)	(6) Women (%)	County Chairs (7) Men (%)	(8) Women (%)	TEST I t	P(t)	II t	P(t)	III t	P(t)
CONSIDER SELF TO BE PARTY REGULAR	77	70	94	95	91	94	96	98	2.7	0.00	-1.3	0.19	2.6	0.01
WORK FOR PARTY OVER CANDIDATE OR ISSUES	72	60	84	90	80	84	83	89	3.2	0.00	0.5	0.60	2.7	0.01
REPRESENT INTEREST GROUP IN PARTY ACTIVITY	41	57	21	29	17	27	16	12	1.4	0.08	-2.6	0.01	1.3	0.10
REPRESENT A WOMEN'S GROUP IN PARTY WORK	1	30	1	16	1	15	0	2	3.4	0.00	-4.5	0.00	4.0	0.00
RECRUITED TO POLITICS THROUGH INTEREST GROUP	9	15	5	2	1	1	2	1	2.2	0.01	0.7	0.46	1.7	0.05
RECRUITED TO POLITICS THROUGH PARTY	9	6	12	9	9	18	10	20	0.0	0.50	-0.1	0.93	-3.1	0.00
TOTALS (N =)	202	262	442	165	288	264	347	118						

women. We provide an alternative explanation for the singular "amateurism" of Democratic delegate women below.

The Artificial Creation of Factions

We now examine interest group activity among party elites. Our analysis of this represents a significant departure from other comparable studies. Warren Miller and M. Kent Jennings (1986:165–67) analyze *evaluations* of thirteen groups on a feeling thermometer in their over-time study of Democratic and Republican nominating convention delegates. The 1980 study of caucus-convention delegates in eleven states (Abramowitz and Stone, 1984; Francis and Benedict, 1986) included a question asking the respondents to indicate which of eleven types of interest group they had been *politically active* in. John Francis and Robert Benedict (1986:105–110) find a strong pattern of overlapping memberships among the state activists, a finding which makes it difficult to assess the potential impact of factions in party activity. Rather than examining group membership, our research focused on perceived and self-identified group representation (see Table 5.3). In the 1984 Party Elite Study, we asked our party elites (in an open-ended question) whether or not they felt that they represented the views of a particular group in party activity and, if so, what that group was. We next inquired how they first became active in politics. If one interest does command the allegiance of a party elite faction, we believe that these questions best tap that orientation.

Interest-Group Representation. The responses to the question on interest group representation were varied, ranging from women's groups, to labor, farm, business, and educational groups. They include both traditional interest groups, and political and social movement groups. Again the Democratic delegates—both men and women—were unlike other elites. Democratic delegates were at least twice as likely to indicate that they represented an interest group as any of the other party elites, Republican or Democratic. The magnitude of gender differences on representing an interest group was not different across elites among the Democrats. In both groups, women were much more likely to represent an interest group than men. Like their counterparts at the 1984 Democratic convention, female county chairs were more likely to represent an interest group than male chairs. Clearly, representation of group interests was evident at both levels of the Democratic party, and not just among the reformed convention delegates.

In comparing Republican and Democratic delegates, the magnitude of gender differences on interest-group representation was similar across party— with women being more likely to indicate ties to interest groups than men. Across the Republican elites however a different pattern emerged—with greater gender differences being found at the delegate level than at the county chair level and with women county chairs being less likely than male ones to indicate that they represent an interest group, the reverse of the pattern found among Republican delegates.

These results support the social movement hypothesis. There are indications of gender differences within the Republican party across elite level. The Republican women delegates—being more metropolitan than the Republican women county chairs—should provide greater evidence of the effects of social change because it would occur earlier and more readily in metropolitan areas.[7] They are more likely to represent an interest group—and the groups that they represent are *women's groups*.

Representation of Women's Groups. Of particular pertinence to our analysis is the proportion of elites identifying themselves as representing social movement groups (as we have defined them)—both specific women's groups (e.g., NOW, NWPC) or more generally "women"—in their party work. Gender differences across elite levels in both parties were of different magnitudes on representation of women's groups. This varied across party delegate groups as well. For *all* men, no more than 1 percent indicated that they represented women's groups. On the other hand, twice the proportion of women Democratic delegates indicated that they represented a women's group than either their same-party same-sex county chairs (30 percent vs. 16 percent) or the other-party, same-sex delegates (30 percent vs. 15 percent). Women Republican county chairs hardly represented women's groups at all (2 percent). Except for this group, all other women, regardless of party or level, were much more likely to represent women than any male elites. This is most marked among the Democratic delegates, but it also is a consistent pattern to be found across level and across party.

These results indicate that women activists who represent women's groups are present in both parties and not just among the reformed Democrats. And it is at the delegate level in each party that proportionately larger numbers of activists representing women are found. Yet, we must still explain why Democratic women delegates exhibited greater group consciousness than Republican women. To do this, we turn to an examination of political recruitment.

Initial Recruitment to Politics. Party elites may be self-recruited (through a strong issue or candidate preference), or they may be recruited to political activism by the party, or an interest or social movement group. We found no sex differences or proportional differences by level on the two most common responses (candidate campaign or issues). However, there were some significant proportional differences on recruitment by party and interest group (shown in Table 5.3). The party represents a fairly major political recruitment vehicle for Republican women: about 20 percent of female Republican delegates and county chairs became active in politics through the party. The party, however, is a less important recruitment vehicle for Republican men and for Democrats as a whole. The magnitude of gender difference on recruitment by party for the Republican delegates was greater than that found on the Democratic side. This finding explains, in part, the higher degree of party ties found among Republican women.

For most of the elite groups, interest groups represent a minor recruitment vehicle. Compared to the Democratic county chairs, Democratic female delegates were more likely to be recruited through an interest group than were male delegates. There were no significant proportional differences among the Republican elites. There were also interparty differences, with the gap between Democratic (delegates) men and women being greater than the comparable Republican one. This represents a particularly interesting finding. While Democratic reform rules do require a fifty-fifty split among delegates at the nominating convention, the rules do not require that the party leadership actively recruit new female party workers. In the words of David Price, "reform commissions cannot change the fact that many of these key people, under present circumstances, are white males; they can only dictate that white males can have so many seats but not more" (1984:201).

Among Republican women in 1984, the party served as an important initial recruitment vehicle. If the party has not served as a major recruitment device for Democratic women, perhaps interest groups serve to fill a void. Indeed, previous research indicated that at least among elected public officials, volunteer or community groups have served as alternative avenues for elite political recruitment among women (e.g., Kirkpatrick, 1974). It may well be that the Democrats need quotas to provide for equal representation of women—the Republicans in 1984 were able to attain a nearly fifty-fifty split without the use of quotas. This also suggests an explanation for the lesser ties to party among Democratic women delegates—the party itself provides a framework for political activism, *but it does not bring new women into the party*. It is this paucity of official Democratic party recruitment that probably contributes to the hypertrophy of female interest-group representation in the Democratic party, with the consequence that women not recruited by the party are less tied to the party.

If men and women differ in their recruitment, how do they compare on the type of interest represented? To answer this, we next examined the modal interest group mentioned by the different party elites (Table 5.4). As might be expected from the major role that organized labor has played in Democratic politics, the modal group represented by male Democratic delegates is labor. Labor was mentioned by one out of ten male delegates, or about one-third of those who expressed an interest-group identification. Among male Republican delegates, the modal group identification was with professional groups (e.g., American Medical Association, American Bar Association). This group identification reflected about one in twenty male delegates, or approximately one-third of those expressing an interest-group identification.

With the exception of female Democratic county chairs, county chairs more often represented farm groups. This is expected given that we do not weigh our sample of county chairs by a population factor and thus rural

Table 5.4

A Comparison of Men and Women on Interest-Group Identification by Party and Elite Level

CRITERIA	DEMOCRATS				REPUBLICANS			
	Delegates		County Chairs		Delegates		County Chairs	
	Men	Women	Men	Women	Men	Women	Men	Women
MODAL INTEREST GROUP IDENTIFICATION	LABOR	WOMEN	FARM	WOMEN	PROFESSIONAL ASSOCIATIONS	WOMEN	FARM	FARM
PERCENT IDENTIFYING WITH MODAL GROUP	12	30	6	16	6	15	5	5
PERCENT OF INTEREST GROUP IDENTIFIERS IN MODAL GROUP	31	53	28	55	36	56	36	40
TOTALS (N =)	202	262	442	165	288	264	347	122

interests are over-represented among the county chairs. About one in twenty male Democratic county chairs and Republican county chairs of both sexes identified with farm groups (the Farm Bureau, as well as other unspecified farm interests). Of those who expressed a group interest, this modal group comprised about one-quarter of male Democratic county chairs, one-third of male Republican county chairs, and two-fifths of female Republican county chairs.

The modal group identified by all Democratic women and by female Republican delegates comprised women's groups. This group identification was expressed by 30 percent of the female Democratic delegates and by about 15 percent of the female Democratic chairs and female Republican delegates. The proportion identifying with women's groups among those with a group identification was relatively large. Fifty-three percent of female Democratic delegates, 55 percent of female Democratic chairs, and 56 percent of female Republican delegates who identified with an interest group indicated that they represented women. It is only among Democratic women that we find a continuity of interest-group representation from county seat to nominating convention—with women's groups being the modal group represented at both levels.

The only group targeted by current Democratic party reform is women. Critics have argued that this targeting has created an artificial group among delegates. Yet, we find women's groups spontaneously mentioned at both levels of the Democratic party and among Republican women delegates. These findings strongly suggest the influence of a social movement affecting both parties, rather than the singular effect of party reform that should only affect the Democratic female delegates.

Do Artificial Groups Have a Disproportional Influence in the Presidential Nominating Process?

We confine our analyses here to only Democratic elites and turn to an examination of preferences for the 1984 Democratic presidential nomination. In order to compare delegates and county chairs, it is necessary to use preference for the 1984 nomination rather than actual vote for the nomination because county chairs have no vote (unlike the delegates).

There were no statistically significant sex differences on the choice for the 1984 Democratic nomination among either the delegates or county chairs. However, this finding itself does not address the reform critics contentions. Rather, if the critics are correct, we should find support for Mondale to be greater among interest-group representatives and particularly among those who represent women's groups.

Interest-Group Representatives and Candidate Preference. In our analyses of candidate preference, we compared (1) women's interest-group representatives, (2) representatives of interest groups other than women, and (3) those who indicated that they did not represent an interest group in their party work among delegates (reformed) and county chairs (unreformed). Table 5.3 indicates that the women delegates are divided 30 percent to 27 percent to 43 percent between the three comparison groups, with the division for the male delegates being 1 percent to 40 percent to 59 percent. The women county chairs are divided 16 percent to 13 percent to 71 and the division for their male counterparts is 1 percent to 20 percent to 79 percent (Table 5.5).

The delegates and county chairs were statistically different in their candidate preferences in all three subgroups but not in ways attributable to quotas for women. Roughly similar proportions of delegates and county chairs preferred Walter Mondale, but the level of that support varied considerably across the comparison groups. Mondale's support was quite weak (ranging from 37.5 percent to 41.1 percent) *except* among those identifying themselves as representatives of traditional interest groups, i.e., other than women's groups (where it ranged from 53.8 percent to 58.4 percent).

Those delegates (almost exclusively women) who identified themselves as representatives of women's groups clearly did not support Mondale, as might have been expected. In fact, the evidence suggests that Gary Hart—the losing candidate—was the candidate preferred by this group. In comparison with similar county chairs, albeit a small group, the main difference between the two groups is the additional support found among the delegates for the two outsider candidates—Hart and Jesse Jackson—a finding possibly attributable to other aspects of reform but not to quotas.

The evidence on candidate preference indicates no undue influence by representatives of women's groups on the nomination process. In fact, it is quite contrary to the reform critics charges. First, Mondale—the nominee— achieved his greatest levels of support among those who the critics charge have been deprived by the reform process, of an adequate say in the nomination process, namely the traditional interest groups (e.g., labor and farm groups). In fact, there was only one other subgroup of delegates that we examined who favored Mondale as strongly—the *ex officio* delegates, an arguably counterreform group, who favored Mondale three to one. Those representing women's groups provide no evidence of any special clout and in fact appeared the least supportive of Mondale of any of the subgroups examined.[8]

CONCLUSIONS

This chapter focused on the controversial issue of party reform in the context of women—the group that has gained the most from reform. Using data from the 1984 election, we inquired whether Democratic party reform, specifically quotas for women at the national convention, has had an artificial effect on the individuals and groups active in the party. By artificial, we

Table 5.5
Preference for Democratic Presidential Nomination by Interest-Group Representation and Elite Level (Democrats Only)

NOMINEE	DELEGATES			COUNTY CHAIRS		
	REPRESENT AN INTEREST GROUP			REPRESENT AN INTEREST GROUP		
	YES		NO	YES		NO
	REPRESENT A WOMEN'S GROUP			REPRESENT A WOMEN'S GROUP		
	YES	NO		YES	NO	
	(%)	(%)	(%)	(%)	(%)	(%)
Mondale	37.5	58.4	40.1	38.7	53.8	41.1
Hart	46.3	21.5	53.9	35.5	27.4	36.5
Jackson	12.5	13.4	2.2	3.2	4.7	0.9
Other	3.8	6.7	5.2	22.6	14.2	20.2
Totals (N =)	80	149	232	31	106	455

DELEGATES: X² = 52.0   P(X²) ≤ 0.00

COUNTY CHAIRS: X² = 82.7   P(X²) ≤ 0.00

mean an effect that could be isolated among female Democratic delegates as compared to the regular party leadership, measured in our study by county chairs. We examined three propositions to assess this.

The first proposition was: does the quota for women result in an artificial increase in influence in party affairs by individuals who are not party supporters? The answer is a qualified yes—with two important qualifications. First, the difference between male and female delegates on this issue is not very large. In fact, all Democratic delegates (whether male or female) were more amateur than other party elite groups—perhaps suggesting some other mechanisms at work. Second, this greater amateurism—and lesser party support—found among women delegates is not accompanied by policy differences. Male and female delegates were in substantial agreement, more so than their counterparts at the county seat.

The second proposition was: does the quota for women create artificial factions in party activity? We think not. It is true that Democratic women delegates indicated that they represented an interest group (actually a social movement group) in their party work more often than their male counterparts—usually NOW and NWPC. However, representatives of these women's groups have moved equally strongly into nonreformed party groups—Democratic county chairs and Republican convention delegates. This finding is more compatible with the social movement hypothesis than the reform hypothesis. Beyond this finding, it was also observed that interest groups were a more significant avenue of recruitment for Democratic women delegates—and there is a least some evidence that the Democratic party has not done much active recruiting of women. This finding is highlighted by an additional finding that the Republican party *is* more actively recruiting women than the Democratic party.

The final proposition was: does the quota for women create a disproportionate influence of these artificial groups on the presidential nominating process? The findings here are quite clear, and the answer is no. Women's group representatives, who are almost exclusively women, were one of Mondale's weakest support groups, and the findings suggest quite cogently that it was the traditional support groups and the counterreform groups who in fact championed Mondale's cause—if anything, over the objections of these women.

Reform critics have argued that the reform rules themselves have been a primary source of Democratic problems at the polls. Our evidence suggests that the results of reform may be less important than that assumed by critics, albeit not the neutral instrument portrayed by many supporters. The reform rules did not create the women's rights movement, nor did we find any evidence of ideological extremity or disproportionate influence by representatives of women and women's groups on the nominating process, quite the contrary. Female Democratic delegates were, however, singularly less supportive of the party.

Reform supporters have argued that the Democratic party was the target of reform because it was the majority party. Our results indicate that the Democrats probably *needed* to require a quota for women. The Republicans, by contrast, have been able to increase their proportion of women in the party without recourse to quotas (although as discussed in Chapter 3, the significance of this is not necessarily greater influence for women in Republican party affairs). It is the Republican party that historically has been most supportive of elite participation among women. It is tempting to speculate that—in addition to the influence of the women's rights movement in both parties (as supported by our findings)—it is the low level of party recruitment that made the Democratic party the target of reform efforts *and* made reform necessary in a party less interested in actively recruiting women.

NOTES

1.   On this point, see Nelson Polsby's expressed support for affirmative action for blacks (Polsby, 1983b). Also, Kirkpatrick (1974) and Romano (1986).

2.   McClosky's study comparing delegates at the 1956 national conventions to their party identifiers and the public indicated that Republican delegates were in substantial disagreement with both their party identifiers and the mass public. A Republican nominee won a substantial victory that year (McClosky, et al. 1960).

3.   The phenomenon of diffusion of reform to the Republican party and local elites is complementary to both hypotheses. The distinction between the two lies not in the Republicans including proportionately more women among their convention delegates, but whether the inclusion of women among the Democrats disproportionately includes advocates of women's rights. Recall that the reform hypothesis is based on an artificial inclusion of extremist elites—not on the increasing representation of disadvantaged groups.

4.   We have selected county chairs for our comparisons because it is the one party elite cadre that remains palpably and without question unreformed. Hauss and Maisel (1986) studied the 1980 caucus-convention delegates from eleven states to assess the validity of the reform critics' position. They justifiably argue that the caucuses were "certainly susceptible to take-over by non-regulars" (1986:217) and, therefore, should provide at least a partial test of what they describe as "neoconservative theory." They found very little evidence of extremist activists or ideologues. While the selection of the Democratic delegates was governed by the national party requirement of proportional representation of presidential preferences, and both parties selected the delegates in open caucuses, the selection of state convention delegates occurred in local party meetings. Therefore, a reform critic might well argue that this null finding proves very little as the study of *state* convention delegates selected at the local level does *not* address the crucial issue of whether or not reforms have resulted in increased extremism among *national* convention delegates.

5.   For a discussion of this statistical technique, see Blalock (1979:234–236). This statistical analysis was performed using SPSSX (1985:467–469).

6.   This item adapted from Soule and Clarke (1970).

7.   The formulas allocating delegates to the national party conventions are popu-

lation sensitive, i.e., delegates are assigned proportional to population. However, counties have but one county chair regardless of population, and thus rural areas and less populated areas are overrepresented.

8. We also examined support for the proposition of a woman vice-presidential candidate. All of the Democratic party elite groups overwhelmingly endorsed the idea of a woman on the ticket. However, as our survey was conducted after the convention and Ferraro was nominated by acclamation with no serious opposition, our data do not address the claims made concerning undue influence in the preconvention selection process for a vice-presidential nominee.

6

Party Reform: The Selective
Alienation of Support

INTRODUCTION

Our position on internal party reform is clear: it represents an attempt to democratize and rejuvenate the party system by incorporating the new social energies of previously neglected groups (e.g., women, youth, and minority groups) into the political process. While reform critics consider party reform to be the cause of deeper maladies, we view it as a response to them and a necessary and desirable one. Final assessments of party reform, however, must include a tally of the costs as well as the benefits. We have thus far stressed the benefits of reduced elite oligarchy and more democratic group representation, and limited our consideration of the potential costs to the selection of presidential candidates. Reform critics—as well as more neutral observers (e.g., Price, 1984)—have argued that the costs of reform have extended far beyond the national nominating conventions. Earlier, we cited research documenting the organizational strength and grass-roots vitality of state and local parties. This does not mean, however, that there have been no costs associated with internal party reform. On the contrary, we hold that there have been costs, and in this chapter we will provide some evidence documenting them.

In this chapter we examine whether internal party reforms are alienating segments of the local-level elite cadres (county chairs), and if so, what are the costs associated with this alienation. The reform issue that we review is the Fifty-Fifty Rule, i.e., the party rule mandating equal representation for women at the Democratic National Convention, and the main costs that we consider concern support for the national party ticket. We use this because it is the "cost" most often highlighted by reform critics. Moreover, it has been shown that "a well organized party that *extends* itself to campaigning for its candidates can have a decided impact on increasing its proportionate share of the vote" (Crotty, 1971:445). We also probe some additional and important related issues—specifically, whether some segments of the local party elite cadres are merely opposed to reform on philosophical grounds, or whether there is a deep-rooted opposition to the goals and agenda of the social movements that we have been discussing. Lastly, we examine whether any dissatisfied elites represent a systematic class in terms of region and ideology.

THE FOCUS ON COUNTY CHAIRS

This analysis is based on a survey of Democratic and Republican county chairs—the party cadres most often assumed to reflect local party activists and supporters. They are not affected by any internal party reform rules either in selection or tenure, and they differ considerably from their respective delegates—especially on the Democratic side (see Tables 5.1 to 5.4). Data from the 1980 Party Elite Study (Jackson et al., 1982) indicate that Democratic county chairs in 1980 very faithfully reflected the views of the mass public as well as their own identifiers on many issues, for example, inflation, unemployment, and support for the ERA. County-level party leaders play an important role in the local party and reflect the attributes of local party organizations. They play a major power role in dispensation of patronage and party responsibilities, and the county convention is the basic represent-ative link of the party with local activists (Eldersveld, 1982). If any elite cadres have been alienated by the reforms, it would more likely be at the state or local level because in some sense they have borne many of the obvious costs (e.g., less latitude of action in the delegate selection process and a diminished role at the national convention, including in the important party rule-making area) while potential benefits (e.g., a broadened party base) are less tangibly theirs.

An analysis of the opinions and characteristics of county chairs ought to provide an indication of some the effects of this mandated equal represen-tation. It certainly is a constraint on them and perhaps contributes to a loss (perceived or genuine) of status. If this is so, we ought to observe an op-position to both the *means* and possibly the *ends* of party reform and the social movement it addresses. This should weaken their support for the *national* party and its presidential nominee.

Support for the reform critics' claims of a disaffected local elite would be seen in a lack of cooperation between the national party organization and state and local party organizations, resulting in the refusal (or more likely, *an absence of enthusiasm*) of subnational level elite cadres to work for the national party candidates. Nelson Polsby, writing about central control of membership criteria for the national conventions suggests that

the net effect on state and local party organizations of this discouragement of grass roots political activity during a presidential election year is hard to assess. At a minimum, it tends to diminish the value of state and local party leaders in their dealings with candidates, thus reinforcing trends that already have ample momentum. Further, on the assumption that presidential campaigns are a good way to build party solidarity at the grass roots, to recruit workers and to reinforce their loyalties and their commitment to the party as an organization, a consequence of party reform might well have been to encourage the atrophy of political parties at the grass roots. (1983a:80–81)

Hence, the reforms may have provided a basis for tension between the different strata as they have established the superiority of national over state party rules and have "imposed on the state parties the national party's conception of 'full and meaningful opportunity' to participate in the delegate selection process" (Hitlin and Jackson, 1979:622). Despite the evident strength and vitality of local parties, a selective alienation of support may undermine traditional relations between national and local parties—particularly for the Democrats. It has been found that Republican *state* party organizations are significantly stronger than Democratic ones, but that Democratic *local* party organizations are stronger than local Republican ones, reflecting the influence of local traditions, resources, and ways of doing things (Gibson et al., 1985). The significance of this is that in local politics, where the reforms have not yet penetrated, the Democratic party organization remains strong, and thus the reform critics' charges of alienation of support are not to be taken lightly if the Democratic party is to remain competitive in presidential elections.

Studies of local party organizational strength also provide some interesting notes on region as a factor. "Region is a significantly better predictor of organizational strength than party" (Gibson et al., 1985:152). For example, the South is the second strongest of eight *state* party regions for the Republican party while it is also the weakest of the eight *local* party regions. Anne Hopkins (1986:65) observes that in many southern states (such as the Nashville community she studied), the Republican party has no geographic organization below the county level.

Concurrently, the *national* Democratic party has been decreasing in strength in the South. Some associate this decline with the lack of support for the new reforms, resulting in an increased loyalty to Republican presidential candidates among conservative white southerners (Price, 1984). The theory about the relationship between region and vote has been that native southern white Democrats opposed the civil rights laws of the 1960s and blamed the national Democratic party for their passage (Kamieniecki, 1985).

To explain the growth in Republican voting in presidential elections in the South, one needs to examine more than party identification, which is more significant in subpresidential voting. Attitudinal factors, party loyalty and issue positions appear to bear the strongest correlation with vote. In the South, economic, racial, and social conservatism tend to determine the vote so a party's appeal depends to a considerable degree on the differential salience of various economic and social issues (Prysby, 1980). As we noted in Chapter 3, the conservative social agenda of the new right was framed to appeal to conservative southern Democrats without an overt appeal to race. The increase in independents, ticket splitting, and heightened awareness of certain salient issues account for the majority of Democratic defections. A continuous realignment of individuals on an *ad hoc* basis is occurring, due to the focus on issues (Sorauf, 1984). The Fifty-Fifty Rule and its association with affirmative action, racial quotas, and feminism relates to both social and economic concerns (and anxieties).

The Republican party is increasingly competitive in the South. This is, we suggest, an inevitable result of the decline of sectional as opposed to national conflict (Schattschneider's [1960] socialization of conflict). With increasing polarization between the two parties nationally (Miller and Jennings, 1986), the Conservative Coalition is less prevalent. Yet, the South remains Democratic. There is evidence that suggests that the impact of party organization on vote is strongest in areas with uneasy majorities, i.e., where the election outcome can be easily influenced (Cutright and Rossi, 1958). Although Phillip Cutright and Peter Rossi's study was not concerned with the South, their findings are pertinent to a South in an uncertain and transitional state. A strong party organization can be expected to enhance competitiveness at the polls, and, furthermore, if the reforms have weakened the commitment to the national party, then they should adversely affect the national party ticket's performance on election day.

ASSESSING THE COSTS OF PARTY REFORM

We assume here that commitment on behalf of the party's national candidates will tend to produce some positive advantage for those candidates. This is important because much of the reform debate centers on the issues of party support (and loyalty), competitiveness, and representativeness. Thus, we again return to those issues discussed in earlier chapters. Given this underlying assumption, we are most concerned then with the factors that have an effect on the degree of commitment to the party's national candidates, as expressed by the county chairs. First, we assess whether the evidence supports an interpretation of alienation from the national party and its candidates. Next, we assess whether this alienation can be attributed to party reforms—specifically party quotas for women. This is an important distinction because if ideological factors account for the decline in presidential vote (for the Democrats) then it is not party reform, per se, but rather the rift between the national Democratic party cadres and certain local Democratic party cadres on issues and philosophy that is the problem. If this is so, then the problem for the Democratic party is one of deciding whether it will accommodate the significant social changes identified and discussed earlier—and incorporate the energies of their accompanying social movements—or fail to do so because of an attendant risk of alienating some elements of local organizational leadership. The debate would then be more openly a policy one, reflecting a clash of interests, rather than an organizational one over form and structure.

In analyzing the intentions and opinions of county chairs, we are assessing local party cadres and activists (at least indirectly), and thus, we should see evidence of negative feelings toward party reform translated into lesser support for the national ticket—both in local organizational efforts and at the polls. In our analyses here, we use ideological self-placement rather than introducing particular policy issues, because party elites have been shown to be capable of correctly placing themselves.[1] Items regarding party organization, rules, positions, and a number of items on personal and background characteristics are also included.

Quotas for women (the Fifty-Fifty Rule). In our analyses here we employ a five-point Likert scale on the Fifty-Fifty Rule. The responses were as expected within and across party (predictive validity) and corresponded to a similar question (interitem reliability) as to whether the national party should mandate quotas for women as opposed to whether this was more reasonably a goal to promote or be left to the states to decide individually.

Support for the national ticket. Our respondents were asked whether they intended to fully and genuinely work for all of the candidates on their party's ticket, local candidates only, or the top of the ticket only. Furthermore, we inquired as to their feelings toward the two 1984 presidential nominees (using standard SRC-NES thermometer scale format). We also inquired as to their preference for their own party's presidential nominee. Because of Ronald Reagan's uniform support in 1984 (and thus an item without variance) we employ a similar inquiry about 1988 for the Republicans.

Presidential vote. Our survey data were supplemented with demographic information about the counties in which our county chair respondents held office. This county-level information included the two-party presidential vote breakdown, population, unemployment rate, black population, proportion rural and farm, median family income, proportion completing high school and college, area of country, and voter turnout. Our measure of the consequences of party reform is county-level presidential vote. Our measure of presidential vote (for Walter Mondale) as well as certain other indicators used here (unemployment, proportion black, etc.) are somewhat less than actual national averages because a number of large cities are not included in our sample as a result of jurisdictional definition, i.e., they are not included in our population of counties.[2] These lower numbers do not materially change our analyses, except insofar as introducing a slight bias toward a view contrary to our own.

Support for the National Party

The first question: is there evidence of alienation (toward the national party) among the Democratic county chairs?[3] There are four pieces of information in Table 6.1 that we believe indicate some alienation from the national Democratic party. First, the distribution of county chairs according to their type of party support shows a large proportion (28.4 percent) of them working only for local candidates. This in itself does not indicate any disaffection, but in conjunction with the other information the pattern is quite clear. Those county chairs working only on local races feel less positive about Mondale and more positive about Reagan than the "national Democrats," i.e., those expressing unequivocal support for the national party. The degree of this difference is considerable—the "local" Democrats rate Mondale less than twenty points higher than Reagan, while the "national" Democrats rate him over sixty points higher. Further, only about one-quarter of the local Democrats indicated that Mondale was their nominee of choice. An even more telling indication of disaffection is the fact that over 30 percent of the local Democrats voiced no support for either of the two main contenders for the 1984 Democratic nomination.

The evidence of local alienation toward the national Democratic party can be seen in further relief when comparing it with similar information from the Republicans in the same table. The Republicans have proportionally fewer local types than do the Democrats (15.0 percent versus 28.4 percent). Furthermore, they were outnumbered by county chairs indicating that they intended to work only for the national ticket (on the Democratic side a local type response was almost three times as likely as a top-of-the-ticket response). Local type Republicans rated Reagan over Mondale by a lesser margin than the other county chairs, but that lesser margin was sixty points. Finally, it is not possible to directly compare Republican preferences for 1988 with Democratic ones for 1984—but it is worth noting that the distribution of responses on this question, including preferences for "other," do not differ markedly depending on support for the national party.

We find that the answer to the first question that we posed is yes, there is evidence suggesting that there are local-level Democratic party cadres who feel some disaffection for the national Democratic party. We do not measure the magnitude of this disaffection in terms of group size—but a rough calculation across party would yield a figure of about 10–18 percent (the difference between the proportion of local Democrats and Republicans, allowing for some statistical margin of error). However, we should not make too much of the magnitude of this difference, as Republican parties in some states (Murray and Tedin, 1986:59) may be exclusively nationally oriented.

Sources of Alienation: Quotas for Women

The second question: do national party quotas contribute to local disaffection? Having concluded that there are alienated local party elites, what

Table 6.1
Assessment of National Party Candidates by Type of Party Support and Party

	DEMOCRATS			REPUBLICANS		
	TYPE OF PARTY SUPPORT			TYPE OF PARTY SUPPORT		
1984 Presidential Candidate Ratings	National Candidates Only	All Party Candidates	Local Candidates Only	National Candidates Only	All Party Candidates	Local Candidates Only
	(%)	(%)	(%)	(%)	(%)	(%)
MONDALE (D)	80	79	53	13	15	21
REAGAN (R)	18	18	36	93	92	81
PREFERENCE FOR 1984(1988) PARTY NOMINATION						
1984						
Mondale	55.2	47.0	25.4			
Hart	27.2	35.0	41.9			
Jackson	1.4	2.9	3.1			
Other	16.1	15.1	29.6			
1988						
Bush				58.0	49.2	52.6
Kemp				13.5	23.8	20.1
Baker				9.8	10.0	7.0
Dole				0.0	3.3	2.3
Other				18.7	14.7	18.0
TOTALS: 1984(1988)	70	313	152	62	273	60
%TOTALS: 1984(1988)	11.0	60.6	28.4	15.8	68.4	15.0

contribution to that disaffection can be attributed to this particular reform, per se? In Table 6.2, we examine the relationship between position on the Fifty-Fifty Rule and support for the national party. There is clear evidence here suggesting that there is a relationship between position on quotas and support for the national Democratic party. By a small margin (49.2–43.0 percent), Democratic county chairs oppose the quotas for women. Among those who favor or are indifferent to them, the proportion of chairpersons working only on local contests is less than one in five. Almost one-half (45.4 percent) of the Democratic county chairs who oppose the equal representation rule respond as local Democrats. The magnitude of this difference is large and, as expected, those who oppose the rule are satisfied to "tend their own gardens." This finding is in sharp contrast to what was observed on the Republican side.

The Republican party has no equal representation provision in its party rules (though 44 percent of their delegates in 1984 were women) and their county chairs do not view this as a party issue. Over 80 percent of the Republicans oppose quotas (a remarkable demonstration of commitment to basic party philosophy, to privatize conflict),and even among the group of county chairs who favor them, support for the national party is strong (only 13.7 percent of those favoring quotas said they would work only on local races).

Competing Explanations: Party Reform versus Ideology

We observed a relationship between national party support and position on quotas among the Democratic county chairs. We now assess whether the disaffection that we observed was primarily a function of mandated representation and other party reforms, or whether it represented a more fundamental opposition to the public policy positions, ideology (socialization of conflict), and the evolving social composition of the national Democratic party. For our part, this distinction is an important one. If this is genuinely a problem of party organization independent of party philosophy, then it involves a complex mix of issues: personal (and private) motivations and intraorganizational competition between elite cadres. Paradoxically, elite competition may increase with increased national-state integration, and therefore, interaction.

Alternatively, since party *elite* cadres, unlike members of the mass public, tend to have highly constrained belief systems (in Converse's [1964] sense), it may be that the organizational dimension here is not independent of the public policy one, and opposition to "party quotas" will closely correspond to opposition to "governmental quotas" (i.e., affirmative action) and expanded government, more generally. If this is so, then what more genuinely is at stake is party philosophy. In this case, because the members of the various social movements (and especially their elites) that we have been

Table 6.2

Type of Party Support by Position on the Fifty-Fifty Rule

TYPE OF PARTY SUPPORT	DEMOCRATS			REPUBLICANS		
	POSITION ON THE 50% RULE			POSITION ON THE 50% RULE		
	Support (%)	Neutral (%)	Oppose (%)	Support (%)	Neutral (%)	Oppose (%)
National Candidates Only	16.9	16.3	7.4	11.7	8.9	16.9
All Party Candidates	64.1	72.1	47.2	74.6	66.3	68.4
Local Candidates Only	19.0	11.6	45.4	13.7	24.8	14.7
TOTALS: %TOTALS:	237 43.0	43 7.8	271 49.2	48 12.1	23 5.8	324 82.1

Table 6.3

A Profile of Democratic County Chairs by Type of Party Support

PROFILE	TYPE OF PARTY SUPPORT		
	National Candidates Only	All Party Candidates	Local Candidates Only
	(%)	(%)	(%)
Ideology			
Left	37.4	36.6	18.9
Center	56.8	54.7	59.4
Right	5.8	8.7	21.8
Women's Rights			
Supports ERA	85.0	84.0	62.0
Gender Distribution			
Men	72.9	69.5	83.4
Women	27.1	30.5	16.6
TOTALS (N =)	70	313	152

discussing, who experience powerlessness and deprivation for group-level reasons, would not readily abide by anything other than the group-level remedies that they seek, their response would be a simple one—basically, them or us.

The third question: the Fifty-Fifty Rule or ideology? We now compare local and national Democrats on ideology and position on the Equal Right's Amendment (ERA). It can be seen in Table 6.3 that the ideological character of the local Democrats does differ considerably from the national ones. There are proportionally half as many self-identified liberals among the local types (only 18.9 percent identify themselves as liberal) and there are between two and three times as many self-identified conservatives among their numbers. Furthermore, the local Democrats are more than 20 percent less likely to support the ERA than those more supportive of the national Democratic party—a clear indication of differences over more than just party rules. The distribution of men and women among each of these groups differs as well, and consistent with our social movement thesis, we find the proportion of women to be considerably higher (about two to one) among those expressing support for the national party. To test these competing explanations of the lack of support by certain local party cadres, we examined the relationship between position on the Fifty-Fifty Rule and support for the national party ticket—this time controlling for the effects of ideology (Fig. 6.1).[4]

This analysis yielded a finding that opposition to party quotas was at least as responsible for lack of support for the national ticket as ideology. While congruence between ideology and position on the Fifty-Fifty Rule magnified the relationship (i.e., there was an interaction between ideology and position

Figure 6.1
Democratic County Chairs: Support for National Party by Position on Fifty-Fifty Rule, Controlling for Ideology

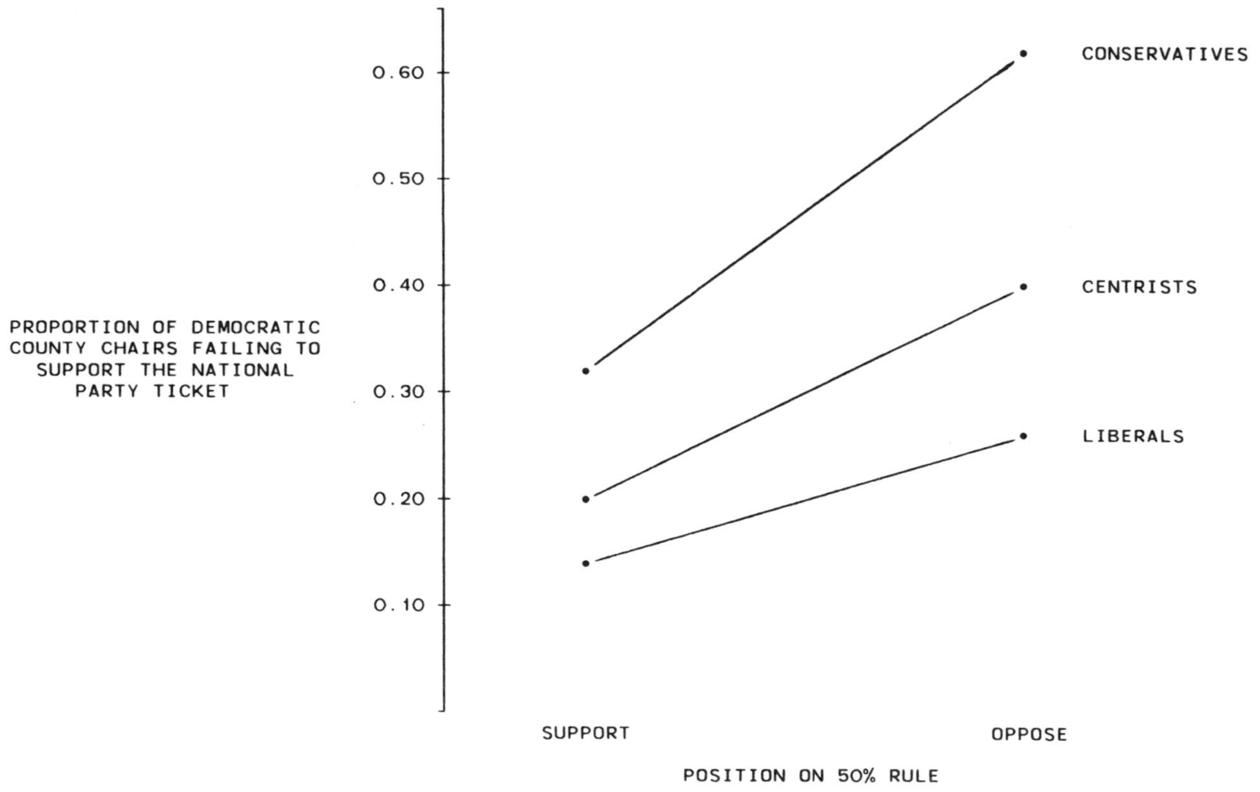

Table 6.4

Democratic County Chairs: Selected County Characteristics by Type of Party Support

COUNTY PROFILE	TYPE OF PARTY SUPPORT		
	National Candidates Only	All Party Candidates	Local Candidates Only
Mondale Vote	39.7%	38.4%	36.8%
Mean Population	143,000	119,700	77,900
Unemployment Rate	7.4%	7.8%	7.3%
Median Family Income (Dollars)	17,328	17,254	16,812
High School Graduates	61.9%	63.8%	61.8%
Black Population	8.3%	6.2%	8.4%
Located in South	38.6%	28.2%	41.2%
TOTALS (N =)	70	313	152

on the Fifty-Fifty Rule—note the differing slopes of the three lines in Figure 6.1), there was nonetheless a clear relationship between position on quotas and working for the national ticket. Liberal county chairs, supported affirmative action for minorities, the ERA, and expanded government (i.e., socialization of conflict), but those who opposed quotas at the national convention were 12.2 percent less likely (86.4 percent–74.2 percent) to support the national ticket. Centrist county chairs, who were on the whole more supportive of government programs (and the ERA) than not, were 20.8 percent less likely to work for the national ticket when opposed to quotas for women. Finally, conservative Democratic county chairs, who could best be described as skeptical about expanded government and lukewarm toward ERA, were 30.7 percent less likely to support the national ticket when in opposition to the Fifty-Fifty Rule.

Party Reform: The Electoral Cost

The last question: do disaffected local party cadres cost the national ticket votes? Our examination of county-level vote for president yielded the not unexpected finding that in counties where the county chair supported the national ticket, the vote was higher than in counties where such support was not forthcoming (Table 6.4).[5] In counties with disaffected county chairs, Mondale's vote was on the average 2.9 percent less than in counties with chairpersons indicating that all of their efforts would go to the national ticket.

The difference in magnitude across these two groups of counties is quite small. Furthermore, Mondale's average vote in counties where the county chair did not support him was no different (statistically) than in those counties where the county chair indicated support for the entire party slate (and thus, of course, for Mondale). However, we do not feel comfortable dismissing the difference for the following reason. The Democratic nominee has won the presidential election only three times since 1960—and there were margins of less than 2.9 percent of the popular vote in two of those three elections.

Because there are many aggregate-level factors that are plausible competing explanations for differences in presidential vote, we decided to compare other possible factors, which we had measured, with support for the national ticket. These differences can be seen in Table 6.4. First, the group of counties with chairpersons who indicated that they would work exclusively for the national ticket were more populous, but otherwise differed little from the other groups of counties. The counties with chairs supporting the entire party slate averaged higher unemployment rates and were proportionally less southern (and hence had a higher proportion of high-school graduates and a lower proportion of black voters). Those counties represented by disaffected county chairs were proportionally more southern (and hence had the lowest proportion of high-school graduates, the lowest median family income, and the highest proportion of black voters). They were also, by a substantial margin, the least populous counties.

In order to sort out the effects of these factors, we performed a stepwise regression analysis to determine which among them best accounted for varying county-level support for the Democratic national ticket. Our results yielded three significant explanatory factors—population, unemployment rate, and proportion of black voters.[6] Thus, for our set of observations, the observed difference in vote for the Democratic ticket across the two sets of counties (one where the county chair worked exclusively for the top of the ticket and the other where the county chair worked only on local races) was actually a function of their differential population size. Each group was similar on unemployment rate and proportion of black voters, but the counties of the disaffected local Democrats were on the average 65,000 persons smaller than the other group of counties. This explained the difference in vote for Mondale. One last observation from our analysis is pertinent given our earlier discussion of region as a factor. While it is true that disaffected local cadres are more concentrated in the South than elsewhere, region was not a significant factor in our analysis of the vote for the Democratic ticket.

A PARTY DILEMMA

We believe that there is a plausible case to be made that party rules mandating equal representation for men and women at the Democratic National Convention has cost the national Democratic party some support. The fact of this disaffection is clearer than its import. There is some loss of support, but of an uncertain and perhaps small magnitude. Support deriving from the relevant social movement (the women's movement) is more tangible, and its demands are entirely consistent with Democratic party philosophy (socialization of conflict). Nonetheless, this loss is perceptible and should not be ignored in assessing reforms. The internal party tension found here testifies strongly to the success of the women's movement; after all, if no party elites were disaffected, one would suspect co-optation of group members.

Disaffected county chairs can usefully be divided into two groups. The first, and smaller, group is comfortable with, and mostly supports, the Reagan agenda. There is no basis for compromise with these elements of local Democratic party leadership. They are ideologically opposed to the ends of the women's movement. They are socially conservative and incapable (or unwilling) of adjusting to the new social reality of the 1980s. They both consciously and unconsciously discriminate against women. In fact, national remedies such as the equal representation provision are necessary because of a strong tradition of local-level group-based discrimination (detailed in Chapter 4). If the national Democratic party is to appeal to these elements, it cannot attract and keep the majority support from the women's movement that it presently enjoys.

The second, and larger, group of disaffected county chairs are not so unsympathetic to the ends of the women's movement. The interests of the women's movement are, like other political interests, recognized and, when relevant, used for political ends. These local elites will work for (and advance) the ends of the women's movement when it is in their personal interest to do so. They will also work against or compromise away those ends when *that* advances their private interests. This is precisely the reason why accommodating new (and out-group) elites is so important. The entrenched elites—regardless of their ideology—are too willing to compromise away the interests of out-groups.

NOTES

1. Our data clearly support this finding. Comparing liberals, moderates, and conservatives as groups within the two parties, we find that on each of six issues—defense spending, detente, job guarantees, national health insurance, affirmative action, and cutting public services—the group means (on a seven-point Likert scale) are *not only* in proper relation to one another but each group was approximately one-step distant from the next, with the liberals to the left, the moderates in the center, and the conservatives to the right. This was a relative placement related to party, and thus Democrats perceiving themselves as conservative voiced conservative policy positions—but they were clearly not as conservative as their ideological brethren in the other party.

2. In the course of our analysis, we tried a number of refinements on this county-level vote in order to more carefully isolate the effects of the county chairs' efforts (or lack of effort) for the presidential vote. These refinements were in addition to the

explicit factors noted above, and they included adjustments for statewide presidential vote, statewide party competitiveness (utilizing both Ranney's [1965] state party index and the Bibby and associates' [1983] update) as well as changes in party competitiveness over time. In each instance, our subsequent interpretation was basically the same as using the unadjusted vote; therefore, in the interest of simplicity, we ultimately relied on that unadjusted vote.

3. It should be assumed that when we state that there is a difference (or a relationship) between identified groups, that difference is statistically significant at a critical level of 0.05. We employ chi-square tests for testing tabular relationships and t-tests for specified group comparisons (when the dependent variable is a continuous one).

4. For this analysis we grouped county chairs neutral toward party quotas with those supporting them because their earlier responses were similar, and more important, neutrality toward the Fifty-Fifty Rule is hardly a reason to forsake the national ticket.

5. The one-tail t-test associated with this 2.9 percent difference was equal to 1.79, $P(t) < 0.04$.

6. The explained variance for the three-variable model was 13 percent.

7

Gauging the Commitment to Party

INTRODUCTION

For the most part, critics of party reform have not been of one mind concerning the *causes* of party reform but have been virtually unanimous in their catalog of consequences for the party system.[1] The party system, and the Democratic party in particular, have become captured and dominated by ideological extremists, candidate factions, and political "amateurs." James Ceaser argues that "there is good reason to believe that any kind of restored party organizations would normally be strongly influenced, and probably dominated, by amateurs" (1980:111). Similarly, Byron Shafer concludes that reform has become so institutionalized that the notion of " 'regularity' itself is a vanishing concept" (1983:537). These assessments have become dogma in political science; yet we now know that party organizations have not declined—either in organizational terms as both amateurs and professionals contribute to organizational strength (e.g., Cotter et al., 1984) or at the grass-roots level (e.g., Eldersveld, 1986). And the two congressional parties are more distinct ideologically, as is true of convention delegates since 1972. However, some theorists have concluded that the parties have become stronger only to surrender "much of this power to the candidates" (Orren, 1982:26). We now turn to an analysis of party commitment in the postreform party era.

DIMENSIONS OF PARTISAN COMMITMENT

As Leon Epstein makes clear, it has been difficult for political scientists to consider political parties apart from their assumed role as "products and agents of American democracy" (1983:128; 1986). Two schools of thought have evolved: the indigenous or conventional American parties school (favored by reform critics) and the responsible party school. The latter position has been associated most prominently with E. E. Schattschneider, who chaired the American Political Science Association committee issuing the report, *Toward a More Responsible Party System* (1950). These two perspectives on parties posit a strong commitment to the party; however, the indigenous party school favors a nonideological and pragmatic compromise on policy between the two parties, whereas the responsible party school advocates ideological parties who ensure the responsibility of their program by instituting sanctions against those that do not support party positions. Many who consider the future prospects of the parties, in particular the increased ideological congruence between partisanship and issue positions among the electorate, do so against the benchmark of the responsible party position (e.g., Pomper, 1971; Orren, 1982).

Yet, these two *scholarly* points of view do not encompass the range of possible orientations among party elites. First, the responsible party position has been largely discredited as impractical due to the distinctive constitutional features of federalism and separation of powers—what Epstein (1986) has referred to as the "American mold." Furthermore, the capacity of congressional party leaders to "punish" straying party members has decreased since the 1970s. Second, the indigenous parties—however institutionalized under the Democratic and Republican labels (Epstein, 1986)—are not, as indicated earlier, immune to ideological political and social movements. Third, amateurs—those with only a weak commitment to party (as their commitment to ideological purity transcends their support of party)—have become more prevalent (Orren, 1982). And fourth, candidate factions (and those with personalistic ties to individual leaders) have become a regular feature of party politics (Salmore and Salmore, 1985).

We conclude, then, that an examination of party commitment should encompass the tie to party versus candidate and a preference for ideological versus pragmatic programs in their appeals for electoral support. Following Gary Orren (1982; see also Sullivan et al., 1976:59), we view these as two independent polarities that result in four major types of partisan commitment (1) Responsible Party, (2) Pragmatic Party, (3) Limited Issue and (4) Personalistic.

Those who favor more ideology in the party appeals (i.e., want the parties to represent programmatic alternatives) and who support the party over individual candidates can be considered the Responsible Party supporters (as described in the APSA committee report). Those who favor more ideology in the party appeals, but support only a particular candidate(s) in the party, are the Limited Issue types. Those who prefer pragmatic appeals to the moderate middle, but support the party over a candidate are the Pragmatic Party supporters (as assumed by the defenders of indigenous institutions). Finally, those who prefer pragmatic appeals, but support only a particular candidate(s) are called Personalistic supporters. Distinct from some (e.g., Price, 1984), we separate the notion of enforcement of party cohesion by a centralized national party from the typology of party types investigated here. Instead, we will examine support for measures of party responsibility as a dependent variable.

Neither previous analyses nor assessments of the party system offer sufficient information to generate firm hypotheses. Gerald Pomper, for example, argues that the "new political energies evident [in 1971] in the United States" made the "nation more ready for responsible parties . . . than in 1950" (1971:940,939). Yet, more than a decade later, Orren offers a grim analysis of the "decline of parties and the rise of personalistic and limited-issue styles of politics" while arguing that responsible parties are unlikely (1982:40). Edward Banfield points to a rise in centralized party authority and candidate-centered "image" politics (1980a). Nelson Polsby identifies a turn to both personality politics and a resuscitation of ideology (1980; 1983a). Thus, these diverse points of view encompass the national party system as a whole, and provide little in the way of comparative expectations other than that the local elites should be more pragmatically oriented.[2] Hence, we conduct no hypothesis testing in this chapter and instead explore the distribution of these party types among Democratic and Republican party elite groups.

THE VIEWS OF THE ELITE CADRES

Our first step in this analysis was to divide the party elites into one of the four groups we identified based on their responses to the following two questions:

- Would you characterize yourself as someone who: (A) works for the party year after year, win or lose and whether or not you like the candidate or issues (Party Orientation); or (B) works for the party only when there is a particularly worthwhile candidate or issue (Amateur Orientation).[3]
- The (Republicans/Democrats) should take issue and ideological stances that make us more clearly the (conservative/liberal) party in this country; (Agree = Ideologue Orientation; Disagree = Pragmatic Orientation).

Our analytic strategy is to compare the changes over time, across party, and within party between these four groups (hereinafter referred to as Responsible Party, Pragmatic Party, Limited Issue and Personalistic). In addition to comparing the proportional group sizes, we also compare the group strength of those within each group who share ideological preferences (i.e., liberal versus conservative) and candidate preferences. Finally, we compare the support within each group for three specific measures tapping national party enforcement or implementation of a responsible party system and one measure assessing political pragmatism.

Republican National Committee Members

The analysis for the Republican National Committee members yields a finding of almost equal proportions of Responsible Party and Pragmatic Party types—with slightly more Responsible Party types. This was the case in both 1980 and in 1984. Not unexpectedly, there were virtually no expressions of support by RNC members for nonparty orientations (i.e., Limited Issue or Personalistic).

The Responsible Party types among the RNC members were self-identified conservatives in both years (83 percent and 87 percent) and the Pragmatists were self- identified moderates. Those Responsible Party types who did not identify themselves as conservative, characterized themselves as moderate, and, except for a few isolated liberals, the Pragmatic Party types who were not self-identified moderates characterized themselves as conservative.

In order to make these groups more tangibly different, we correlated party orientation with candidate preference (for president) for both 1980 and 1984. In 1984, we actually used Republican presidential preference for 1988 because Ronald Reagan was a near unanimous favorite in 1984. Our divisions corresponded quite nicely to the earlier cleavages. In 1980, Reagan, as the conservative candidate, was the favorite of the Responsible Party types and George Bush, as the moderate alternative, was the favorite of the Pragmatic Party types. In 1984, not unexpectedly, the favorite of both groups for 1988 was Bush. However, expressions of support for him were greater among the Pragmatic Party types, and while the conservative alternative, U.S. Representative Jack Kemp (R-NY), had some support among the Responsible Party types (12 percent), he had none among the Pragmatic Party types.

The last items that we correlated with party orientation were the responsible party model's implementing recommendations. These included support for a strong national party, support for national party loyalty test (to vote in the Republican primary), and support for the establishment by the national committee (i.e., the RNC) of criteria for participation in Republican party affairs. Along with these items, we included one other (assessing pragmatism) inquiring whether ensuring winning candidates was the main job of the Republican National Committee.

There was little or no support to be found for a strengthened national party at the expense of the states. Both Responsible Party and Pragmatic Party types were uniformly opposed to this initiative. The conservativism expressed by the Responsible Party types would hardly be consistent with support for a large centralized party structure that would dominate state and local institutions. The Pragmatic Party types could hardly be expected to support this either because the pragmatic school, identified earlier, stresses the importance of the fragmented federal system where local initiative is such a deep-rooted part of the American political system.

Support for a party loyalty test to vote in the Republican primary differed considerably from 1980 to 1984, probably due to the John Anderson (R-IL) candidacy in 1980. In 1980, the conservative Responsible Party types witnessed a considerable number of voters participating in the Republican primaries solely to express support for John Anderson and his ideas. Given that they heartily opposed his candidacy, the idea of restricting access to the Republican primaries probably seemed like a good thing to do—and about half of the national committee members responding indicated just that. The Pragmatic Party types, believing quite differently, gave only slight support to this initiative (20 percent). In 1984, when this issue had no immediate referent, these two party types expressed similar levels of support for the loyalty test, with approximately one-third responding positively. Arguably, the 1984 results are more indicative of an underlying philosophical commitment to this position than are the 1980 ones.

There was very little difference between the Pragmatic Party and Responsible Party types on support for the national party setting up criteria for participation in party affairs. As with the earlier item on strong national parties, there was little inclination to vest more power in a centralized party structure.

The last of these items was one on choosing winning candidates, that is, that the main responsibility of RNC members is to promote winning candidates. This position is contrary to the Responsible Party position and should (and does) receive more support from the Pragmatic Party types. In 1980 and 1984, about one-half of the Pragmatic Party types supported this position. In 1980, about one-quarter of the Responsible Party types supported this position—slightly more than half the support found among the Pragmatic Party types. In 1984, that proportion ballooned to 51 percent. This inconsistency may be attributable to waning ideological commitment or, more likely, to the fact that in 1984 the winning candidate was the conservative candidate—and thus choosing the winning candidate was also choosing the responsible (i.e., conservative) candidate.

The examination of the Republican National Committee members yields mixed findings on support for the responsible party system. However, it does not yield mixed findings on the question of whether these two positions characterize the RNC members. They clearly do. The RNC members are a mix of Responsible Party and Pragmatic Party types, and that division nicely captures the variation in the character of its members.

Republican National Convention Delegates

The analysis for the Republicans indicates that at least one-half of their national convention delegates fell in the Responsible Party category (Table 7.1). There was a slight decline from 1980 to 1984 (about 5 percent). The second largest group of Republican convention delegates were Pragmatic Party supporters (approximately 30 percent each year with a higher propor-

Table 7.1
Ideology by Party Orientation, Party and Elite Level, 1980 and 1984

DEMOCRATS

IDEOLOGY	Delegates				County Chairs				National Committee			
	I	II	III	IV	I	II	III	IV	I	II	III	IV
	%	%	%	%	%	%	%	%	%	%	%	%
LIBERAL												
1980	72	22	87	31	55	6	47	0	80	30	50	*
1984	78	33	88	30	70	12	61	10	73	16	*	43
CENTRIST												
1980	26	70	13	59	43	76	33	51	20	66	50	*
1984	20	63	13	53	25	73	35	57	24	84	*	57
CONSERVATIVE												
1980	2	8	0	9	3	18	20	49	0	4	0	*
1984	3	4	0	17	5	15	4	33	3	0	*	0
TOTALS: 1980	153	126	76	32	134	212	15	41	45	53	6	0
TOTALS: 1984	103	133	66	56	147	258	23	49	29	51	*	7
%TOTAL: 1980	40	33	20	8	33	53	4	10	43	51	6	0
%TOTAL: 1984	29	37	18	16	31	54	5	10	32	57	*	8

REPUBLICANS

IDEOLOGY	Delegates				County Chairs				National Committee			
	I	II	III	IV	I	II	III	IV	I	II	III	IV
	%	%	%	%	%	%	%	%	%	%	%	%
LIBERAL												
1980	0	5	0	8	0	2	3	8	0	*	3	*
1984	0	2	0	10	1	2	0	0	0	*	7	*
CENTRIST												
1980	16	66	18	65	19	62	15	42	14	*	76	*
1984	15	55	4	68	14	56	8	58	17	*	69	*
CONSERVATIVE												
1980	84	30	83	27	81	36	82	50	87	*	21	*
1984	85	43	86	23	85	42	93	42	83	*	24	*
TOTALS: 1980	224	108	40	26	287	121	35	13	31	30	0	0
TOTALS: 1984	234	146	59	31	223	101	40	12	37	29	2	0
%TOTAL: 1980	56	27	10	7	63	26	8	3	51	49	0	0
%TOTAL: 1984	50	31	13	6	59	27	11	3	54	43	3	0

PARTY ORIENTATION:
I   RESPONSIBLE PARTY
II   PRAGMATIC PARTY
III LIMITED ISSUE
IV   PERSONALISTIC

tion in 1984 corresponding to a similar size decline in the Responsible Party group). The two categories combined accounted for over 80 percent of the delegates in both years, a reasonable indication of strong support for the Republican *party*. As expected, the Responsible Party group was overwhelmingly "conservative" (over 80 percent) and the Pragmatic Party group was overwhelmingly "moderate" in their self-characterization. The secondary ideological characterization for each group (Responsible Party versus Pragmatic Party) was the adjacent position (our data indicate that there are few self-identified liberals left in the Republican party).

The remaining two groups for the Republicans (comprising less than 20 percent of the total number of delegates) were the Limited Issue types (the larger of the two groups), who were as conservative as the Responsible Party group, and the Personalistic types, who were predominantly "moderate" in their self-characterization. The second of these two groups did not change from 1980 to 1984, but the Limited Issue types did increase a small percentage of the total (2.5 percent; proportionately, that is a 25 percent increase in size). For the Republicans, from 1980 to 1984, the loss in Responsible Party delegates was split between Pragmatic Party types (4 percent) and Limited Issue types.

In an effort to make the differences between these groups more tangible, we again correlated party orientation with candidate preference (for president) for 1980 and 1984 (1988 for the Republicans) and these data are presented in Table 7.2. Our divisions corresponded quite nicely to individual preferences for president. In 1980, Reagan received overwhelming support from the Responsible Party delegates and the Limited Issue types because both groups are conservative ones. The Pragmatic Party delegates in 1980 actually preferred Bush to Reagan by a substantial margin, and Reagan's support among the Personalistic types was matched by the combined support for Bush and Anderson. In 1984 (1988), Bush received support from about half the Responsible Party group with Kemp running a not-so-distant second. Bush was the clear favorite of the Pragmatic Party people, and he had the support of half of the delegates in the Personalistic category (while Kemp had no support among these delegates). Kemp's support group clearly fell into the Limited Issue category, where he received majority support.

We again correlated party orientation with the responsible party model's implementing recommendations as we had done for the RNC members (Table 7.3). There were no substantial differences across party groups on support for a strong national party among the Republican delegates in either 1980 or 1984. In fact, in 1984 among the predominant Republican groups (Responsible Party and Pragmatic Party) there were no differences at all. As noted earlier (in regard to RNC members), this finding comes as no surprise.

On support for a party loyalty test to vote in the primary, the delegates differed in that the more conservative categories (i.e., the Responsible Party category and the Limited Issue category) supported a party loyalty test more

Table 7.2
Presidential Preference by Party Orientation, Party and Elite Level, 1980 and 1984 (1988)

DEMOCRATS

PREFERENCE	Delegates I	II	III	IV	County Chairs I	II	III	IV	National Committee I	II	III	IV
	%	%	%	%	%	%	%	%	%	%	%	%
1980												
REAGAN (R)												
BUSH (R)												
OTHER (R)												
CARTER (D)	45	78	23	59	58	74	47	68	51	83	60	*
KENNEDY(D)	52	16	75	25	36	15	53	5	36	8	40	*
OTHER (D)	3	6	2	16	6	11	0	27	13	9	0	*
1984(1988)												
BUSH (R)												
KEMP (R)												
OTHER (R)												
MONDALE(D)	51	53	29	26	51	40	26	26	54	80	33	50
HART (D)	40	35	52	58	32	35	52	41	18	6	33	17
OTHER (D)	9	12	19	16	17	25	22	33	28	14	33	33
TOTALS: 1980	153	126	76	32	134	212	15	41	45	53	6	0
TOTALS: 1984	103	133	66	56	147	258	23	49	29	51	3	7
%TOTALS: 1980	40	33	20	8	33	53	4	10	43	51	6	0
%TOTALS: 1984	29	37	18	16	31	54	5	10	32	57	3	8

REPUBLICANS

PREFERENCE	Delegates I	II	III	IV	County Chairs I	II	III	IV	National Committee I	II	III	IV
	%	%	%	%	%	%	%	%	%	%	%	%
1980												
REAGAN (R)	88	45	88	48	58	27	59	8	60	19	*	*
BUSH (R)	5	37	5	20	18	39	15	8	20	69	*	*
OTHER (R)	7	18	7	32	24	34	26	0	20	12	*	*
CARTER (D)												
KENNEDY(D)												
OTHER (D)												
1984(1988)												
BUSH (R)	51	74	38	65	44	67	52	46	71	81	*	*
KEMP (R)	34	11	50	4	30	9	34	9	9	0	*	*
OTHER (R)	15	15	12	31	27	24	14	45	17	19	*	*
MONDALE(D)												
HART (D)												
OTHER (D)												
TOTALS: 1980	224	108	40	26	287	121	35	13	31	30	0	0
TOTALS: 1984	234	146	59	31	223	101	40	12	37	29	2	0
%TOTALS: 1980	56	27	10	7	63	26	8	3	51	49	0	0
%TOTALS: 1984	50	31	13	6	59	27	11	3	54	43	3	0

PARTY ORIENTATION:
I RESPONSIBLE PARTY
II PRAGMATIC PARTY
III LIMITED ISSUE
IV PERSONALISTIC

Table 7.3
Support for Responsible Party Initiatives by Party Orientation, Party and Elite Level, 1980 and 1984

	DEMOCRATS												REPUBLICANS											
	Delegates				County Chairs				National Committee				Delegates				County Chairs				National Committee			
INITIATIVES	I	II	III	IV	I	II	III	IV	I	II	III	IV	I	II	III	IV	I	II	III	IV	I	II	III	IV
	%	%	%	%	%	%	%	%	%	%	%	%	%	%	%	%	%	%	%	%	%	%	%	%
FAVORS STRONG NATIONAL PARTY																								
1980	30	10	25	19	18	7	20	2	30	13	50	*	8	12	6	4	10	11	6	15	0	3	*	*
1984	35	21	29	16	24	16	22	8	48	36	*	14	7	7	4	10	11	11	8	0	3	3	*	*
FAVOR PARTY LOYALTY TEST																								
1980	53	37	37	22	51	47	20	20	53	43	50	*	19	16	21	4	26	26	26	8	48	20	*	*
1984	51	37	35	13	51	49	30	27	69	58	*	29	32	19	27	7	28	18	13	17	33	31	*	*
NATIONAL PARTY DEFINED CRITERIA																								
1980	35	26	31	19	31	22	33	17	55	42	50	*	8	12	3	4	10	11	6	15	19	13	*	*
1984	36	39	21	23	33	17	22	10	62	47	*	0	23	14	24	10	21	10	8	25	16	14	*	*
ENSURE WINNING CANDIDATES																								
1980	29	31	17	23	40	38	53	29	28	37	36	*	40	33	29	31	47	36	33	23	26	47	*	*
1984	32	33	15	19	39	34	41	37	21	38	*	29	36	27	29	36	48	42	50	33	51	45	*	*
TOTALS: 1980	153	126	76	32	134	212	15	41	45	53	6	0	224	108	40	26	287	121	35	13	31	30	0	0
TOTALS: 1984	103	133	66	56	147	258	23	49	29	51	*	7	234	146	59	31	223	101	40	12	37	29	2	0
%TOTALS: 1980	40	33	20	8	33	53	4	10	43	51	6	0	56	27	10	7	63	26	8	3	51	49	0	0
%TOTALS: 1984	29	37	18	16	31	54	5	10	32	57	*	8	50	31	13	6	59	27	11	3	54	43	3	0

PARTY ORIENTATION:
I   RESPONSIBLE PARTY
II PRAGMATIC PARTY
III LIMITED ISSUE
IV PERSONALISTIC

than the delegates in the Pragmatic Party category in both 1980 and 1984. All groups were more supportive of a party loyalty test in 1984 than they were in 1980 (which was surprising given the Anderson candidacy in 1980), with between one-fifth and one-third of each group supporting this position *except* among the Personalistic types. It is reasonable to assume that in neither supporting the party, per se, nor wanting the party to espouse a more conservative platform, the delegates in this group would not desire a party loyalty test.

As with RNC members, the level of support for RNC-established criteria for participation in party affairs was similar to support for a strong national party—a generally negative response uniform across party orientation. In 1984, there was more support for this initiative than in 1980 (about one-quarter of the Responsible Party and Limited Issue types versus about 10 percent for the Pragmatic Party and Personalistic types), and this support differentiated the more conservative (i.e., Responsible Party and Limited Issue) from the less conservative types, with the former being more supportive of this change.

Somewhat unexpectedly, those delegates in the Responsible Party category were more in agreement with the pragmatic proposition that their main job was to ensure (the selection of) winning candidates than any other group. There was slightly less support for this position in 1984 than in 1980 (contrary to what was found with the RNC members), but in both years the Responsible Party types were more supportive of it than were the Pragmatic Party types (by margins of 7–9 percent). The small group of Personalistic types was as supportive of "winning candidates" as any other group of Republican delegates.

Democratic National Committee Members

The Democratic National Committee members were, like their Republican counterparts, mostly party types. More than half of the responses in 1980 and 1984 were Pragmatic Party types (more in 1984 than 1980). The proportion of Responsible Party types was over 40 percent in 1980 but fell to only slightly more than 30 percent in 1984. Part of this decline was a shift to the Pragmatic Party side but there was also a fairly steep increase in the proportion of nonparty types from 1980 to 1984 (from 6 percent to 11 percent). The proportion of nonparty types among the DNC members was much higher than among RNC members but still less than that of any of the other Democratic cadres. This is consistent with the overall pattern of Republican cadres being more party oriented than Democratic cadres.

The Responsible Party types on the DNC are mostly self-identified liberals as expected. Also as expected, the Pragmatic Party types more often identify themselves as moderate than as liberal. That order reverses for the second most frequent characterization. Those few Limited Issue and Personalistic types among the DNC members are divided in a similar fashion.

In 1980, those DNC members responding indicated their support for then President Jimmy Carter. However, there were clear differences across party orientation with over one-third of the Responsible Party and Limited Issue types expressing their preference for Senator Edward Kennedy (D-MA), whereas less than one-tenth of the Pragmatic Party types supported him.

There was quite a different dynamic in 1984. First, there were greater numbers preferring someone other than the two front-runners (Walter Mondale and Gary Hart) than in 1980. Next, Senator Hart, the second-place candidate, had very little support among the DNC members (as opposed to Kennedy in 1980). Finally, while Mondale support among the party types was proportionally very similar to Carter's in 1980, there was no apparent liberal-moderate split among the national committee members.

The DNC members expressed much greater support for implementing the procedures called for in the responsible party model in 1984 than in 1980. Furthermore, there was a consistent pattern of Responsible Party types favoring implementation of responsible party procedures more than Pragmatic Party types. By 1984, half of the Responsible Party types favored a strong national party (at the expense of the states), over two-thirds favored a party loyalty test to vote in the Democratic primary, close to that number favored the DNC setting up criteria for participation in Democratic party affairs, and only one in five was primarily concerned with choosing winning candidates. There was considerably less support for these positions in 1980 by DNC members who responded as Responsible Party types. It could not even be said that the Pragmatic Party types in the DNC were (at least by 1984) all that unfavorable to these initiatives—with over one-third favoring a strong national party, close to three-fifths favoring party loyalty tests, and about one-half favoring DNC defined criteria for participation in party affairs. They were, however, more favorably disposed to selecting candidates based on their electability.

The DNC members expressed themselves (much like their Republican counterparts) such that two predominant types can be isolated—the Responsible Party and the Pragmatic Party. While there are more Pragmatic Party types, this disparity between the two must be considered in light of the considerable support for implementing the responsible party model's procedures found among these Pragmatic Party types.

Democratic National Convention Delegates

The analysis for the Democrats indicates that a considerably smaller proportion of the delegates were Responsible Party types than was the case for the Republicans (see Table 7.1). In 1980, slightly more delegates were in this category than in the Pragmatic Party category (40–35 percent), but by

1984 this circumstance had changed to the extent that the predominant type for the Democratic delegates was Pragmatic Party. Compared to the Republicans, the "party" people among the Democratic delegates represented a smaller proportion of the total delegate pool (three-quarters in 1980 and only two-thirds in 1984). As with the Republicans, the ideological makeup of these categories was as expected, with the Responsible Party group being primarily liberal with a small proportion of self-identified moderates and with the Limited Issue types similarly distributed. The Pragmatic Party types were primarily moderate in ideology with a slight number of conservatives (overall our assessment of the Democratic delegates reveals that conservative is about as unpopular an identification here as is liberal among the Republicans). The clear movement from 1980 to 1984 for the Democratic delegates was from liberal to pragmatic categories (i.e., from Responsible Party and Limited Issue to Pragmatic Party and Personalistic).

As with the Republicans, we correlated the different party orientation groups with candidate preference (see Table 7.2). In 1980, the more liberal types (i.e., the Responsible Party and Limited Issue groups) preferred Kennedy to Carter—by a small margin in the first group and by a large margin in the second. Pragmatic Party types and the Personalistic types, in 1980, preferred Carter to Kennedy—by a substantial margin. Thus, support for Kennedy versus Carter was not a party versus amateur split, but rather a liberal versus moderate split.

In 1984, Mondale was preferred over Hart in both party groups (Responsible Party and Pragmatic Party) by similar margins, with Mondale having the support of about one-half of each group and Hart having the support of slightly more than one-third of the delegates in these groups. Conversely, Hart was preferred over Mondale in both the amateur groups. Thus, the split between Hart and Mondale was one that was less ideologically based and more one reflecting party-amateur cleavages. With respect to 1984, one other aspect of candidate preference is significant for the Democrats—namely, the fairly large number of delegates who preferred neither Hart nor Mondale. This was true not only in the amateur categories, but in the party categories as well.

When we correlated party orientation with the items assessing support for strong national parties, a party loyalty test, DNC-defined criteria for party participation, and ensuring winning candidates, we observed that support for a strong national party increased from 1980 to 1984 among all groups except for the Personalistic types (see Table 7.3). The evidence suggests concern by some for a *strong* national party by the 1984 election. The Personalistic types were the exception to this pattern. This is consistent with their being less party oriented and in opposition to the Democratic party being the liberal alternative.

Support for a party loyalty test (to vote in the primary) changed little from 1980 to 1984 with the Responsible Party group being the most supportive of this (over 50 percent) and with the Pragmatic Party and Limited Issue types following behind (about 15 percent). The Personalistic types again betrayed the trend, probably for the same reasons as indicated above. Support for the establishment of partisan criteria by the DNC followed a different pattern. First, both pragmatic groups expressed increased support from 1980 to 1984. The Responsible Party group changed little, and the Limited Issue types expressed 10 percent less support. For some reason, perhaps changes in the DNC, the evidence suggests that the less liberal delegates felt more comfortable with the DNC—and the more liberal amateurs felt less confident about entrusting new powers to the national party committee.

Those delegates falling in the Pragmatic category were more supportive of the position that their main job was to ensure winning candidates (by a small margin over the ideological groups) and there was relatively little change from 1980 to 1984. The Democratic convention delegates who fell into the Responsible Party category for both years were the most supportive of the responsible party positions.

Republican and Democratic County Chairs

There is some general correspondance between the patterns observed for the Republican and Democratic delegates and those for their respective county chairs. However, there are also some consistent differences that are worth noting (see Table 7.1). Both Republican and Democratic county chairs—probably because of their functional role—are more party oriented than are their respective convention delegates. Close to 90 percent of each identify themselves as party supporters rather than amateurs. The two party groups differ in that the Republican county chairs are predominantly Responsible Party and secondarily Pragmatic Party, while the reverse holds true for the Democrats. Here, we find the unreformed party *more* ideologically oriented than the reformed party, a result clearly contrary to the reform critics expectations. Yet, the strong support of party evidenced here also undermines assertions that the local parties may have declined in party commitment.

As expected, those few Republican county chairs who are candidate-oriented (amateur) are ideologues and conservatives, while Personalistic types on the Democratic side tend to be less liberal than their party-oriented compatriots. There are very few Limited Issue types among the Democratic county chairs and similarly few Personalistic types on the Republican side. The Republican county chairs are slightly more conservative in their self-identification than are their corresponding delegates. The Democratic county chairs are more moderate (and conservative) than the Democratic delegates (and to a greater degree than is true on the Republican side). Even among the Responsible Party types, county chairs are more likely to characterize themselves as moderate than liberal (this is while advocating that the party represent the liberal alternative).

With respect to candidate support, the county chairs—both Republican and Democratic—are less supportive of any given candidate than are the convention delegates, which is not surprising since most of the delegates are selected to support some specific candidate (see Table 7.2). On the Republican side, the Responsible Party types preferred Reagan to any other candidate; at least one-third of them, however, preferred other candidates (with Bush a distant second). The Pragmatic Party types among the Republican county chairs preferred Bush to Reagan. It is interesting to note that shortly after the 1980 Republican National Convention (when our 1980 observations were made), the Republican county chairs were, as a group, rather divided as to their preferred presidential nominee. The same was true in 1984 (1988)—especially in comparison with other elite cadres—with Bush being the leading candidate with each type, but with less than majority support except among the Pragmatic Party and Limited Issue types.

The Democratic county chairs, in 1980, generally preferred Carter to all alternatives regardless of party orientation. Kennedy had some support among county chairs in both the Responsible Party and Pragmatic Party categories, but Carter was preferred by a majority in both groups. The Personalistic types favored Carter by a large margin. In 1984, Mondale had less support than Carter (in 1980) across all categories. Mondale was preferred by a small majority of county chairs in the Responsible Party category, but nowhere else. He had more support than Hart among the county chairs, but this represented only 40 percent of the total. What is most striking in both 1980 and 1984 is the degree to which the Democratic county chairs preferred a different candidate for president from the one eventually nominated by the party.

On the responsible party positions on strong national party, party loyalty tests, DNC/RNC-defined criteria for party participation, and the pragmatic position on ensuring winning candidates, we observed that the Republican county chairs were similar to their delegate counterparts in lack of support for strong national parties, probably for the same reason (it is not a conservative position) (see Table 7.3).

A party loyalty test (to vote in the GOP primary) was more agreeable to the county chairs than to the delegates in 1980—26 percent for the county chairs who were homogeneous across party orientation categories, to about 18 percent for the delegates, where the conservative orientations (Responsible Party and Limited Issue) are more favorable to party loyalty tests than the Pragmatic Party group. By 1984, the GOP county chairs were virtually indistinguishable from their delegates on party loyalty tests with individuals in the Pragmatic Party category (for both county chairs and delegates), being less supportive of party loyalty tests than those delegates and county chairs who fell into the Responsible Party category.

On RNC-defined criteria for participation in party affairs, the Republican county chairs in the Responsible Party category expressed twice as much support for this position in 1984 as they did in 1980 (21 percent versus 10 percent). The support for this position among the county chairs in the Pragmatic Party category remained unchanged (about 10 percent).

Finally, the Republican county chairs in the Responsible Party category were the most supportive of the pragmatic proposition on ensuring winning candidates of the four types (as was the case with the Republican delegates). Unlike the Republican delegates, the county chairs from 1980 to 1984 changed in a direction more supportive of this position. Again, unexpectedly, the more ideological groups were generally more supportive of this pragmatic position.

For the Republicans, delegates and county chairs alike, a pattern had emerged by 1984 on party loyalty tests and RNC-defined criteria for participation in party affairs. In each instance, the Republicans who we classified in the Responsible Party category also supported the responsible party ideal (from the 1950 APSA committee report) on these other issues more so than did any of the other categories (i.e., Pragmatic Party or Limited Issue). However, it is worth noting that even in the Responsible Party category, only between one-fifth and one-third of the delegates and county chairs gave responses consistent with the responsible party model, and they expressed more concern for ensuring the selection of winning candidates (a pragmatic position) than any other group.

The pattern for the Democratic county chairs on these items were likewise consistent. Those who fell into the Responsible Party category consistently favored a strong national party, party loyalty tests, and DNC-defined criteria for party participation more than those who fell into either the Pragmatic Party category or either of the amateur categories. There was some variation in support for the proposition on ensuring winning candidates with the more ideological groups being slightly more concerned with selecting winning candidates. There was little change from 1980 to 1984. Of the four items, party loyalty tests to vote in the Democratic primary received the most support (over half), followed by DNC-defined criteria (about one-third support), and lastly support for a strong national party (one-quarter).

The main change that occurred for the Democratic county chairs from 1980 to 1984 was in the expression of increased support for a strong national party. This support has not reached the level found among the Democratic convention delegates, but it moved in a direction of increased consistency between delegates and county chairs. There were roughly similar levels of support for party loyalty tests and DNC-defined criteria for both the delegates and county chairs.

CONCLUSIONS

Changes in party organization (particularly among the Democrats) have incorporated several of the necessary conditions for the responsible party model outlined by the APSA committee (Ranney, 1975; Everson, 1980; Price, 1984). The data discussed here provide little support for the causal influence of these reform measures in increasing party unity and responsibility. While party discipline has increased in the U.S. Congress (particularly since 1980), support for a responsible party system has decreased. Yet, Democratic elites do continue to support increased party centralization. What we do not have data on is the extent to which these shifts and findings are due to actual reassessment of the electoral advantage to certain partisan appeals, or to the important personnel changes from 1980 to 1984.[4] The responsible party model provides some insight into comparative differences between the parties, but there is limited support in the real world for the tenets of the model.

Party elites remain a diverse mix of types in their support for party. In both parties and among all elite cadres, we find that party supporters out-number the nonparty types by at least two to one. It is of note that it is the unreformed Republican party, not the reformed Democratic party, that yielded proportionately more Responsible Party types. From 1980 to 1984, the proportion of Responsible Party types (as we have defined them here) decreased among all four sets of party elites. It was only among the Democrats that we find the local party elites *more* pragmatic (and moderate) than the national party elites. Among both Democrats and Republicans, the conven-tion delegates were relatively more candidate oriented. Finally, while the proportion adopting a Responsible Party orientation decreased from 1980 to 1984, there was an overall increase in support for related measures that would enforce party responsibility over the same time period. This support was considerably higher among the Democrats than among the Republicans at comparable levels of the party.

In the period of our study (1980–1984), we find a Republican party at both national and local levels that is more comfortable than the Democratic party in representing their end of the ideological spectrum. The local Democratic elite cadres are more often pragmatic and moderate compared to their more ideological and liberal national elite cadres. In part, these findings may be a reflection of the Reagan presidency. Yet, these findings are also consonant with the observations that the local Republican party organizations have more often been exclusively concerned with national issues, which are necessarily more ideologically based (Murray and Tedin, 1986:59) and less rooted in local organization, than comparable Democratic parties (Hopkins, 1986:65). It is tempting to speculate that the reform critics preferred the hegemony of the old local Democratic parties because they provided a bulwark against social change. Some intriguing evidence for this can be found in William Crotty's 1981 survey of Chicago ward committee members. Seventy-five per-cent of the Democratic ward committee members were married to full-time homemakers, compared to only 46 percent of the Republican ward committee members—this in an era when only 49.8 percent of all married American women are full-time homemakers and only 45.8 percent of married women with children under eighteen occupy that role (Taeuber and Valdisera, 1986:7). Thus, the underrepresentation of women and blacks in the Democratic party prior to reform probably resulted in a less liberal party (Sullivan et al., 1974:34), while the Republican party comprised a party more fully reflective of its conservative base. To the extent that reform critics have celebrated a pluralist "consensus," it has been an artificial one built on the exclusion of the more liberal elements of the Democratic coalition.

The politicization of contemporary social movements and Democratic party reforms have indeed resulted in a Democratic party more fully representative of its constituent elements. Yet, at base, we find a strong commitment to party among all cadres of contemporary party elites—and certainly little indication of the loss of party regularity assumed by many political scientists. Judged in this light, the postreform party system is in robust health.

NOTES

1. While critics of reform do agree that the reforms were an unnecessary and irrational response by party regulars to the breakdown of consensus, they have diverged in their explanation as to why party leaders chose to acquiesce in their loss of power. Some critics have chosen to treat the reforms as an accident occurring in an emotional context (e.g., Banfield, 1980a; Polsby, 1980), others stress the unintended consequence of Pragmatic Party regulars seeking to appease an unappeasable minority within the party (e.g., Shafer, 1983), while some identify "social engineering" in the manipulation of party rules by frustrated (minority) party activists who cannot influence public opinion or groups (e.g., labor) within the party (e.g., Ranney, 1975:209). Of course, viewing party reform as irrational is made all the easier because there has been no clear philosophy of *contemporary* party reform that articulates the public responsibilities of a political party. Supporters of the reforms (e.g., Bode and Casey, 1980; Crotty, 1983; Crotty and Jackson, 1985) have described the reforms as a practical response to a practical problem. Donald M. Fraser (1980:126) summarizes this view in concluding "that once the legitimacy of the old ways was challenged, the national party had little choice but to acquiesce in a movement toward procedures that were more defensible under the values of a democratic society."

2. While critics (e.g., Kirkpatrick, 1979) stress the role of party rules in causing party decomposition, others (Orren, 1982) conclude that the major causes lie elsewhere (e.g., long-term trends of increasing education, geographic mobility, growth of television, and increased government regulation of parties, for example, FECA). These factors should act on both parties.

3. This question was drawn from John Soule and James Clarke's (1970) original typology of amateurs and professionals.

4. The proportion of female Democratic delegates increased 1 percent (from 49 percent to 50 percent) from 1980 to 1984, female Republican delegates increased 15 percent (29 percent to 44 percent), female Democratic county chairs increased 5 percent (22 percent to 27 percent) and female Republican county chairs 6 percent (20 percent to 26 percent).

8

Representing the Public in Party Politics

PARTY COALITIONS AND LINKAGE IN A DEMOCRATIC SOCIETY

Political parties are described by most party theorists as democratic agencies of collective representation—a mechanism that links elite policy representation to mass preferences (Epstein, 1983; 1986). Not only are political parties the only institution whose function is to aggregate diverse political interests, but parties also represent those who have no other representation (i.e., through their elite position or through interest groups). More generally, the relationship between public opinion and popular government remains one of the more enduring issues in both normative theory and empirical research (e.g., Pateman, 1970; Weissberg, 1976; Luttbeg, 1981).

Representation has many meanings (Pitkin, 1967). We focus in this chapter on the meaning commonly relied on by reform critics: representation of the American public—the shifting mass center of gravity. We defined democracy as liberty for all groups—a definition based on substantive results, rather than democracy as a mechanism or a process of competition for political leadership (e.g., Schumpeter, 1950). Reform critics may well grant us this point and accept that social movements have indeed resulted in a more extensive ideological conflict between the parties. However, the critical question is whether elites, in their reflection of group interests, are insensitive to those *not* an active part of their party coalition. Reform critics have predicted that an increase in amateurs and in ideology will "force an unwanted extremism on the American electorate" (Ceaser, 1980:111). In this chapter we examine in what sense the party elite cadres represent public opinion and, more generally, their responsiveness to it.[1] In doing so, we extend our Party Elite Theory of Democracy from our earlier focus on interest intermediation *within* the party to issues of popular representation.

THE PARTY ELITE THEORY OF DEMOCRACY AND OPINION REPRESENTATION

Our Party Elite Theory of Democracy incorporates three elements pertinent to popular representation (1) the ways in which elites differ from nonelites, (2) the moderating effects of two-party competition, and (3) the
dynamic nature of party conflict and polarization.

Elites Differ from Nonelites

Our Party Elite Theory of Democracy is predicated on a fundamental
distinction between elites and nonelites. First, elites and nonelites are interdependent, yet retain their own independent spheres of action. It is the elites
who decide party organizational policy, write party platforms, and act to
secure the nomination of one of their own for a party office. Traditional party
theory has stressed voting as the primary mechanism through which nonelites
may exercise influence on elite behavior (e.g., Schattschneider, 1942; Key,
1964; 1966). We have stressed social movements as a mechanism through
which nonelites act to secure social change. If nonelites (or the mass public)
do act independently (particularly through their groups), then it is reasonable
to expect mass opinion to be responsive to political events.

Second, elites do share a common background. A common conclusion of
studies of party elites is that, at least in terms of status, profession, educational
background, and income, elites of both parties have more in common with
each other than they do with the mass public (e.g., McClosky et al., 1960;
Kirkpatrick, 1976; Rapoport et al., 1986). These similarities in education,
status, and background have important effects on elite versus nonelite differences. Elite attitudes are considered to be more stable than those of the
mass public (Kinder, 1983:397) and are relatively "constrained" when considered as a belief system (Converse, 1964). Elites thus tend to be more
extreme ideologically and more consistent in their belief systems. This elite-
mass difference was first delineated within the party system by Herbert
McClosky, Paul J. Hoffman, and Rosemary O'Hara in 1960, and has been
replicated in many subsequent studies (Montjoy et al., 1980; Jackson et al.,
1982; Miller and Jennings, 1986). We term this the McClosky distribution.

Elites differ from the mass public as well in their media use. A major
research finding is that the ability to acquire and use information differs
between the elites (generally higher income and better educated) and the
mass public (generally lower income and less educated). Elites are more likely
to rely on multiple media sources for their information and to rely more
heavily on the print media than is true of the mass public (Graber, 1984:136,
145). Compared to the broadcast media, the print media provides more and
more current information. With the *increasing* amount of information now
available, the result is an increasing gap in knowledge between elites and the

mass public (Tichenor et al., 1984). This allows elites, who have access to more information and a greater variety of information, to respond more immediately to changes in government policy. The similarities that elites share in terms of attitudinal constraint, information access, and processing vis-à-vis nonelites results in a secular phenomenon known as elite agenda-setting (Graber, 1984). Thus, we conclude that for some issues, elites, regardless of party, may move in similar directions in response to changes in government policy in advance of the mass public. This effect is probably most pronounced in foreign policy issues, which are relatively remote from the everyday lives of nonelites, and least evident in domestic issue areas, which have more immediate significance for both elites and nonelites through their group memberships.

Party Competition

Fundamental to an understanding of party competition in the United States is the constraint imposed by two-party competition (Downs, 1957; Schlesinger, 1966). As party identifiers are more extreme and less moderate than independents, those seeking to win elections must appeal to a differently constituted electorate in the general election than during the nomination process. Party competition thus tends to moderate party appeals. This represents a moderating effect imposed by party competition. In adapting the Downsian model of two-party competition, we expand this moderating effect to encompass not only public officials and candidates, but those diverse cadres of party elites who recruit and nominate their party candidates.

The Downsian model and Joseph Schlesinger's ambition theory both presume a consensual center to American public opinion—an assumption that we diverge from as well. First, the decline of the third party option has intensified competition between the two parties. Groups have developed closer partisan ties with one party; it is increasingly difficult for groups to "hedge their bets" by working with both parties. And second, recent research challenges the traditional consensual understanding of partisan cleavage at the mass level. Warren E. Miller concludes that shifting party loyalties in the period from 1980 to 1984 (comparable to the period of increased party cohesion at the elite level) provides "the first substantial indications . . . of party realignment along ideological fault lines" (1987:293). Among those entering the electorate in 1964 or more recently, Miller found a realignment of party identification increasingly congruent with prior ideology. That is, conservatives became more Republican in their loyalties, while liberals shifted toward the Democratic party. "All told, among the younger half of the voting populace, 1984 did see a rather massive realignment of party loyalties, which strengthened markedly the association between ideology and partisanship" (Miller, 1987:307). Miller argues that the fact that these potential voters comprise over half of the electorate and that partisanship has risen since 1976

indicate the need for a reconceptualization of partisan identification and undermines the notion of a consensual public (1987:304, 307). Therefore, we
would expect that party competition would *not* lead to convergence (i.e.,
toward a mythical consensus); however, we expect that the party with the
more extreme position would move closer to the shifting mass center to reduce
any competitive disadvantage. We term this mezzotropic opinion change.

The Dynamic Nature of Party Conflict

The fact that economic and social change is continuous, and the capacity
of nonelites to respond behaviorally and attitudinally, provides substantial
fodder for party conflict. We stressed earlier the scope of conflict—the opposition between the privatization versus the socialization of conflict
(Schattschneider, 1975). Yet this does not circumscribe the nature of conflict.
In his classic analysis of the displacement of conflict in politics, E. E.
Schattschneider stresses that *"people must choose among conflicts. In other
words, conflicts compete with each other"* (1975:63). Parties seek power. To
do so, they must define the nature of the "conflict of conflicts," and *"the
definition of the alternatives is the supreme instrument of power"* (Schattschneider,
1975:66; emphasis in original).

These aspects of power and conflict are dynamic. As parties compete with
each other for the electoral success that leads to power, they continuously
seek to substitute submerged conflicts in order to exploit weaknesses in their
opponent's coalition. While the parties may be differentiated along a liberal-
conservative dimension, the search for partisan advantage comprises a constant competition for wider electoral support. Because each party is constrained in its competition by the established loyalties and preferences of
their party identifiers and party activists, partisan cleavage and polarization
is most likely to occur on those issues in which Democratic and Republican
coalitions are most homogeneous within each party and heterogeneous between parties. We term the phenomenom of Democratic and Republican
party elites moving further apart (polarization) as an instance of partisan
opinion change. This is most likely to occur when elites are able to exploit
a weakness and gain a partisan advantage (i.e., when this moves one party
closer to the mass public).

Theoretical Expectations

In this chapter, we examine the closeness of opinion and the change over
time (1980 to 1984) in position of party elite cadres and the mass public,
based on our comprehensive definition of political party elites. This period
is of particular interest to us because it substantially overlaps the period when
the Republican party was turning away from the interests of a social move-

ment—the women's movement—and toward the interests of a political movement—the new right.

Previous research has yielded an incomplete body of knowledge, based as it is on particular election years and limited definitions of party elites. McClosky and his associates (1960) found the Democratic convention delegates of 1956 to be closer to the mass public than were the Republican delegates. A similar study conducted in 1972, following the institution of Democratic reform, found the Democratic delegates to be more out of step with their mass base than was true of the Republican delegates and identifiers (Kirkpatrick, 1976). A study of county chairs in office in 1972 came to the opposite conclusion—that the Republican county chairs were more extreme and out of step than their Democratic counterparts (Montjoy et al., 1980). These results considered in tandem do appear to support the arguments of reform critics, although a study of the 1972 Democratic convention concluded that the group quotas comprised only one factor resulting in the greater liberalism of the 1972 convention, a factor greatly reinforced by the McGovern insurgency, the weakness of the centrist forces in 1972, and the McClosky elite-mass model (Sullivan et al., 1974:34). If Sullivan and his associates are correct, then the resulting more liberal convention would likely have occurred without quotas, while the impact of the quotas was to make the party more fully reflective of its base (i.e., that women tend to be more liberal than men, blacks are more liberal than whites, younger activists are more liberal than older ones).

Ironically, support for Sullivan and his associates' position is provided by the Miller and Jennings (1986) extension of the original Kirkpatrick (1976) study of 1972 convention delegates. Warren Miller and M. Kent Jennings found that it was the *unreformed* Republican party that, by 1980, was seriously out of step with its own rank and file. They conclude that "rules do make a difference, but it is quite clear that additional forces, such as ideology, candidate coalitions, mobilization, and strategies—and perhaps chance—contribute heavily to the nature of mass-elite relationships accompanying the nomination process" (1986:219). As a result, the Ronald Reagan supporters "were as much out of step with their mass supporters as the McGovernites had been with theirs" (Miller and Jennings, 1986:237).

Despite this vast gulf, the Reagan forces were victorious in 1980. Miller and Jennings believe that electoral victory under these circumstances raises concern for representation. After all, both the Goldwater insurgent candidacy in 1964 and the McGovern insurgency resulted in electoral defeat. In this context, Miller and Jennings assume that "mass preferences and behavior change with almost glacial slowness over time" (1986:250). Thus, this "reveals a certain looseness or weakness in the institutional linkage that is supposed to ensure representation of mass demands through the workings of the competitive two-party system" (1986:249).

We believe our comprehensive definition of party elite cadres to be best situated to resolve the contradictions raised by these earlier studies. We include both local (e.g., county and state chairs) and national (e.g., committee members and convention delegates) party elites. Our data cover the period from 1980 to 1984, perhaps a limited period of time, but sufficient, we believe, to assess the capacity for institutional representation of popular preferences. Even more important, the time span under study here is one of dramatic change in government policy presided over by the Reagan administration (as well as party position changes for both the Democrats and Republicans). Domestic policy changes include a consolidation and reduction in social programs, antilabor policies, and a slashing of federal income tax rates with the tax rate now indexed to inflation (Greenstein, 1983). These policy changes have been linked to an increased income inequality (Moon and Sawhill, 1984). Foreign policy changes include the longest stalemate in arms control negotiations with the Soviets in fifteen years—effectively reversing the policy of detente, accompanied by a sharp increase in defense spending (Talbott, 1984).

To what extent have elites (of both parties) and the mass public responded to these changes? While a mezzotropic model of representation would predict the elites furthest away from the mass public moving closer, an elite-agenda setting model of representation would predict that, at least on some foreign policy issues, elites (of both parties) would respond in the same direction in advance of the mass public (who would be slower to perceive changes in government policy). Finally, a partisan model of opinion change would result in an increased polarization between the parties, but one that yields a partisan advantage to one party.

In our analyses, we assume that the Republican and Democratic party elites together with their followers and the mass public will form a continuum of opinion on any given policy issue with the Republicans on the right, the Democrats on the left, and the mass public centrally located (the McClosky distribution). We base our expectations on the mezzotropic opinion model. Those party elite groups further from the mass public's position (or their respective party identifiers' position) on salient policy issues than their equivalent elites in the opposite party will be located (in their expressions of opinion) nearer the mass public's position (and their respective identifiers' position), relative to their counterparts, at some later point in time (our two time points are 1980 and 1984). We find that the agenda-setting model is a credible one for foreign policy issues, but do not offer it in juxtaposition, because we do not judge it to be at variance with the mezzotropic model.

We expect partisan opinion change (with increased partisan polarization) to be confined to a limited subset of issues and to result in a partisan advantage accruing to one party. Our expectations diverge from reform critics. If the two parties have become *too* extremist, then there would be little evidence of mezzotropic opinion change, while partisan opinion change would be evident regardless of issue. It should be clear here that we distinguish between democracy and representation—certainly there may be a representation of issues advocated by a political movement. However, social and political movements and their influence within parties should be subject to the same institutional constraints of two-party competition.

POLICY ISSUES AND OPINION REPRESENTATION, 1980-1984

Our analysis here will focus on five separate policy issues that we measured in both election years and at both the elite and mass level. The opinion items selected for examination are measured using standard National Election Study question design and include items on defense spending, relations with the Soviet Union (detente), government services and spending, affirmative action for minority groups, and government job guarantees. We rely on an analysis of individual issues rather than a summative measure for four reasons. (1) While elites may be relatively consistent on ideology, public opinion at the mass level is quite diverse and may be formed through multiple sources other than deduction from ideological principle (Kinder, 1983). (2) A summary measure, while perhaps useful in highlighting gross ideological changes (e.g., Price, 1984:195–198), masks individual movement on separate issues and policy changes in distinct policy areas (i.e., foreign versus domestic issues). (3) An ideological scale prejudges the question of interest here: the extent to which outlying groups of party elites move to a more favorable position vis-à-vis the mass public. If we used a summary measure, we would be implicitly assuming that parties represent only coherent ideological alternatives, rather than the mezzotropic model that we wish to assume. (4) Finally, the use of a summative measure does not allow for a pure case of elite agenda-setting— in which elites in both parties move in a similar direction. An ideologically based summative measure would mute the elite-mass distinction that is the centerpiece of our design.[2]

The analyses are based on simultaneous relational comparisons of linear position, e.g., comparing the closeness of Democratic county chairs to Democratic identifiers on defense spending *relative* to the closeness of the Republican county chairs to their party identifiers on the same issue. We use the difference of differences in means test (see Table 5.2) to test for simultaneous relative group differences.[3]

Democrats and Republicans on Foreign Policy Issues: 1980-1984

A comparison of opinions on defense-spending in 1980 and 1984 indicates that support for defense spending increases in 1980 had seriously eroded by 1984 (Fig. 8.1). In both years, groups were arranged as expected with Democratic elites on the left (less support for defense spending or support for spending cuts), identifiers and the mass public in the center (in 1980 the

Figure 8.1
Placement of Party Elite Cadres, Identifiers, and the Mass Public on Defense Spending, 1980 and 1984

	1980		1984	
REPUBLICAN DELEGATES	5.7			
REPUBLICAN NATIONAL COMMITTEE				
REPUBLICAN COUNTY CHAIRS	5.6			
Republican Identifiers				
Mass Public	5.2			
Democratic Identifiers	5.0			
			4.8	REPUBLICAN DELEGATES
				REPUBLICAN COUNTY CHAIRS
DEMOCRATIC COUNTY CHAIRS	4.5		4.5	REPUBLICAN NATIONAL COMMITTEE
				Republican Identifiers
DEMOCRATIC NATIONAL COMMITTEE	4.0	-NEUTRAL-	4.0	Mass Public
DEMOCRATIC DELEGATES	3.8			
			3.6	Democratic Identifiers
			3.3	DEMOCRATIC COUNTY CHAIRS
			3.0	DEMOCRATIC NATIONAL COMMITTEE
			2.7	DEMOCRATIC DELEGATES

For this and Figures 8.4 to 8.7, party cadres, identifiers, and the mass public are located based on group means from seven-point Likert items (4 = neutral). Low means correspond to more liberal positions and higher means to more conservative ones.

"center" was for defense spending increases; in 1984 it was neutral), and the Republican elites were on the right (greater levels of defense spending). For all party elite groups, identifiers, and the mass public, there were statistically significant declines in support for defense spending over this period. This movement can be synoptically characterized as one from support for defense increases in 1980 to a neutral position in 1984, with Democrats moving toward a position favoring defense cuts; Republicans toward what is, at best, lukewarm support for further increases; and with the mass public averaging a genuinely neutral position.

This decline in support of defense spending is particularly interesting in comparison to the period from 1978 to 1980.[4] Doris Graber (1984:330) indicates that support for defense spending more than doubled in the two years prior to 1980—probably as a result of televised foreign news. While we have no data as to the source of the consistency of elite and mass responses to the 1980–1984 defense buildup, the strikingly similar responses of party elites and the mass public suggest that both groups were simultaneously responding to similar stimuli, clearly not an instance of elite agenda-setting.

In 1980 the Republican elites were more favorably situated than their Democratic counterparts. The top national party leadership for the Republicans—the national committee members, state chairs, and the national convention delegates—expressed opinions on defense spending closer to those of the mass public than did their Democratic counterparts. The Democratic and Republican local party elites were equidistant from the mass public in their opinions on defense spending.

The configuration of opinion on defense spending remained the same in 1984 as it was in 1980, with the exception of the leftward movement noted above. The Republican national elites' opinions on this issue were closer to the public center of gravity than were the national Democrats, and the local elites were again symmetrically arrayed about the center. However, while the configuration remained the same, the national Democrats moved closer to the mass public than before because they did not collectively move leftward as much as the general public did (Fig. 8.2).[5]

The configuration described above for the mass public also held in separate analyses for party identifiers. In 1980, Republican elite groups were much more in agreement with their followers on defense spending than was true for the Democrats. This still held in 1984, but again with the Democratic elites being more proximate to their identifiers than in 1980 (Figs. 8.2 and 8.3).

The net result of the leftward movement of the party elites and the mass public was that the party elite group (the Democrats) who were positioned unfavorably in 1980, were more favorably situated on the issue of defense spending in 1984, thus supporting the mezzotropic model of representation.

Opinions toward relations with the Soviet Union (detente) were distributed in an unexpected fashion (Fig. 8.4). First, in 1980, the mass public was not located in between the party elites but rather with the Democrats on the left—with Republican party identifiers being to the left of all other groups. In 1984, again unexpectedly, a substantial shift occurred, with the mass public moving from a position indistinguishable from the Democratic elites on the left, to one indistinguishable from the Republicans, slightly to the right of

Figure 8.2
Mezzotropic Change on Five Policy Issues, 1980–1984

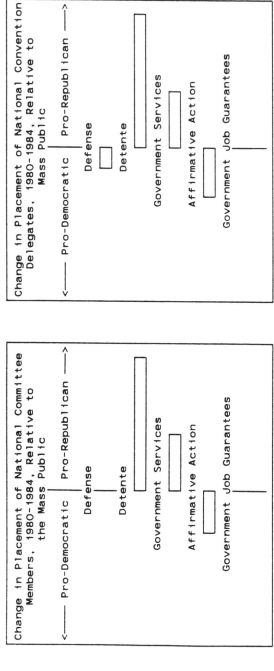

(a)

(b)

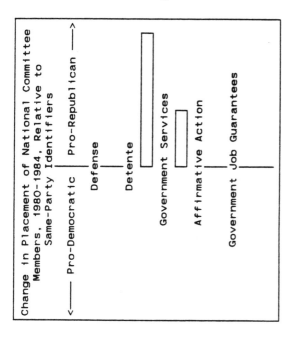

Change in Placement of National Committee
Members, 1980–1984, Relative to
Same-Party Identifiers

<—— Pro-Democratic | Pro-Republican ——>

Defense

Detente

Government Services

Affirmative Action

Government Job Guarantees

(d)

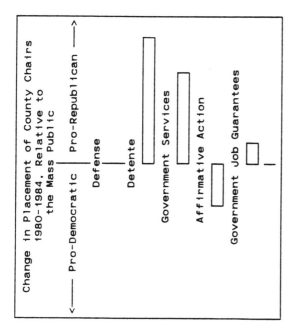

Change in Placement of County Chairs
1980–1984, Relative to
the Mass Public

<—— Pro-Democratic | Pro-Republican ——>

Defense

Detente

Government Services

Affirmative Action

Government Job Guarantees

(c)

Figure 8.3
Mezzotropic Change on Five Policy Issues, 1980–1984

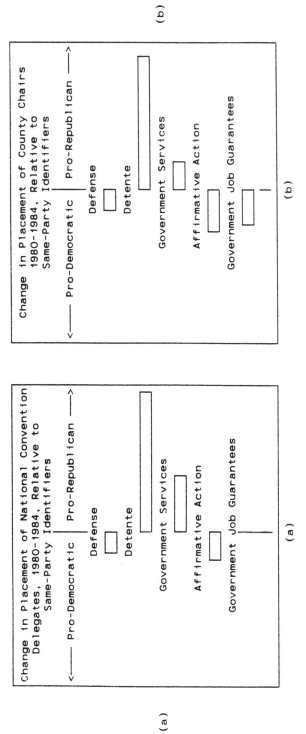

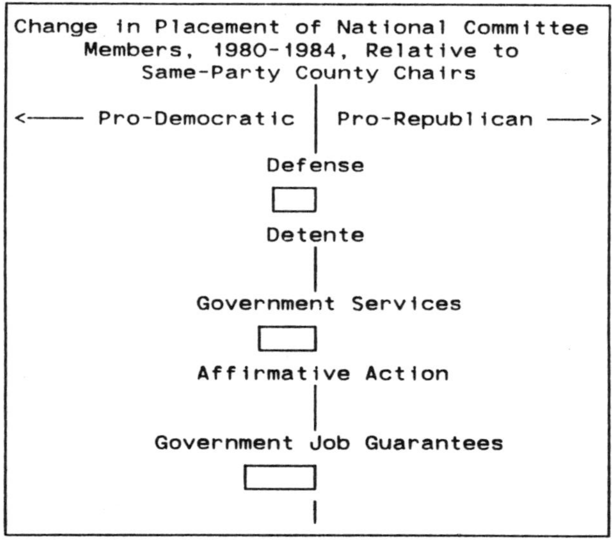

Change in Placement of National Committee Members, 1980-1984, Relative to Same-Party County Chairs

<----- Pro-Democratic | Pro-Republican ----->

Defense

Detente

Government Services

Affirmative Action

Government Job Guarantees

(c)

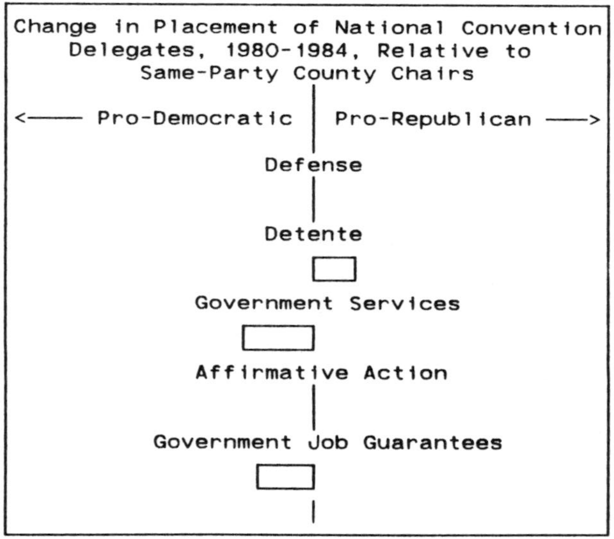

Change in Placement of National Convention Delegates, 1980-1984, Relative to Same-Party County Chairs

<----- Pro-Democratic | Pro-Republican ----->

Defense

Detente

Government Services

Affirmative Action

Government Job Guarantees

(d)

197

Figure 8.4
Placement of Party Elite Cadres, Identifiers, and the Mass Public on Detente,
1980 and 1984

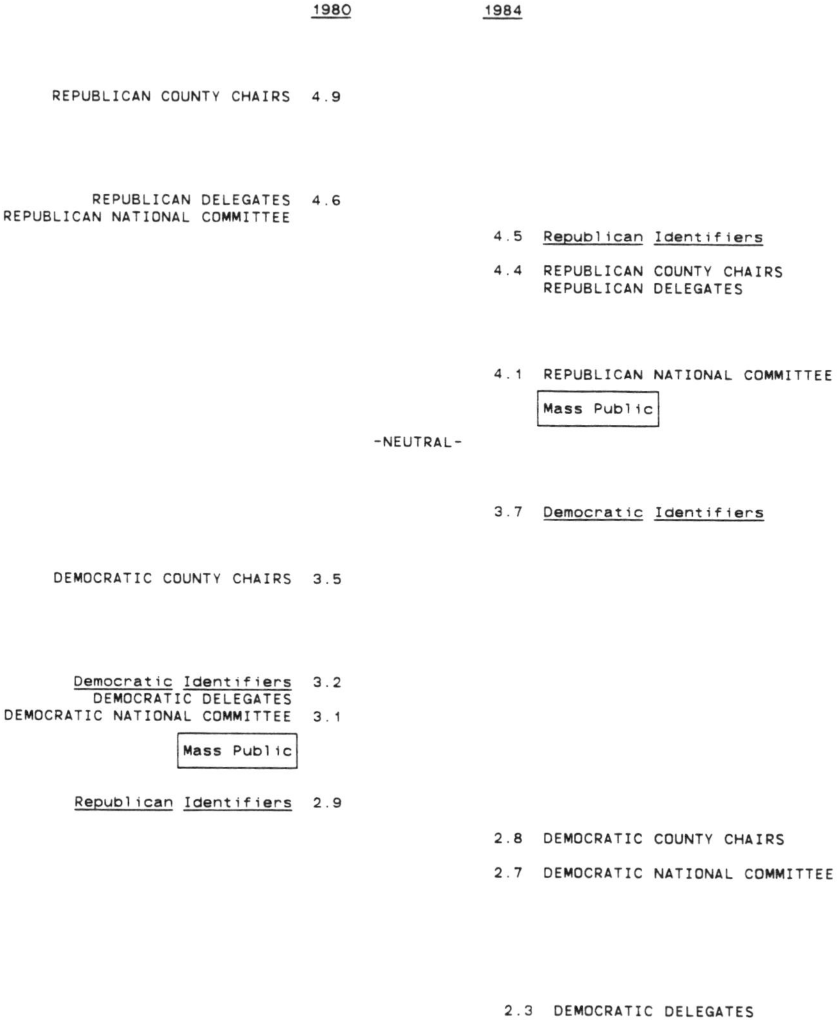

1980   1984

REPUBLICAN COUNTY CHAIRS   4.9

REPUBLICAN DELEGATES   4.6
REPUBLICAN NATIONAL COMMITTEE

                                    4.5   Republican Identifiers

                                    4.4   REPUBLICAN COUNTY CHAIRS
                                          REPUBLICAN DELEGATES

                                    4.1   REPUBLICAN NATIONAL COMMITTEE
                                          | Mass Public |

                    -NEUTRAL-

                                    3.7   Democratic Identifiers

DEMOCRATIC COUNTY CHAIRS   3.5

Democratic Identifiers   3.2
DEMOCRATIC DELEGATES
DEMOCRATIC NATIONAL COMMITTEE   3.1
                    | Mass Public |

Republican Identifiers   2.9

                                    2.8   DEMOCRATIC COUNTY CHAIRS

                                    2.7   DEMOCRATIC NATIONAL COMMITTEE

                                    2.3   DEMOCRATIC DELEGATES

a neutral position. The Republican party identifiers—as a self-identified group—moved from being the anchor group on the left to a similar position on the right. This dramatic change for the Republican identifiers is probably a function of Reagan's appeal to the new right and his attracting evangelicals, or rather televangelicals, especially from the South to the Republican ranks. This is less a change of position on the part of traditional Republicans and more a change of composition among party identifiers. All elite groups—

Democratic and Republican—moved in a leftward direction from 1980 to 1984, while the mass public—including Democratic identifiers—moved in a rightward direction (essentially toward a neutral position on detente). Despite these changes and differences between groups, it should be noted that opinions on relations with the Soviet Union, nonetheless, remain rather restrained and collectively never far from a neutral position.

The finding that the two elite groups move in a similar direction (viz., more favorable toward detente) while the mass public uniformly become less favorable toward detente suggests some elite agenda-setting.While we have no direct evidence here of elite-mass influence, the fact that the elites (who are more informed about foreign policy) were, as a whole, generally more favorable toward better relations with the Soviet Union in 1984 than in 1980 suggests an immediate response by elites to the Reagan administration's reluctance to negotiate an arms treaty in the first term; the opposite movement by the public probably reflects a lagged response to real changes in policy versus supporting arguments for them.

Those elites situated furthest from the public on detente in 1980 (Republican elites) were better situated—in fact, statistically closer to the mass public than the Democrats—in 1984 (see Figs. 8.2 and 8.3). In 1980, the public, and all party identifiers—including Republican ones—were in close proximity with the Democratic elites on opinions toward relations with the Soviet Union. From 1980 to 1984, the Republican and Democratic elites moved in a leftward direction—while the public and all partisan identifiers moved to the right—leaving a configuration with the Republican national elites and local elites more proximate to the public and their identifiers than were comparable Democratic elite groups (the reverse of the 1980 case).

While we found that elites of both parties moved in the same direction (elite agenda-setting), we still found support for our expectation for the mezzotropic model of representation. As with defense spending, the partisan group which was furthest away from the mass public in 1980 moved closer to the mass center of gravity in 1984.

Democrats and Republicans on Domestic Policy Issues: 1980–1984

We now turn to a basic issue of domestic policy: opinions on whether the national government should cut services and spending versus maintaining services (without spending cuts). The party elites and the mass public were again distributed as expected—with the mass public in the center, the Democratic elites on the left, and the Republicans on the right (Fig. 8.5). The Republican elites strongly supported service cuts, the Democratic elites opposed those cuts (except for the county chairs), and the mass public occupied an essentially neutral position. From 1980 to 1984, the national Democratic elites and the Republican identifiers (who had mildly supported cuts) re-

Figure 8.5
Placement of Party Elite Cadres, Identifiers, and the Mass Public on
Maintenance of Government Services, 1980 and 1984

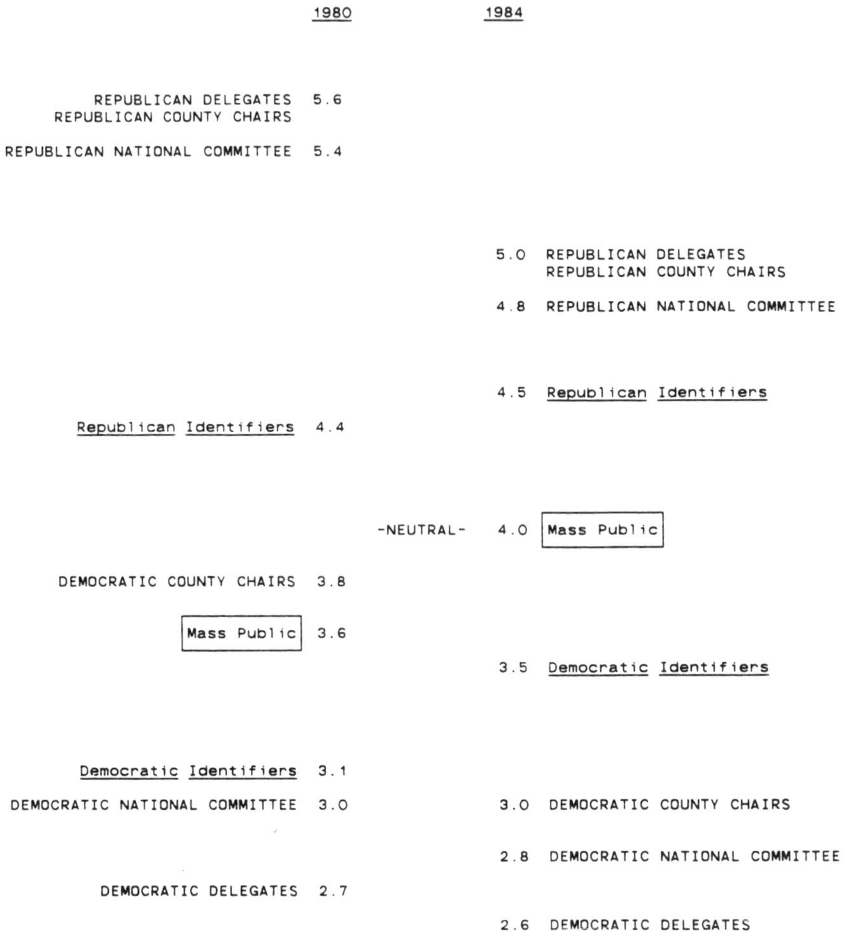

```
                              1980              1984


          REPUBLICAN DELEGATES   5.6
         REPUBLICAN COUNTY CHAIRS

   REPUBLICAN NATIONAL COMMITTEE  5.4



                                         5.0   REPUBLICAN DELEGATES
                                               REPUBLICAN COUNTY CHAIRS

                                         4.8   REPUBLICAN NATIONAL COMMITTEE



                                         4.5   Republican Identifiers

         Republican Identifiers   4.4



                          -NEUTRAL-     4.0  ┌─────────────┐
                                             │ Mass Public │
                                             └─────────────┘
      DEMOCRATIC COUNTY CHAIRS   3.8
              ┌─────────────┐
              │ Mass Public │    3.6
              └─────────────┘
                                         3.5   Democratic Identifiers



         Democratic Identifiers   3.1

  DEMOCRATIC NATIONAL COMMITTEE  3.0     3.0   DEMOCRATIC COUNTY CHAIRS

                                         2.8   DEMOCRATIC NATIONAL COMMITTEE

         DEMOCRATIC DELEGATES   2.7

                                         2.6   DEMOCRATIC DELEGATES
```

'mained unchanged. The elites who had expressed more conservative opinions in 1980—all of the Republican elites and the Democratic county chairs— were less conservative, i.e., were no longer so supportive of (or in actual opposition to) service cuts. The mass public and the Democratic party identifiers in the mass public expressed slightly more conservative opinions in 1984, and the mass public averaged a neutral position on this issue.

Overall, from 1980 to 1984, elites of both parties either remained the same or adopted a more liberal position on the question of cutting services and spending versus maintaining services without cutting spending, while party identifiers and the mass public either remained the same or adopted a more conservative position.

In 1980, the mass public was statistically more proximate to the Democratic elites on this issue. All of the Republican elite groups were enthusiastically supportive of domestic spending cuts while the mass public was slightly to the left of center (maintain services) and the Democratic elites were somewhat to the left of the mass public (except for the Democratic county chairs who were actually slightly to the right of the mass public). The Democratic elite groups were also much closer to their party identifiers relative to the Republicans—whose identifiers were not so enthusiastic about spending cuts as their party leaders.

By 1984, the party elites were situated such that the configuration of party elites was no longer unfavorable to the Republicans, and, in one instance, was actually more favorable to the Republicans relative to the Democrats (see Figs. 8.2 and 8.3). The Republican National Convention delegates expressed opinions on government services more proximate to the mass public than did their Democratic counterparts—with the other elites of each party equidistant from the mass public relative to one another. This same situation held in 1984 with respect to party identifiers as well, i.e., Republican convention delegates were more in step with their identifiers on this issue than Democratic convention delegates with theirs, but with all other party elites being equally distant (left or right) from their respective identifiers. On the issue of spending versus services, we again find support for the mezzotropic model of opinion change, even while elites of both parties tend to move in the same direction when compared to the mass public.

In both 1980 and 1984, opinions of the party elites on affirmative action (for minority groups) were distributed about the mass public, left and right (Fig. 8.6). The national Democratic elites and one element of the national Republican leadership (RNC and state chairs) did not change from 1980 to 1984 on this issue, the remaining Republican elites became slightly more conservative, and all other groups expressed less conservative opinions. In 1980 and 1984, there was little support for affirmative action, with only national Democratic party elites expressing support for government help for minority groups. The mass public averaged lukewarm opposition in 1980 and an essentially neutral position in 1984.

This was the one policy issue that we examined where Republican party elites changed in a more conservative direction from 1980 to 1984. From 1980 to 1984, the Democratic party elites and the mass public moved in the same direction—toward a more liberal position on the government responsibility toward minority groups. The divergent movement of Republican and Democratic party elites suggests that the issue of affirmative action became more of a defining partisan issue over the four year period and one, of course, consonant with our earlier arguments about social movements and party reforms.

Figure 8.6
Placement of Party Elite Cadres, Identifiers, and the Mass Public on
Government Help for Minority Groups, 1980 and 1984

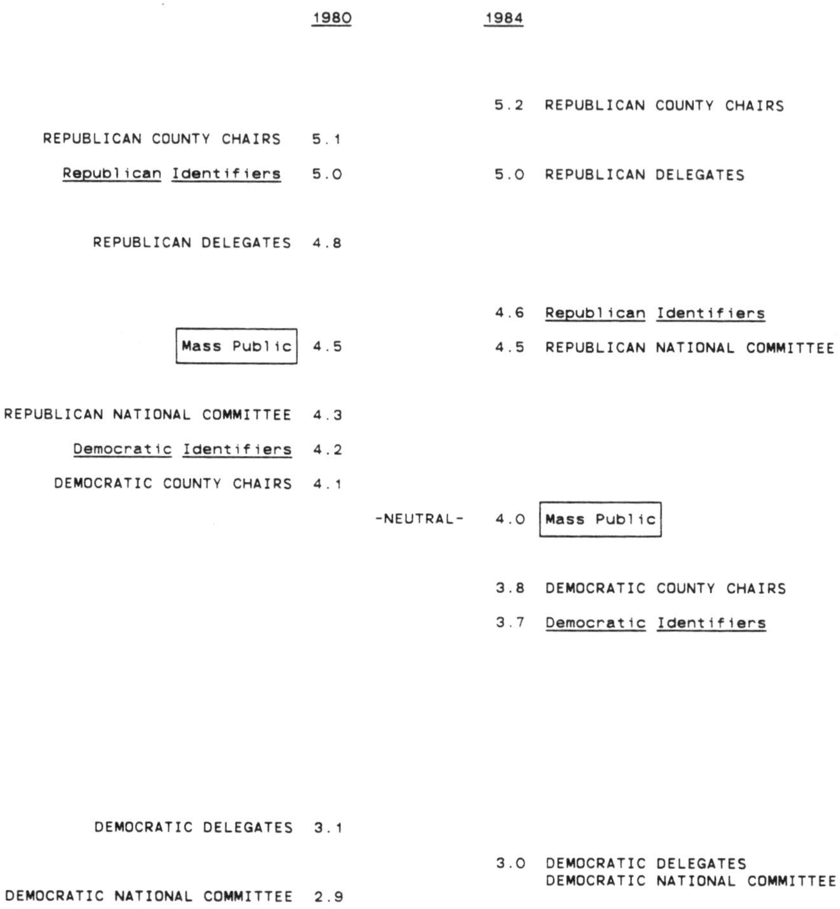

```
                        1980                    1984


                                        5.2   REPUBLICAN COUNTY CHAIRS

 REPUBLICAN COUNTY CHAIRS    5.1

    Republican Identifiers   5.0        5.0   REPUBLICAN DELEGATES


    REPUBLICAN DELEGATES      4.8


                                        4.6   Republican Identifiers

              Mass Public     4.5       4.5   REPUBLICAN NATIONAL COMMITTEE


 REPUBLICAN NATIONAL COMMITTEE  4.3
       Democratic Identifiers   4.2
    DEMOCRATIC COUNTY CHAIRS     4.1

                     -NEUTRAL-  4.0     Mass Public


                                        3.8   DEMOCRATIC COUNTY CHAIRS

                                        3.7   Democratic Identifiers




    DEMOCRATIC DELEGATES      3.1

                                        3.0   DEMOCRATIC DELEGATES
                                              DEMOCRATIC NATIONAL COMMITTEE
 DEMOCRATIC NATIONAL COMMITTEE  2.9
```

The national Republican party elites were closer to the mass public and their identifiers on this issue than were their Democratic counterparts in 1980. The local party elites were situated similarly to one another relative to the mass public and their identifiers on government help. Changes from 1980 to 1984 found the Democratic elites more optimally situated with respect to the mass public (vis-à-vis comparable Republican groups) and their identifiers on this issue. Republican National Committee members and state chairs remained closer to the mass public and their identifiers than their Democratic counterparts—as they were in 1980. This was primarily because the RNC members expressed the least conservative opinions on this issue of all Republican elite groups. The Democratic National Convention delegates were symmetrically opposite from their Republican reference group in 1984, after being further from the mass public (and their identifiers) relative to the RNC in 1980. Finally, the Democratic county chairs were closer to their identifiers and the mass public than were the comparable Republican elites in 1984. Again, as expected, the elite groups most distant from the mass public in 1980, relative to their opponents, find themselves nearer in 1984.

While the affirmative action issue became one of increased partisan definition from 1980 to 1984, the net result of the increased conflict over the issue was to benefit the Democrats (see Figs. 8.2 and 8.3). In 1984, the Democratic party elites were situated more favorably than they were in 1980. Consistent with our model of partisan opinion change, the mass public moved in a more liberal direction consonant with the Democrats—with the result that the Democratic elites were significantly closer in 1984 as a result.

On the issue of (federal) government job guarantees (Fig. 8.7), Republican and Democratic party elites, identifiers, and the mass public were arrayed from left to right, as expected, in 1980 and 1984. There was a slight change from 1980 to 1984 toward the center (i.e., leftward). The Republicans (elites and identifiers) were opposed to government job guarantees; the mass public, local Democratic elites, and Democratic identifiers averaged positions around the neutral position; and the national Democratic elites generally favored government job guarantees.

As the only party group showing any substantial change, the Democratic county chairs moved from opposition in 1980 to a more neutral position comparable to Democratic identifiers in 1984.

The configuration of groups on this issue favored the Democratic elites in 1980 with all Democratic elite groups being relatively closer to the mass public and their party identifiers than were their Republican counterparts. This was again true in 1984, but with the Republican elite groups—except the national convention delegates—being more favorably situated than in 1980, and the RNC and state chair group was actually as close to the mass public and their identifiers as was the DNC and state chair group. The change from 1980 to 1984 (see Figs. 8.2 and 8.3) was thus in a direction consistent with our expectations except, for the Republican delegates. The Republican delegates moved, albeit very little, toward the center (as expected) but the public moved faster, such that, the Republican delegates were actually less proximate to the mass public and their identifiers relative to the Democratic delegates in 1984 than in 1980. This was the only instance where we observed responses contrary to our expectations on the relative movements of elites over time based on the mezzotropic representation model.

PARTY ELITE CADRES AND MEZZOTROPIC OPINION CHANGE

Our analysis provides evidence of the continuing role of parties (and elite cadres) as mediating (and moderating) institutions in a two-party system. We

Figure 8.7
Placement of Party Elite Cadres, Identifiers, and the Mass Public on
Government Job Guarantees, 1980 and 1984

1980   1984

REPUBLICAN DELEGATES   6.1

REPUBLICAN COUNTY CHAIRS   6.0
REPUBLICAN NATIONAL COMMITTEE

                              5.9   REPUBLICAN DELEGATES

                              5.8   REPUBLICAN COUNTY CHAIRS

                              5.5   REPUBLICAN NATIONAL COMMITTEE

Republican Identifiers   5.0

                              4.7   Republican Identifiers

DEMOCRATIC COUNTY CHAIRS   4.5

                Mass Public   4.3

                              4.2   Mass Public

                   -NEUTRAL-

Democratic Identifiers   3.8   3.8   DEMOCRATIC COUNTY CHAIRS

                                   3.7   Democratic Identifiers

DEMOCRATIC NATIONAL COMMITTEE   3.4

DEMOCRATIC DELEGATES   3.2   3.2   DEMOCRATIC NATIONAL COMMITTEE

                                   3.1   DEMOCRATIC DELEGATES

find substantial evidence of the movement of elites of both parties toward
the shifting mass center of gravity—in a direction to reduce any real (or
perceived) disadvantage in opinion representation. This movement left the
Republicans somewhat better situated in 1984 than in 1980 relative to the
Democrats. In 1980, all three cadres of Democratic party elites were significantly closer to the mass public and their own identifiers on three of the five
issues (detente, job guarantees, and government services). By 1984, the Republican party elites had moved to reduce their disadvantage on these same
three issues by reducing their distance from the mass public relative to the

Democrats. We observed a similar movement by Democratic party elites on the two issues (defense spending, aid to minorities) that favored the Republicans in 1980.

Second, we found considerable differences across individual issues. On two issues (detente and government services), we found evidence that opinion change over time found elites of both parties moving *in the same direction*, while the mass public either did not change or moved in the opposite direction. On some issues, then, there is a secular movement of elite opinion (or elite agenda-setting) that may occur alongside the mediating role of party elites in articulating public opinion as expected. On only one issue—aid to minorities—did we find evidence of increasing partisan definition (i.e., elites of different parties moving in opposite directions) and polarization. While our results indicate an overall advantage to the Republican party, it was an advantage that accrued primarily through decreasing distance from the public (relative to the Democrats), *not* through heightened partisanship. On the one issue (detente) in which Republican cadres were significantly closer to the mass public in 1984—after being significantly more distant in 1980—the flip-flop in party representation occurred not through increased partisan definition (elites of both parties became more liberal on this issue), but because the public soured on good relations with the Soviet Union. These results indicate that an increasingly ideology-based party system is not necessarily incompatible with representation of public opinion.

NOTES

1. We wish to note the contributions of John S. Jackson III to this chapter, both as the senior member of the Party Elite Study and, more important, as a keen observer and supporter of party reform.

2. There have been a number of different approaches used in analyzing elite-mass representational issues. McClosky and his associates employed what they termed support ratios (1960:408–410). Philip Converse and Roy Pierce (1986) use and defend correlation coefficients as proximity measures in making elite-mass comparisons. Miller and Jennings (1986:199–200) also employ correlation techniques. We employ a visual approach suggested by Edward Tufte (1983:158–159). In our figures, we visually display the means of both elite and mass groups, over time and with the names of the groups spaced in proportion to one another. Tufte writes of this approach, "the information shown is both integrated and separated: integrated through its connected content, separated in that the eye follows several different and uncluttered paths in looking over the data . . . " (1983:159). We suggest that this approach conveys more information than correlation techniques, which inevitably involve some loss of information.

3. In our discussions, reference to a group difference or a multigroup relational difference indicates that it is a statistically significant relationship at the 5 percent level. No difference (or equidistance from a single or dual central reference point) indicates otherwise. In these analyses, missing data were negligible for the elite samples. Group sizes for the mass public vary by issue from 1,028 to 1,944, group sizes

for the Democratic party identifiers vary by issue from 518 to 925, and the comparable figures for the Republicans are 380 and 802.

4. We examined self-identified ideology in 1980 and 1984 and found that the Democratic elites are divided between self-identified liberals and moderates with moderates being the more numerous. Republicans identified themselves mostly as conservatives with a minority of moderates. The mass public fell between the two with moderate being the modal self-identification and conservative more popular than liberal. This distribution remained essentially unchanged from 1980 to 1984. These self-characterizations do not correspond particularly well with issue positions, and, in fact, the over-time changes run counter to issue changes over time.

5. The analysis in Figures 8.2 and 8.3 is based on the group means presented in Figures 8.1 and 8.4 to 8.8. See Table 5.2 for the general form of the hypotheses used in the t-test analysis. There were twenty-nine statistically significant instances of relevant position change from 1980 to 1984—all in a mezzotropic direction.

APPENDIX A

Group Comparisons on Age, Gender, Race, and Education: 1980–1984

	AGE (Years)		% FEMALE		% BLACK		EDUCATION (Years)	
	1980	1984	1980	1984	1980	1984	1980	1984
DNC & State Chairs	49.3	50.6	50.0	50.0	7.6	7.3	----	16.7
Dem. Delegates	43.0	43.0	49.0	50.0	9.6	10.4	----	16.7
Dem. County Chairs	48.0	47.8	23.8	27.3	1.7	4.1	----	15.8
Dem. Identifiers	45.7	45.0	59.9	58.2	18.1	17.9	11.9	12.1
Mass Public	44.6	44.4	56.9	56.2	11.6	11.1	12.2	12.3
GOP Identifiers	45.4	44.8	55.0	53.8	2.8	2.7	12.9	12.8
GOP County Chairs	49.7	50.6	20.4	25.8	0.6	0.6	----	15.4
GOP Delegates	48.2	50.4	29.0	44.0	1.0	2.7	----	15.9
RNC & State Chairs	52.2	51.1	36.8	36.6	2.3	0.0	----	16.3

We do not have 1980 average education for elite groups since we observed only categorical information that year.

APPENDIX B

Sampling Information and Return Rates

The Party Elite Study is a research project on the elite cadres in the two major parties dating from 1974. The principal investigator is John S. Jackson III of Southern Illinois University at Carbondale. Barbara L. Brown was coinvestigator in 1980, and the authors were coinvestigators in 1984. During the period 1980–1984 various funds were provided by the National Science Foundation, Southern Illinois University at Carbondale, Hobart and William Smith Colleges in Geneva, New York, and the George Washington University in Washington, D.C.

The sample populations for this study included all those holding official party offices in the summers of 1980 and 1984. The RNC and the DNC provided official party lists of all delegates to their respective party conventions along with lists of RNC and DNC members and state party chairpersons. The RNC was also able to provide an official list of all of their county chairs. The DNC had no such list, and in consequence, the authors assembled this list by contacting each state party and requesting a list of their county chairs. This proved to be a tedious process, but all of the state Democratic parties eventually complied except Alaska (which technically does not have counties) and Nebraska. Accordingly, the overall county chair list for the Democrats was deficient for those two states.

For the national convention delegates of both parties, a systematic random sample was drawn from the official party lists. This procedure was also repeated for all of the county chairs once those lists were available. The entire population of RNC and DNC members and state party chairs was included in the study.

Those elites sampled were mailed questionnaires with a cover letter explaining the nature of the survey and requesting cooperation. The questionnaires were mailed (first wave) to all party groups in the two week period following their respective national conventions. The Democrats met in New York in mid-August 1980 and in San Francisco in mid-July 1984. The Republicans met in Detroit in mid-July 1980 and in Dallas in mid-August 1984. In September and October 1980 and 1984 a second mailing was sent to all those who had not yet responded and the survey was complete by election day each year.

Statistical tests have been performed to check the representativeness of our samples where we had known population characteristics available to us. The parameters included age, sex, and, for the delegates, how they were selected. Our tests yielded unsatisfactory results in only one instance. Our sample of Democratic delegates in 1984 contained too high a proportion of women. In an effort to understand this disparity, we examined other available information about our sample and population, and believe that the cause of this disparity lies with the superdelegates. The *ex officio* delegates were underrepresented in our sample though not to a statistically significant degree (one-tail test, $Z = 1.56$). 14 percent of the population of 1984 Democratic delegates were *ex officio* while only 11 percent of our sample was selected thusly. This imbalance occurred because the superdelegates were overwhelmingly male (75 percent to 25 percent; source: the Democratic National Committee). The gender division at the 1984 Democratic Convention was Fifty-Fifty (as mandated by party rules), but the division of those selected by means other than their *ex officio* status was actually 54 percent female and 46 percent male. With this division, our sample was satisfactorily representative (in a statistical sense, i.e., the null hypothesis that our sample came from the given population could not be rejected; one-tail test, $Z = 1.17$). We believe that the lower response rate for the superdelegates is not systematically related to anything other than gender and primarily reflects the fact that prominent public figures are less likely to respond to a mail survey than the less visible elites.

DEMOCRATS

	Completed Questionnaires 1980 (N)	Completed Questionnaires 1984 (N)	Mailed Questionnaires 1980 (N)	Mailed Questionnaires 1984 (N)	Return Rate 1980 %	Return Rate 1984 %
Convention Delegates	497	470	1085	986	46	48
County Chairs	535	619	951	1160	56	53
State Chairs	27	15	50	50	54	30
National Committee	110	95	247	247	45	38
Totals	1169	1199	2333	2440	50	49

REPUBLICANS

	Completed Questionnaires 1980 (N)	Completed Questionnaires 1984 (N)	Mailed Questionnaires 1980 (N)	Mailed Questionnaires 1984 (N)	Return Rate 1980 %	Return Rate 1984 %
Convention Delegates	509	566	1003	1020	51	51
County Chairs	551	473	1137	860	48	55
State Chairs	35	21	50	50	70	42
National Committee	55	50	107	145	51	34
Totals	1150	1110	2297	2173	50	51

References

Abramowitz, Alan I., and Walter J. Stone. 1984. *Nomination Politics*. New York: Praeger.

Abzug, Bella, and Mim Kelber. 1984. *Gender Gap: Bella Abzug's Guide to Political Power for American Women*. Boston: Houghton Mifflin.

Adamany, David. 1975. "Introduction." In *The Semisovereign People*, by E. E. Schattschneider, pp. ix–xxxi. Hinsdale, Ill.: The Dryden Press.

Alinsky, Saul. 1969. *Reveille for Radicals*. New York: Vintage Books.

———. 1972. *Rules for Radicals: A Pragmatic Primer for Realistic Radicals*. New York: Vintage Books.

APSA Committee on Political Parties. 1950. "Toward a More Responsible Party System." *American Political Science Review* 44 (Supplement).

Arendt, Hannah. 1954. *The Origins of Totalitarianism*. New York: Harcourt, Brace Jovanovich, Inc.

Arterton, G. Christopher. 1982. "Political Money and Political Strength." In *The Future of American Political Parties*, edited by Joel L. Fleishman, pp. 101–139. Englewood Cliffs, N.J.: Prentice-Hall.

Asher, Herbert B. 1983. "Voting Behavior Research in the 1980s: An Examination of Some Old and New Problem Areas." In *Political Science: The State of the Discipline*, edited by Ada W. Finifter, pp. 339–388. Washington, D.C.: The American Political Science Association.

Bachrach, Peter. 1966. *The Theory of Democratic Elitism*. Boston: Little, Brown & Co. Inc.

Baer, Denise L., and John S. Jackson III. 1985. "Are Women Really More Amateur in Politics Than Men?" *Women and Politics*, 5: 79–92.

Banfield, Edward C. 1980a. "Party 'Reform' in Retrospect." In *Political Parties in the Eighties*, edited by Robert M. Goldwin, pp. 20–33. Washington, D.C.: American Enterprise Institute.

———. 1980b. "In Defense of the American Party System." In *Political Parties in the Eighties*, edited by Robert A. Goldwin, pp. 133–149. Washington, D.C.: American Enterprise Institute.

Baxter, Sandra, and Marjorie Lansing. 1984. *Women and Politics: The Invisible Majority*, 2nd ed. Ann Arbor, Mich.: University of Michigan Press.

Benson, Peter L., and Dorothy L. Williams. 1982. *Religion on Capitol Hill: Myths and Realities.* New York: Harper & Row, Publishers Inc.

Berelson, Bernard R., Paul F. Lazarsfeld, and William N. McPhee. 1954. *Voting.* Chicago: University of Chicago Press.

Berry, Jeffrey. 1984. *Interest Group Society.* Boston: Little, Brown & Co., Inc.

Bibby, John F., Cornelius P. Cotter, James L. Gibson, and Robert J. Huckshorn. 1983. "Parties in State Politics." In *Politics in the American States: A Comparative Analysis,* 4th ed., edited by Virginia Gray, Herbert Jacob, and Kenneth N. Vines, Chapter 3. Boston: Little, Brown & Co. Inc.

Blalock, Hubert M., Jr. 1979. *Social Statistics,* 2nd ed., rev. New York: McGraw-Hill Inc.

Blumberg, Rhoda L. 1980. "White Mothers in the American Civil Rights Movement." In *Research in the Interweave of Social Roles: Women and Men,* edited by Helen Z. Lopata, pp. 33–50. Greenwich, Conn.: JAI Press.

Blumenthal, Sidney. 1982. *The Permanent Campaign,* rev. ed. New York: Touchstone.

Bode, Kenneth A., and Carol F. Casey. 1980. "Party Reform: Revisionism Revisited." In *Political Parties in the Eighties,* edited by Robert A. Goldwin, pp. 3–19. Washington, D.C.: American Enterprise Institute.

Broder, David. 1971. *The Party's Over.* New York: Harper & Row, Publishers Inc.

Bromley, David G., and Anson D. Shupe, Jr. 1983. "Repression and the Decline of Social Movements: The Case of the New Religions." In *Social Movements of the Sixties and Seventies,* edited by Jo Freeeman, pp. 335–347. New York: Longman.

Burnham, Walter D. 1969. "The End of American Party Politics." *Transaction* 7: 12–22.

———. 1970. *Critical Elections and the Mainsprings of American Party Politics.* New York: W.W. Norton & Co. Inc.

———. 1982. *The Current Crisis in American Politics.* New York: Oxford University Press.

———. 1985. "The 1984 Election and the Future of American Politics." In *Election 84,* edited by Ellis Sandoz and Cecil V. Crabb, Jr., pp. 204–260. New York: Mentor.

Burton, Michael G., and John Higley. 1987. "Invitation to Elite Theory: The Basic Contentions Reconsidered." In *Power Elites and Organizations,* edited by G. William Domhoff and Thomas R. Dye, pp. 219–238. Beverly Hills: Sage.

Campbell, Angus, Philip E. Converse, Warren E. Miller, and Donald E. Stokes. 1960. *The American Voter.* New York: John Wiley & Sons Inc.

Campbell, Bruce A., and Richard J. Trilling. 1979. *Realignment in American Politics: Toward a Theory.* Austin, Tex.: University of Texas Press.

Cantor, Joseph. 1979. "Single Issue Politics in the United States." *Report No. 79–151.* Washington, D.C.: Congressional Research Service (The Library of Congress).

Cardwell, Jerry D. 1984. *Mass Media Christianity: Televangelism and the Great Commission.* New York: University Press of America.

Carmines, Edward G., and James A. Stimson. 1984. "The Dynamics of Issue Evolution." In *Electoral Change in Industrial Democracies,* edited by Russel Dalton, Paul Allen Beck, and Scott Flanagan, pp. 134–158. Princeton, N.J.: Princeton University Press.

Ceaser, James W. 1980. "Political Change and Party Reform." In *Political Parties in the Eighties*, edited by Robert M. Golwin, pp. 97–115. Washington, D.C.: American Enterprise Institute.

———. 1982. *Reforming the Reforms*. Cambridge, Mass.: Ballinger.

Chafe, William. 1977. *Women and Equality: Changing Patterns in American Culture*. New York: Oxford University Press.

Chambers, William N. 1967. "Party Development and The American Mainstream." In *The American Party System: Stages of Political Development*, edited by William N. Chambers and Walter D. Burnham, pp. 3–32. New York: Oxford University Press.

Cigler, Allan J., and John M. Hansen. 1983. "Group Formation Through Protest: The American Agriculture Movement." In *Interest Group Politics*, edited by Allan J. Cigler and Burdett A. Loomis, pp. 84–109. Washington, D.C.: CQ Press.

Clark, Peter B., and James Q. Wilson. 1961. "Incentive Systems: A Theory of Organizations." *Administrative Science Quarterly*, 6: 129–166.

Clausen, Aage R. 1973. *How Congressmen Decide*. New York: St. Martin's Press.

Conlan, Timothy, Ann Martino, and Robert Dilger. 1984. "State Parties in the 1980s: Adaption, Resurgence and Continuing Constraints." *Intergovernmental Perspective* 10: 6–13.

Converse, Philip E. 1964. The Nature of Belief Systems in Mass Publics. In *Ideology and Discontent*, edited by David E. Apter, pp. 206–261. New York: The Free Press.

———. 1976. *The Dynamics of Party Support: Cohort Analyzing Party Identification*. Beverly Hills: Sage.

Converse, Philip E., and George Dupeux. 1966. "The Politicization of the Electorate in France and the United States." In *Elections and the Political Order*, edited by Angus Campbell, Philip Converse, Warren Miller and Donald Stokes, pp. 269–291. New York: John Wiley & Sons.

Converse, Philip, and Roy Pierce. 1986. *Political Representation in France*. Cambridge, Mass: Harvard University Press.

Conway, Margaret M. 1985. *Political Participation in the United States*. Washington, D.C.: CQ Press.

Conway, Margaret M., and Frank B. Feigert. 1968. "Motivation, Incentive Systems and the Political Party Organization." *American Political Science Review*, 62: 1169–1183.

Cook, Timothy E. 1986. "The Electoral Connection in the 99th Congress." *PS*, 19: 16–22.

Cooper, Joseph, and Louis Maisel. 1978. "Problems and Trends in Party Research: An Overview." In *Political Parties: Development and Decay*, edited by Louis Maisel and Joseph Cooper, pp. 7–30. Beverly Hills, Sage.

Costain, Anne N. 1982. "Representing Women: The Transition from Social Movement to Interest Group." In *Women, Power and Policy*, edited by Ellen Boneparth, pp. 19–37. New York: Pergamon.

Cotter, Cornelius P. 1986. "A Book Review of Xandra Kayden and Eddie Mahe, Jr., *The Party Goes on: The Persistence of the Two-Party System in United States*." *American Political Science Review* 80: 671–673.

Cotter, Cornelius P., and John F. Bibby. 1980. "Institutional Development and the Thesis of Party Decline." *Political Science Quarterly* 95: 1–27.

Cotter, Cornelius P., James L. Gibson, John F. Bibby, and Robert J. Huckshorn. 1984. *Party Organizations in American Politics. New York: Praeger.*

Cotter, Cornelius P., and Bernard Hennessy. 1964. *Politics without Power.* New York: Atherton Press.

Crotty, William J. 1967. "The Social Attributes of Party Organizational Activists in a Transitional Political System." *Western Political Quarterly* 20: 669–681.

————. ed. 1968. *Approaches to the Study of Party Organization.* Boston: Allyn & Bacon.

————. 1971. "Party Effort and Its Impact on the Vote." *American Political Science Review* 65: 439–450.

————. 1977. *Political Reform and the American Experiment.* New York: Harper & Row, Publishers Inc.

————. 1978. *Decision for the Democrats.* Baltimore, Md.: Johns Hopkins University Press.

————. 1980. *The Party Symbol: Readings on Political Parties.* San Francisco: W.H. Freeman & Co. Publishers.

————. 1983. *Party Reform.* New York: Longman.

————. 1985. *The Party Game.* San Francisco: W.H. Freeman & Co. Publishers.

————. 1986. "Local Parties in Chicago: The Machine in Transition." In *Political Parties in Local Areas*, edited by William J. Crotty, pp. 157–196. Knoxville: The University of Tennessee Press.

Crotty, William J., and John S. Jackson III. 1985. *Presidential Primaries and Nominations.* Washington, D.C.: CQ Press.

Crotty, William, and Gary C. Jacobson. 1984. *American Parties in Decline, 2nd ed. Boston: Little Brown & Co. Inc.*

Cutright, Phillip, and Peter Rossi. 1958. "Grass Roots Politicians And The Vote." *American Sociological Review* 64: 171–79.

Dahl, Robert A. 1961a. "The Behavioral Approach in Political Science: Epitaph for a Monument to a Successful Protest." *American Political Science Review* 55: 763–772.

————. 1961b. *Who Governs?* New Haven, Conn.: Yale University Press.

David, Paul T., Ralph Goldman, and Richard C. Bain. 1960. *The Politics of National Nominating Conventions.* Washington, D.C.: Brookings.

Dennis, Jack. 1975. "Trends in Public Support for the American Party System." *British Journal of Political Science 5: 187–230.*

Diamond, Irene. 1977. *Sex Roles in the State House.* New Haven, Conn.: Yale University Press.

Di Bianchi, Suzanne M., and Daphne Spaine. 1983. *American Women: Three Decades of Change. Special Demographic Analyses, CDS–80–8.* Washington, D.C.: U.S. Bureau of the Census.

Downs, Anthony. 1957. *An Economic Theory of Democracy.* New York: Harper & Row, Publishers Inc.

Duverger, Maurice. 1954. *Political Parties.* New York: John Wiley & Sons Inc.

Dwyer, Lynn E. 1983. "Structure and Strategy in the Antinuclear Movement." In *Social Movements of the Sixties and Seventies*, edited by Jo Freeman, pp.148–161. New York: Longman.

Edsall, Thomas Byrne. 1984. *The New Politics of Inequality*. New York: W. W. Norton & Co. Inc.

Edwards, Richard, and Michael Podgursky. 1986. "The Unraveling Accord: America Unions in Crisis." In *Unions in Crisis and Beyond*, edited by Richard Edwards, Paolo Garonna, and Franz Todtling, pp. 14–60. Dover, Mass.: Auburn House Publishing Co.

Ehrenhalt, Alan. 1987. "Changing South Perils Conservative Coalition." *CQ Weekly Report* 45: 1699–1705.

Ehrenreich, Barbara. 1984. *The Hearts of Men*. Garden City, N.Y.: Anchor Books.

Eisenstadt, Sigmund N. 1965. *From Generation to Generation*. Glencoe, Ill.: The Free Press.

Eldersveld, Samuel. 1964. *Political Parties: A Behavioral Analysis*. Chicago: Rand McNally.

———. 1982. *Political Parties in American Society*. New York: Basic Books Inc., Publishers.

———. 1986. "The Party Activist in Detroit and Los Angeles: A Longitudinal View," 1956–1980. In *Political Parties in Local Areas*, edited by William J. Crotty, pp. 89–120. Knoxville, Tenn.: University of Tennesee Press.

Epstein, Leon D. 1967. *Political Parties in Western Democracies*. New York: Praeger.

———. 1983. "The Scholarly Commitment to Parties." In *Political Science: The State of the Discipline*, edited by Ada Finifter, pp. 127–153. Washington, D.C.: American Political Science Association.

———. 1986. *Political Parties in the American Mold*. Madison, Wisc.: University of Wisconsin Press.

Evans, Sara. 1980. *Personal Politics*. New York: Vintage Books.

Everson, David H. 1980. *American Political Parties*. New York: Franklin Watts.

———. 1982. "The Decline of Political Parties." In *The Communication Revolution in Politics*, edited by Gerald Benjamin, pp. 49–60. New York: Academy of Political Science.

Fenno, Richard F., Jr. 1978. *Home Style: House Members in Their Districts*. Boston: Little, Brown & Co. Inc.

Fiorina, Morris. 1980. "The Decline of Collective Responsibility in American Politics." *Daedalus* 105: 25–45.

Francis, John G., and Robert C. Benedict. 1986. "Issue Group Activists at the Conventions." In *The Life of the Parties: Activists in Presidential Politics*, edited by Ronald B. Rapoport, Alan I. Abramowitz, and John McGlennon, pp. 99–125. Lexington, Ky.: The University of Kentucky Press.

Frantzich, Stephen. 1986. "Republicanizing the Parties: The Rise of the Service-Vendor Party." Paper presented at the Annual Meeting of the Midwest Political Science Association, Chicago, Ill.

Fraser, Donald M. 1980. "Democratizing the Democratic Party." In *Political Parties in the Eighties*, edited by Robert M. Goldwin, pp. 116–132. Washington, D.C.: American Enterprise Institute.

Freeman, Jo. 1975. *The Politics of Women's Liberation*. New York: Longman.

———. 1983a. "On the Origins of Social Movements." In *Social Movements of the Sixties and Seventies*, edited by Jo Freeman, pp. 8–32. New York: Longman.

———. 1983b. "A Model for Analyzing the Strategic Options of Social Movement

Organizations." In *Social Movements of the Sixties and Seventies*, edited by Jo
Freeman, pp. 193–210. New York: Longman.

———. 1986. "The Political Culture of the Democratic and Republican Parties."
Political Science Quarterly, 101: 327–356.

Fromm, Erich. 1945. *Escape from Freedom*. New York: Rinehart.

Fulenwider, Claire Knoche. 1980. *Feminism in American Politics: A Study of Ideological
Influence*. New York: Praeger.

Gamson, William. 1975. *The Strategy of Social Protest*. Homewood, Ill.: The Dorsey
Press.

Garner, Roberta A. 1977. *Social Movements in America*, 2nd. ed. Chicago: Rand
McNally.

Garrow, David J. 1986. *Bearing the Cross*. New York: William Morrow & Co. Inc.

Gerlach, Luther P. 1983. "Movements of Revolutionary Change: Some Structural
Characteristics." In *Social Movements of the Sixties and Seventies*, edited by Jo
Freeman, pp. 133–147. New York: Longman.

Gerlach, Luther P., and Virginia H. Hine. 1970. *People, Power, Change: Movements
of Social Transformation*. Indianapolis, Ind.: Bobbs-Merrill.

Gerth, Hans, and C. Wright Mills. 1953. *Character & Social Structure: The Psychology
of Social Institutions*. New York: Harcourt, Brace Jovanovich, Inc.

Gertzog, Irwin N. 1984. *Congressional Women*. New York: Praeger.

Gibson, James L., Cornelius P. Cotter, John F. Bibby, and Robert J. Huckshorn.
1985. "Whither the Local Parties?: A Cross-Sectional and Longitudinal Analysis of the Strength of Party Organizations." *American Journal of Political
Science* 29: 139–160.

Ginsberg, Benjamin, and Martin Shefter. 1985. "A Critical Realignment? The New
Politics, the Reconstituted Right, and the Election of 1984." In *The Elections
of 1984*, edited by Michael Nelson, pp. 1–25. Washington, D.C.: CQ Press.

Githens, Marianne, and Jewell L. Prestage. 1977. "Introduction." In *A Portrait of
Marginality*, edited by Marianne Githens and Jewell L. Prestage, pp. 1–10.
New York: David McKay.

Gold, Doris B. 1971. "Women and Volunteerism." In *Women in Sexist Society*, edited
by Vivian Gornick and Barbara K. Moran, pp. 533–554. New York: Basic
Books.

Goldenberg, Edie N., and Michael W. Traugott. 1984. *Campaigning for Congress*.
Washington, D.C.: CQ Press.

Goodman, T. William. 1951. "How Much Political Party Centralization Do We
Want?" *Journal of Politics*, 13: 536–561.

Graber, Doris A. 1984. *Mass Media and American Politics*, 2nd ed. Washington, D.C.:
CQ Press.

Greenstein, Fred I. 1983. *The Reagan Presidency: An Early Assessment*. Baltimore,
Md.: Johns Hopkins University Press.

Greenstein, Fred I., and Nelson W. Polsby. 1975. *Nongovernmental Politics*. Reading,
Mass.: Addison-Wesley Publishing.

Greenwood, Michael J. 1981. *Migration and Economic Growth in the United States*.
New York: Academic Press.

Gurr, Ted R. 1969. *Why Men Rebel*. Princeton, N.J.: Princeton University Press.

Gusfield, Joseph R. 1962. "Mass Society and Extremist Politics." *American Sociological Review* 27: 19–30.

Guth, James L. 1983. "The Politics of the Christian Right." In *Interest Group Politics*, edited by Allan J. Cigler and Burdett A. Loomis, pp. 60–83. Washington, D.C.: CQ Press.

Hammond, John L. 1979. *The Politics of Benevolence: Revival Religion and American Voting Behavior*. Norwood, N.J.: Ablex Publishing Co.

Hargrove, Erwin C. 1985. "The Presidency: Reagan and the Cycle of Politics and Policy." In *The Elections of 1984*, edited by Michael Nelson, pp. 189–213. Washington, D.C.: CQ Press.

Hargrove, Erwin C., and Michael Nelson. 1984. *Presidents, Politics and Policy*. Baltimore, Md.: Johns Hopkins University Press.

Hartz, Louis. 1955. *The Liberal Tradition in America*. New York: Harcourt, Brace Jovanovich, Inc.

Hauss, Charles S., and L. Sandy Maisel. 1986. "Extremist Delegates: Myth and Reality." In *The Life of the Parties: Activists in Presidential Politics*, edited by Ronald B. Rapoport, Alan I. Abramowitz, and John McGlennon, pp. 215–226. Lexington: University of Kentucky Press.

Hayes, Michael T. 1983. "Interest Groups: Pluralism or Mass Society?" In *Interest Group Politics*, edited by Allan J. Cigler and Burdett A. Loomis, pp. 110–125. Washington, D.C.: CQ Press.

———. 1986. "The New Group Universe." In *Interest Group Politics*, 2nd. ed., edited by Allan J. Cigler and Burdett A. Loomis, pp. 133–145. Washington, D.C.: CQ Press.

Heberle, Rudolf. 1949. "Observations on the Sociology of Social Movements." *American Sociological Review* 14: 346–357.

———. 1955. "Ferdinand Tonnies's Contributions to the Sociology of Political Parties." *American Journal of Sociology* 61: 216–217.

Hennessy, Bernard. 1968. "On the Study of Party Organization." In *Approaches to the Study of Party Organization*, edited by William J. Crotty, pp. 1–44. Boston: Allyn and Bacon.

Herrnson, Paul. 1986. "National Party Organizations and Congressional Campaigning: National Parties as Brokers." Paper presented at the Annual Meeting of the Midwest Political Science Association, Chicago, Ill.

Hershey, Marjorie Randon. 1984. *Running for Office: The Political Education of Campaigners*. Chatham, N.J.: Chatham House.

Hill, David B., and Norman R. Luttbeg. 1983. *Trends in American Electoral Behavior*, 2nd ed. Itasca, Ill.: F.E. Peacock.

Hitlin, Robert, and John S. Jackson III. 1979. "Change and Reform in the Democratic Party." *Polity* 11: 617–633.

Hopkins, Anne H. 1986. "Campaign Activities and Local Party Organization in Nashville." In *Political Parties in Local Areas*, edited by William J. Crotty, pp. 65–88. Knoxville, Tenn.: The University of Tennessee Press.

Horsfield, Peter G. 1984. *Religious Television: The American Experience*. New York: Longman.

Huckshorn, Robert J., James L. Gibson, Cornelius P. Cotter, and John F. Bibby. 1986. "Party Integration and Party Organizational Strength." *Journal of Politics*, 48: 976–991.

Inglehart, Ronald. 1971. "The Silent Revolution in Europe: Intergenerational Change in Post-Industrial Societies." *American Political Science Review* 65: 991–1017.

———. 1979. "Political Action: The Impact of Values, Cognitive Level, and Social Background." In *Political Action*, edited by Samuel H. Barnes and Max Kaase, pp. 370–377. Beverly Hills: Sage.

———. 1981. "Post-Materialism in an Environment of Insecurity." *American Political Science Review*, 75: 880–889.

———. 1986. "The Changing Structure of Political Cleavages in Western Society." In *Electoral Change in Advanced Industrial Democracies: Realignment or Dealignment*, edited by Russell J. Dalton, Scott C. Flanagan and Paul Allen Beck, pp. 25–69. Princeton, N.J.: Princeton University Press.

Jackson, John S. III, Jesse C. Brown, and Barbara Leavitt Brown. 1978. "Recruitment, Representation and Political Values: The 1976 Democratic National Convention Delegates." *American Politics Quarterly*, 6: 187–212.

Jackson, John S. III, Barbara Leavitt Brown, and David A. Bositis. 1982. "Herbert McClosky and Friends Revisited: 1980 Democratic and Republican Elites Compared to the Mass Public." *American Politics Quarterly* 10: 158–180.

Jacobson, Gary C. 1983. *The Politics of Congressional Elections*. Boston: Little, Brown & Co. Inc.

Janda, Kenneth. 1983. "Cross-National Measures of Party Organizations and Organizational Theory." *European Journal of Political Research* 11: 319–332.

Jaquette, Jane S. 1974. "Introduction." In *Women in Politics*, edited by Jane S. Jaquette, pp. xiii–xxxvii. New York: John Wiley.

Jennings, M. Kent, and Barbara Farah. 1981. "Social Roles and Political Resources: An Over-Time Study of Men and Women in Party Elites." *American Journal of Political Science* 25: 462–481.

Jensen, Richard. 1969. "American Election Analyses." In *Politics and the Social Sciences*, edited by Seymour M. Lipset, pp. 226–243. New York: Oxford University Press.

Jewell, Malcolm E. 1986. "Future Directions for Research on State and Local Political Parties." *PS*, XIX: 862–864.

Jewell, Malcolm E., and David M. Olson. 1978. *American State Political Parties and Elections*. Homewood, Ill.: The Dorsey Press.

Johnson, Stephen D., and Joseph B. Tamney. 1982. "The Christian Right and the 1980 Presidential Election." *Journal for the Scientific Study of Religion*, 21: 123–131.

Judd, Dennis R. 1984. *The Politics of American Cities: Private Power and Public Policy*, 2nd ed. Boston: Little, Brown & Co. Inc.

Judkins, Bennett M. 1983. "Mobilization of Membership: The Black and Brown Lung Movements." In *Social Movements of the Sixties and Seventies*, edited by Jo Freeman, pp. 35–51. New York: Longman.

Kamieniecki, Sheldon. 1985. *Party Identification, Political Behavior and the American Electorate*. Westport, Conn.: Greenwood Press.

Kayden, Xandra, and Eddie Mahe, Jr. 1985. *The Party Goes on: The Persistence of the Two-Party System in the United States*. New York: Basic Books Inc., Publishers.

Keeter, Scott, and Cliff Zukin. 1983. *Uninformed Choice*. New York: Praeger.

Keniston, Kenneth. 1968. *Young Radicals: Notes on Committed Youth*. New York: Harcourt, Brace Javonovich, Inc.

Key, V. O., Jr. 1950. *Southern Politics in State and Nation*. New York: Alfred A. Knopf Inc.

———. 1955. "A Theory of Critical Elections." *Journal of Politics* 17: 5–18.

———. 1959. "Secular Realignment and the Party System." *Journal of Politics* 21: 198–210.

———. 1961. *Public Opinion*. New York: Alfred A. Knopf Inc.

———. 1964. *Politics, Parties & Pressure Groups*, 5th ed. New York: Thomas Y. Crowell.

———. 1966. *The Responsible Electorate*. Cambridge, Mass.: Harvard University Press.

———. 1967. *Public Opinion and American Democracy*. New York: Alfred A. Knopf Inc.

Kinder, Donald R. 1983. "Diversity and Complexity in American Public Opinion." In *Political Science: The State of the Discipline*, edited by Ada W. Finifter, pp. 389–425. Washington, D.C.: American Political Science Association.

King, Anthony. 1969. "Political Parties in Western Democracies." *Polity*, 2: 112–141.

———, ed. 1983. *Both Ends of the Avenue: The President, The Executive Branch and Congress in the 1980's*. Washington, D.C.: The American Enterprise Institute.

Kingdon, John W. 1981. *Congressmen's Voting Decisions*, 2nd ed. New York: Harper & Row, Publishers.

Kirkpatrick, Evron M. 1971. "Toward a More Responsible Two-Party System: Political Science, Policy Science or Pseudo Science?" *American Political Science Review* 65: 965–990.

Kirkpatrick, Jeane Jordan. 1974. *Political Woman*. New York: Basic Books Inc., Publishers.

———. 1976. *The New Presidential Elite*. New York: Russell Sage Foundation.

———. 1979. *Dismantling the Parties: Reflections on Party Reform and Party Decomposition*. Washington, D.C.: American Enterprise Institute.

Klein, Ethel. 1984. *Gender Politics*. Cambridge: Harvard University Press.

Kornhauser, William. 1959. *The Politics of Mass Society*. Glencoe, Ill.: The Free Press.

Kweit, Robert W., and Mary Grisez Kweit. 1986. "The Permeability of Parties." In *The Life of the Parties: Activists in Presidential Politics*, edited by Ronald B. Rapoport, Alan I. Abramowitz, and John McGlennon, pp. 188–214. Lexington: University of Kentucky Press.

Ladd, Everett Carll, Jr. 1970. *American Political Parties*. New York: W.W. Norton & Co. Inc.

———. 1977. "'Reform' is Wrecking the U.S. Party System." *Fortune* (November): 177–88.

———. 1978. *Where Have All the Voters Gone?* New York: W. W. Norton & Company, Inc.

———. 1981. "Party 'Reform' Since 1968: A Case Study in Intellectual Failure." In *The American Constitutional System Under Strong and Weak Parties*, edited by Patricia Bonomi, James MacGregor Burns, and Austin Ranney, pp. 81–95. New York: Praeger.

———. 1982. "Does Reagan Have a Problem with Women?" *Public Opinion* (January): 48–49.

Ladd, Everett Carll, Jr., with Charles D. Hadley. 1975. *Transformations of the American Party System*. New York: W.W. Norton & Co. Inc.

Lasswell, Harold D. 1958. *Politics: Who Gets What, When, How*. New York: Meridian Books.

Lawson, Kay. 1978. "Constitutional Change and Party Development in France, Nigeria and the United States." In *Political Parties: Development and Decay*, edited by Louis Maisel and Joseph Cooper, pp. 145–178. Beverly Hills: Sage.

———. 1980. "Political Parties and Linkage." In *Political Parties and Linkage: A Comparative Perspective*, edited by Kay Lawson, pp. 3–24. New Haven, Conn.: Yale University Press.

Lawson, Ronald. 1983. "A Decentralized But Moving Pyramid: The Evolution and Consequences of the Structure of the Tenant Movement." In *Social Movements of the Sixties and Seventies*, edited by Jo Freeman, pp. 119–132. New York: Longman.

Lazarsfeld, Paul F., Bernard R. Berelson, and Hazel Gaudet. 1944. *The People's Choice*. New York: Duell, Sloan and Pearce.

LeBon, Gustave. 1879. *The Crowd: A Study of the Popular Mind*. London: T.F. Unwin.

Lengle, James I. 1981. *Representation and Presidential Primaries*. Westport, Conn.: Greenwood Press.

Lipset, Seymour M., Martin Trow, and James Coleman. 1956. *Union Democracy*. New York: The Free Press.

Longely, Charles. 1980. "Party Reform and Party Nationalization: The Case of the Democrats." In *The Party Symbol: Readings on Political Parties*, edited by William J. Crotty, pp. 359–75. San Francisco: W.H. Freeman & Co. Publishers.

Lowi, Theodore J. 1985. "An Aligning Election: A Presidential Plebiscite." In *The Election of 1984*, edited by Michael Nelson, pp. 277–302. Washington, D.C.: CQ Press.

Luker, Kristin. 1984. *Abortion and the Politics of Motherhood*. Berkeley, Calif.: University of California Press.

Luttbeg, Norman. 1981. *Public Opinion and Public Policy*, 3rd ed. Itasca, Ill.: F.E. Peacock Publishers, Inc.

Lynn, Naomi. 1979. "American Women and the Political Process." In *Women: A Feminist Perspective*, edited by Jo Freeman, pp. 364–385. Palo Alto, Calif.: Mayfield.

McAdam, Douglas. 1983. "The Decline of the Civil Rights Movement." In *Social Movements of the Sixties and Seventies*, edited by Jo Freeman, pp. 279–319. New York: Longman.

McCarthy, John D., and Meyer N. Zald. 1973. *The Trends of Social Movements in America: Professionalization and Resource Mobilization*. Morristown, N.J.: General Learning Press.

———. 1977. "Resource Mobilization and Social Movements: A Partial Theory." *American Journal of Sociology*, 32: 1212–1241.

McClosky, Herbert, Paul J. Hoffman, and Rosemary O'Hara. 1960. "Issue Conflict and Consensus Among Party Leaders and Followers." *American Political Science Review*, 54: 406–427.

McClosky, Herbert and Alida Brill. 1983. *Dimensions of Tolerance*. New York: Russell Sage Foundation.

McConnell, Grant. 1966. *Private Power and American Democracy*. New York: Alfred A. Knopf Inc.

McCormick, Richard L. 1984. *Political Parties and the Modern State*. New Brunswick, N.J.: Rutgers University Press.

McFarland, Andrew S. 1983. "Public Interest Lobbies Versus Minority Faction." In *Interest Group Politics*, edited by Allan J. Cigler and Burdett A. Loomis, pp. 324–353. Washington, D.C.: CQ Press.

————. 1984. *Common Cause: Lobbying in the Public Interest*. Chatham, N.J.: Chatham House.

McGlen, Nancy E., and Karen O'Connor. 1983. *Women's Rights: The Struggle for Equality in the 19th and 20th Century*. New York: Praeger.

McLoughlin, William G. 1978. *Revivals, Awakening & Reform: An Essay on Religion and Social Change in America, 1607 to 1977*. Chicago: University of Chicago Press.

MacPherson, Myra. 1984. "GOP Women in the Age of Ferraro." *Washington Post*, August 25, sec. G., p. 2, col. A.

Maisel, Louis, and Joseph Cooper, eds. 1978. *Political Parties: Development and Decay*. Beverly Hills: Sage.

Malbin, Michael. 1981. "The Conventions, Platforms and Issue Activists." In *The American Elections of 1980*, edited by Austin Ranney, pp. 99–141. Washington: American Enterprise Institute.

Mann, Judy. 1984. "GOP Women." *Washington Post*, February 15, sec. B, p. 1.

Mannheim, Karl. 1940. *Man and Society in an Age of Reconstruction*. London: Routledge and Kegan Paul.

Marvick, Dwaine. 1986. "Stability and Change in the Views of Los Angeles Party Activists, 1968–1980." In *Political Parties in Local Areas*, edited by William J. Crotty, pp. 121–156. Knoxville, Tenn.: University of Tennessee Press.

Marx, Gary T. 1979. "External Efforts to Damage or Facilitate Social Movements: Some Patterns, Explanations, Outcomes, and Complications." In *The Dynamics of Social Movements*, edited by Mayer N. Zald and John D. McCarthy, pp. 94–125. Cambridge, Mass.: Winthrop Publishers, Inc.

Matthews, Donald R., and James W. Prothro. 1966. *Negroes and the New Southern Politics*. New York: Harcourt, Brace & World, Inc.

Mayhew, David. 1974. *Congress: The Electoral Connection*. New Haven: Yale University Press.

Mead, Margaret. 1978. *Culture and Commitment: The New Relationships Between the Generations in the 1970s*. New York: Doubleday Publishing Co.

Merriam, Charles. 1922. *The American Party System*. New York: Macmillan Publishing Co.

Michels, Robert. [1915] 1962. *Political Parties: A Sociological Study of the Oligarchical Tendencies of Modern Democracy*. New York: Crowell-Collier.

Milbrath, Lester W., and M. L. Goel. 1977. *Political Participation*, 2nd ed. Chicago: Rand McNally.

Miller, Warren E. 1987. "The Election of 1984 and the Future of American Politics." In *Elections in America*, edited by Kay Lehman Schlozman, pp. 293–320. Boston: Allen & Unwin.

Miller, Warren E., and M. Kent Jennings. 1986. *Parties in Transition*. New York: Russell Sage Foundation.

Mills, C. Wright. 1959. *The Power Elite*. New York: Oxford University Press.

Moe, Terry M. 1980. "A Calculus of Group Membership." *American Journal of Political Science*, 24: 593–632.

———. 1981. "Toward a Broader View of Interest Groups." *Journal of Politics* 43: 531–543.

Molotch, Harvey. 1977. "Media and Movements." In *The Dynamics of Social Movements*, edited by Mayer N. Zald and John D. McCarthy, pp. 71–93. Cambridge, Mass. Winthrop Publishers, Inc.

Montjoy, Robert S., William R. Shaffer, and Ronald E. Weber. 1980. "Policy Preferences of Party Elites and Masses: Conflict or Consensus?" *American Politics Quarterly*, 8: 319–343.

Moon, Marilyn, and Isabel V. Sawhill. 1984. "Family Incomes: Gainers and Losers." In *The Reagan Record: An Assessment of America's Changing Domestic Priorities*, edited by John L. Palmer and Isabel V. Sawhill, pp. 317–346. Cambridge, Mass.: Ballinger.

Mosca, Gaetano. 1939. *The Ruling Class*. New York: McGraw-Hill Inc.

Murray, Richard W., and Kent L. Tedin. 1986. "The Emergence of Two-Party Competition in the Sunbelt: The Case of Houston." In *Political Parties in Local Areas*, edited by William J. Crotty, pp. 39–64. Knoxville, Tenn.: The University of Tennessee Press.

Myrdahl, Gunnar, Richard Sterner, and Arnold Rose. 1944. *An American Dilemma: The Negro Problem and American Democracy*. New York: Harper & Row, Publishers Inc.

Nagel, Jack H. 1987. *Participation*. Englewood Cliffs, N.J.: Prentice-Hall.

Nakamura, Robert T. 1983. "The Reformed Nominating System: Its Critics and Uses." *PS*, 16: 667–672.

Natchez, Peter B. 1985. *Images of Voting/Visions of Democracy*. New York: Basic Books Inc., Publishers.

Nelson, Michael, ed. 1985. *The Elections of 1984*. Washington, D.C.: CQ Press.

Nie, Norman H., Sidney Verba, and John R. Petrocik. 1976. *The Changing American Voter*. Cambridge, Mass.: Harvard University Press.

Nisbet, Robert. 1953. *The Quest for Community*. New York: Oxford University Press.

Oberschall, Anthony. 1973. *Social Conflict and Social Movements*. Englewood Cliffs, N.J.: Prentice-Hall.

Olson, Mancur. 1965 (1971). *The Logic of Collective Action*. Cambridge, Mass.: Harvard University Press.

Orren, Gary R. 1982. "The Changing Styles of American Party Politics." In *The Future of American Party Politics*, edited by Joel L. Fleishman, pp. 4–41. Englewood Cliffs, N.J.: Prentice-Hall.

———. 1985. "The Nomination Process: Vicissitudes of Candidate Selection." In *The Elections of 1984*, edited by Michael Nelson, pp. 27–82. Washington, D.C.: CQ Press.

Parkin, Frank. 1968. *Middle Class Radicalism*. New York: Praeger.

Pateman, Carol. 1970. *Political Participation and Democracy*. Cambridge, UK: Cambridge University Press.

Perrow, Charles. 1977. "The Sixties Observed." In *The Dynamics of Social Movements*, edited by Mayer N. Zald and John D. McCarthy. Cambridge, Mass.: Winthrop.

Petrocik, John R. 1981. *Party Coalitions*. Chicago: University of Chicago Press.

Pinard, Maurice. 1971. *The Rise of a Third Party: A Study in Crisis Politics*. Englewood Cliffs, N.J.: Prentice-Hall.

Pitkin, Hannah F. 1967. *The Concept of Representation*. Berkeley: University of California Press.

Piven, Frances F., and Richard A. Cloward. 1971. *Regulating the Poor*. New York: Pantheon Books.

———. 1977. *Poor People's Movements*. New York: Pantheon Books.

Polsby, Nelson W. 1980. "The News Media as an Alternative to Party in the Presidential Selection Process." In *Political Parties in the Eighties*, edited by Robert A. Goldwin, pp. 50–66. Washington, D.C.: American Enterprise Institute.

———. 1983a. *Consequences of Party Reform*. New York: Oxford University Press.

———. 1983b. "The Reform of Presidential Selection and Democratic Theory." *PS*, 16: 695–698.

Polsby, Nelson W., and Aaron B. Wildavsky. 1971. *Presidential Elections*, 3rd ed. New York: Charles Scribner's Sons.

Pomper, Gerald. 1967. "Classification of Presidential Elections." *Journal of Politics* 29: 535–566.

———. 1971. "Toward a More Responsible Party System? What, Again?" *Journal of Politics* 33: 916–940.

———. 1975. *Voter's Choice: Varieties of American Electoral Behavior*. New York: Dodd, Mead & Co.

———, ed. 1980. *Party Renewal in America: Theory and Practice*. New York: Praeger.

Porter, Mary Cornelia, and Ann B. Matasar. 1974. "The Role and Status of Women in the Daley Organization." In *Women in Politics*, edited by Jane S. Jaquette, pp. 85–108. New York: John Wiley & Sons Inc.

Preston, Michael B. 1987. "The Election of Harold Washington: An Examination of the SES Model in the 1983 Chicago Mayoral Election." In Michael B. Preston, Lenneal J. Henderson, Jr. and Paul L. Puryear (eds.), *The New Black Politics*, 2nd ed., New York: Longman, pp. 139–171.

Prewitt, Kenneth. 1970. *The Recruitment of Political Leaders*. Indianapolis: Bobbs-Merrill.

Prewitt, Kenneth, and Alan Stone. 1973. *The Ruling Elites: Elite Theory, Power and American Democracy*. New York: Harper and Row.

Price, David E. 1984. *Bringing Back the Parties*. Washington, D.C.: CQ Press.

Prysby, Charles. 1980. "Electoral Behavior in the South." In Robert Steed, Laurence Moreland and Tod Baker (eds.), *Party Politics in the South*. New York: Praeger, pp. 101–126.

Ranney, Austin. 1951. "Toward A More Responsible Two-Party System: A Commentary." *American Political Science Review*, 45:488–499.

———. 1965. "Parties in State Politics." In Herbert Jacob and Kenneth L. Vines (eds.), *Politics in the American States*. Boston: Little, Brown.

———. 1975. *Curing the Mischiefs of Faction*. Berkeley: University of California Press.

———. 1978. *The Federalization of Presidential Primaries*. Washington, D.C.: American Enterprise Institute.

Rapoport, Ronald B., Alan I. Abramowitz, and John McGlennon, eds. 1986. *The Life of the Parties: Activists in American Politics*. Lexington: University of Kentucky Press.

Rehmus, Charles M. 1978. "Labor as a Pressure Group." In Charles M. Rehmus,

Doris B. McLaughlin and Frederick H. Nesbitt (eds.), *Labor and American Politics*, Revised Edition. Ann Arbor: University of Michigan Press, pp. 24–26.

Rehmus, Charles. M., and Frederick H. Nesbitt. 1978. Epilogue. In Charles M. Rehmus, Doris B. McLaughlin and Frederick H. Nesbitt (eds.), *Labor and American Politics*, Revised Edition. Ann Arbor: University of Michigan Press, pp. 421–433.

Reichley, A. James. 1985. "The Rise of National Parties." In John E. Chubb and Paul E. Peterson (eds.), *The New Direction in American Politics*. Washington, D.C.: Brookings, pp. 175–200.

Reinhard, David W. 1983. *The Republican Right Since 1945*. Lexington: University of Kentucky Press.

Rieselbach, Leroy N. 1986. *Congressional Reform*. Washington, D.C.: CQ Press.

Roback, Thomas H. 1975. "Amateurs and Professionals: Delegates to the 1972 Republican Convention." *Journal of Politics*, 37:436–468.

Romano, Lois. 1986. "Women in the Reagan Administration." *Washington Post* (February 4), sec. A, p. 1, col. 1; sec. A, p. 12, col. 1.

Rosenstone, Steven J., Roy L. Behr and Edward H. Lazarus. 1984. *Third Parties in America: Citizen Response to Major Party Failure*. Princeton: Princeton University Press.

Rosenstone, Steven J. and Raymond E. Wolfinger. 1984. "The Effect of Registration Laws on Voter Turnout." In Richard G. Niemi and Herbert F. Weisberg (eds.), *Controversies in Voting Behavior*, 2nd. ed. Washington, D.C.: CQ Press, pp. 54–86.

Sabato, Larry J. 1981. *The Rise of Political Consultants*. New York: Basic Books.

———. 1984. *PAC Power: Inside the World of Political Action Committees*. New York: W.W. Norton.

Salisbury, Robert M. 1969. "An Exchange Theory of Interest Groups." *Midwest Journal of Political Science*, 13:1–32.

Salmore, Stephen and Barbara Salmore. 1985. *Candidates, Parties and Campaigns*. Washington, D.C.: CQ Press.

Saloma, John S., III, and Frederick H. Sontag. 1973. *Parties: The Real Opportunity for Effective Citizen Politics*. New York: Vintage Press.

Sandoz, Ellis and Cecil V. Crabb, Jr., eds. 1985. *Election 84*. New York: Mentor.

Sanford, Terry. 1981. *A Danger of Democracy*. New York: Westview.

Sapiro, Virginia. 1983. *The Political Integration of Women*. Urbana: University of Illinois Press.

Sapiro, Virginia and Barbara G. Farah. 1980. "New Pride and Old Prejudice: Political Ambition and Role Orientations Among Female Partisan Elites." *Women and Politics* 1:13–36.

Sartori, Giovanni. 1976. *Parties and Party Systems*. Cambridge, U.K.: Cambridge University Press.

Scammon, Richard M. and Ben J. Wattenberg. 1970. *The Real Majority*. New York: Coward, McCann and Geoghegan.

Schattschneider, E. E. 1942. *Party Government*. New York: Farrar and Rinehart.

———. 1960. *The Semisovereign People*. New York: Holt, Rinehart and Winston.

———. 1975. *The Semisovereign People*. (Reissue). Hinsdale, Ill.: The Dryden Press.

Schlesinger, Arthur Jr. 1984. "The Crisis of the American Party System." In Richard

L. McCormick (ed.), *Political Parties and the Modern State*. New Brunswick, N.J.: Rutgers University Press, pp. 71–85.

Schlesinger, Joseph A. 1966. *Ambitiion and Politics: Political Careers in the United States*. Chicago, Rand McNally.

———. 1984. "On the Theory of Party Organization." *Journal of Politics*, 46:369–400.

———. 1985. The New American Political Party. *The American Political Science Review*, 79:1152–1169.

Schlesinger, Stephen. 1975. *The New Reformers: Forces for Change in American Politics*. Boston: Houghton, Mifflin.

Schubert, Glendon. 1985. "Religious Interest Group Politics in the Constitutional Market Place: From Jeannette to Jonestown." *Journal of Law and Politics*, 2:201–238.

Schumpeter, Joseph A. 1950. *Capitalism, Socialism and Democracy*. New York: Harper & Row.

Sears, David O. and John B. McConahay. 1973. *The Politics of Violence*. Boston: Houghton Mifflin, Co.

Selznick, Phillip. 1952. *The Organizational Weapon*. New York: McGraw-Hill.

Shafer, Byron E. 1983. *Quiet Revolution: The Struggle for the Democratic Party and the Shaping of Post-Reform Politics*. New York: Russell Sage Foundation.

Shefter, Martin. 1978. "Party, Bureaucracy, and Political Change in the United States." In Louis Maisel and Joseph Cooper (eds.), *Political Parties: Development and Decay*. Beverly Hills: Sage, pp. 211–265.

Simons, Herbert W. and Elizabeth W. Mechling. 1981. "The Rhetoric of Political Movements." In Dan D. Nimmo and Keith R. Sanders (eds.), *The Handbook of Political Communication*. Beverly Hills: Sage, pp. 417–444.

Sinclair, Barbara Deckard. 1977. "Party Realignment and the Transformation of the Political Agenda:The House of Representatives, 1925–1938." *American Political Science Review*, 71:940–953.

———. 1983. *Majority Leadership in the U.S. House*. Baltimore: Johns Hopkins University Press.

Smallwood, Frank. 1983. *The Other Candidates: Third Parties in Presidential Elections*. Hanover: University Press of New England.

Smelser, Neil J. 1963. *Theory of Collective Behavior*. New York: The Free Press of Glencoe.

Smith, Steven S. and Christopher J. Deering. 1984. *Committees in Congress*. Washington, D.C.: CQ Press.

Sonthoff, Herbert. 1951. "Party Responsibility: A Critical Inquiry." *Western Political Quarterly*, 4:454–468.

Sorauf, Frank J. 1967. "Political Parties and Political Analysis." In William Nisbet Chambers and Walter Dean Burnham (eds.), *The American Party System*. New York: Oxford University Press, pp. 33–55.

———. 1968. *Party Politics in America*. Boston: Little, Brown & Co., Inc.

———. 1984. *Party Politics in America*, 5th. ed. Boston: Little, Brown & Co., Inc.

Soule, John W. and James W. Clarke. 1970. "Amateurs and Professionals: A Study of Delegates to the 1968 Democratic Convention." *American Political Science Review*, 19:888–898.

Soule, John W. and Wilma E. McGrath. 1975. "A Comparative Study of Presidential Nomination Conventions: The Democrats 1968 and 1972." *American Journal of Political Science*, 19:501–517.

SPSSX, INC. 1985. *SPSSX Users Guide*, 2nd. ed. New York: McGraw-Hill Inc., pp. 467–469.

Stedman, Murray S., Jr. and Herbert Sonthoff. 1951. "Party Responsibility—A Critical Inquiry." *Western Political Quarterly*, 4:454–468.

Stimpson, Catharine. 1971. " 'Thy Neighbor's Wife, Thy Neighbor's Servants' ": Women's Liberation and Black Civil Rights." In Vivian Gornick and Barbara K. Moran (eds.), *Women in Sexist Society*. New York: Basic Books, pp. 452–479.

Stone, Walter J. 1984. "Prenomination Candidate Choice and General Election Behavior: Iowa Presidential Activists in 1980." *American Journal of Political Science*, 28:361–378.

Stoper, Emily. 1983. "The Student Nonviolent Coordinating Committee: Rise and Fall of a Redemptive Organization." In Jo Freeman (ed.), *Social Movements of the Sixties and Seventies*. New York: Longman, pp. 320–334.

Sullivan, Denis G., Jeffrey L. Pressman, and F. Christopher Arterton. 1976. *Explorations in Convention Decision Making*. San Francisco: W.H. Freeman.

Sullivan, Denis G., Jeffrey L. Pressman, Benjamin I. Page and John J. Lyons. 1974. *The Politics of Representation: The Democratic Convention 1972*. New York: St. Martin's Press.

Sundquist, James L. 1973. *The Dynamics of the Party System*. Washington, D.C.: Brookings.

Taeuber, Cynthia M. and Victor Valdisera. 1986. "Women in the American Economy." *Current Population Reports Special Studies Series P–23, No. 146*. Washington, DC: Bureau of the Census.

Talbott, Strobe. 1984. *Deadly Gambits: The Reagan Administration and the Stalemate In Nuclear Arms Control*. New York: Alfred A. Knopf, Inc.

Tesh, Sylvia. 1984. "In Support of 'Single Issue' Politics." *Political Science Quarterly*, 99:27–44.

Thelen, David P. 1981. "Two Traditions of Progressive Reform, Political Parties, and American Democracy." In Patricia Bonomi, James M. Burns and Austin Ranney (eds.), *The American Constitutional System Under Strong and Weak Parties*. New York: Praeger, pp. 37–63.

Tichenor, Phillip J., George A. Donohue and Clarice N. Olien. 1984. "Communication and Community Conflict." In Doris A. Graber (ed.), *Media Power in Politics*. Washington, D.C.: CQ Press.

Tilly, Charles. 1979. *Repertoires of Contention in America and Britain, 1750–1830*. Cambridge:, Mass. Winthrop Publishers, pp. 126–155.

———. 1983. "Speaking Your Mind Without Elections, Surveys, or Social Movements." *Public Opinion Quarterly*, 47:461–478.

Tolchin, Susan and Martin Tolchin. 1974. *Clout: Womanpower and Politics*. New York: Coward, McCann and Geoghegan.

Truman, David B. 1958. *The Governmental Process*, 2nd. ed. New York: Alfred A. Knopf, Inc.

Tufte, Edward R. 1983. *The Visual Display of Quantitative Information*. Cheshire, CT: Graphics Press.

Turner, Ralph H. and Lewis M. Killian. 1972. *Collective Behavior*, 2nd. ed. Englewood Cliffs, N.J.: Prentice-Hall.

U.S. Bureau of the Census. 1984. *Voting and Registration Highlights from the Current Population Survey: 1964 to 1980, Series P–23, No. 131*. Washington, D.C.: U.S. Department of Commerce.

Verba, Sidney and Norman H. Nie. 1972. *Participation in America: Political Democracy and Social Equality*. New York: Harper & Row.

Vogel, David. 1980. "The Public Interest Movement and the American Reform Tradition." *Political Science Quarterly*, 95:607–627.

Vose, Clement E. 1972. *Constitutional Change*. Lexington, Mass.: Lexington Books.

Wahlke, John C. 1979. "Pre-Behavioralism in Political Science." *American Political Science Review*, 73:9–31.

Wald, Kenneth D. 1987. *Religion and Politics in the United States*. New York: St. Martin's Press.

Walker, Jack L. 1983. "The Origins and Maintenance of Interest Groups in America." *American Political Science Review*, 77:390–406.

Walton, Hanes Jr. 1972. *Black Political Parties: An Historical and Political Analysis*. New York: The Free Press.

Ware, Alan. 1985. *The Breakdown of Democratic Party Organization, 1940–1980*. New York: Oxford University Press.

Wattenberg, Martin P. 1986. *The Decline of American Political Parties, 1952–1984*. Cambridge: Harvard University Press.

Weissberg, Robert. 1976. *Public Opinion and Popular Government*. Englewood Cliffs, N.J.: Prentice-Hall.

Weyrich, Paul M. 1987. "The Reagan Revolution That Wasn't." *Policy Review*, 41:50–53.

Wildavsky, Aaron. 1971. *The Revolt Against the Masses*. New York: Basic Books.

Wilkinson, Paul. 1971. *Social Movements*. New York: Praeger.

Williams, Linda. 1987. "Black Political Progress in the 1980s: The Electoral Arena." In Michael B. Preston, Lenneal J. Henderson, Jr., and Paul L. Puryear (eds.), *The New Black Politics: The Search for Political Power*, 2nd ed. New York: Longman, pp. 97–135.

Wilson, Graham K. 1981. *Interest Groups in the United States*. New York: Oxford University Press.

Wilson, James Q. 1962. *The Amateur Democrat*. Chicago: University of Chicago Press.

———. 1973. *Political Organizations*. New York: Basic Books.

Author Index

Subject Index

About the Authors

DENISE L. BAER is Assistant Professor of Political Science at Northeastern University. She is a co-investigator with The Political Party Study and Professional Pairs in Political Science research projects. Her articles have been published in *Women and Politics, Political Behavior, International Political Science Review,* and *Politics and the Life Sciences.*

DAVID A. BOSITIS is Assistant Professor in the Department of Political Science at the George Washington University. He is a co-investigator on The Party Elite Study and presently at work on a book about research design. His articles have appeared in *Political Behavior, American Politics Quarterly, Women and Politics, Politics and the Life Sciences,* and *International Political Science Review.*